A GIRL CALLED
DUSTY

This is dedicated to Dusty Springfield

May she now rest in peace

A GIRL CALLED DUSTY

An intimate portrait of
Dusty Springfield

SHARON DAVIS

ANDRE
DEUTSCH

First published in Great Britain in 2008 by
André Deutsch
an imprint of the
Carlton Publishing Group
20 Mortimer Street
London W1T 3JW

A CIP catalogue record for this book is available from the British Library

ISBN 978 0 233 00237 8

The publishers would like to thank the following sources for their kind
permission to reproduce the pictures in this book.

Page 1: (top) Private Collection; (bottom) Popperfoto/Getty Images
Page 2: (both) Michael Ochs Archive/Getty Images
Page 3: (both) Dezo Hoffmann/Rex Features
Page 4: (top) Dezo Hoffmann/Rex Features; (bottom) King Collection/Retna Pictures Ltd
Page 5: (top) Dezo Hoffmann/Rex Features; (bottom) David Redfern/Redferns Music Picture Library
Page 6: (top) BBC Photo Library/Redferns Music Picture Library; (bottom)
      Terry O'Neill/Getty Images
Page 7: Michael Putland/Retna Pictures Ltd
Page 8: (both) Private Collection

Every effort has been made to acknowledge correctly and contact the source
and/or copyright holder of each picture and Carlton Books Limited apologises
for any unintentional errors or omissions, which will be corrected in future
editions of this book.

Typeset by Adrian at microguides.net
Printed and bound in the UK by CPI Mackays, Chatham, ME5 8TD

CONTENTS

INTRODUCTION

I owe much to Dusty. Not only did I follow her lead by back-combing my hair and plonking black spit mascara on my eyelids, but with her encouragement I ventured into the then unknown world of black music which led me to Motown Records. There was then no turning back. I also became an active member of her fan club in East Sussex and entertained many fan club members in my parents' house in Uckfield. Being part of the club meant I got to see Dusty easily, so I met her at all her shows in my area, and at the occasional performance in London. The Drury Lane concert in April 1979 was the last.

While I collected Motown material over the years, I also hoarded Dusty memorabilia and this formed the background to this book, which has been on the back-burner for far too long. And here's how it came about. Mine was the last interview of the day and the hotel manager wanted to reclaim the conference room Dusty had used all day for interviews. So off we trotted to her hotel room and, as we walked along the corridor, I said I'd love to write her life story and would she mind? Or, more importantly, would she help? "I've got tunnel vision just now and as there's much of my life I can't remember, I wouldn't be much help with the details. I won't stop you writing about me. In fact," she smiled, "I'd like to read what you've got to say. So be kind." That was during the nineties. Sadly, Dusty's not here to read it. We chatted for hours; I got my interview for *Blues & Soul*, and much of what wasn't used is printed here for the first time. One of her biggest moments was being featured in the magazine and she said, "It'll be quite an achievement. I'm hardly a soul singer, or a blues singer if it comes to that, but it's interesting to finally get there."

Several uncanny things happened during the year I wrote this book. Whenever I turned on the radio a Dusty song was being, or was about to be played. In a restaurant the background music would always include one of her greatest hits compilations. And my lovely great nephew Oliver James Eagle was born on her birthday, 16 April.

One thing I've noticed since Dusty's death is how regularly her music is featured on television programmes. One-off dramas, sitcoms and "soaps" like *Coronation Street* and *Emmerdale*, and in particular *Eastenders*, play her music on a regular basis. For instance, when the screen character Pat Butcher (played by Pam St Clements) was grieving for her recently deceased screen husband, she hugged the album cover of Dusty's "Greatest Hits" while "I Just Don't Know What To Do With Myself" played in the background. And I'm sure this use of her music will continue for years to come because she was so much a part of the British way of life.

This book would not have been possible without the dedication of certain wonderful people. And my heartfelt thanks, with love and hugs, to Gerry Constable who kept the project together under less than perfect working conditions. To Pat Rhodes, whom I've known since we had small beehive hairstyles, for believing in me and inviting me into her friend's world. To Carole Gibson and Paul Howes who travelled with me on this journey, unravelling my muddled thoughts and astounding me with their knowledge. To Martha Reeves, my lifelong friend, for her huge contribution to black music and unwavering loyalty to Dusty. To Lorna and Gib Hancock for sharing their precious memories. And to Simon Bell for his support, not only now but in the past. You all gave your time and knowledge so freely that it's an honour to include you here.

However, that's not all. Other people generously gave their time – Leon Shaier (such wonderful stories he shared); William Naylor (and his treasure trove of multi-coloured press clippings); Vicki Wickham (for her honesty); Daryl Easlea (for the splendid music); Dave Randle (for his assistance in sorting out the musicians); Jayne Jolliffe and Vivian Copeland (for help with the food and fauna);

Norman Scott, Julie Rough and Maria Williams; Mike Gilbert, Tony Leong and Dusty's fans who contacted me to wish me well and offer help with pictures and memories.

Finally, to Dave Godin, who died in 2004. He had founded the first Tamla Motown Fan Club in Britain, of which Dusty was a member, and was a forerunner in promoting Motown music in this country. Among his many talents he was a journalist, ran his own record store in London, spearheaded his own record label and quickly earned the title of a black music historian. He was also my dearest friend and mentor. Months before his death he wrote an essay about Dusty and gave it to me for safekeeping in the knowledge that I would one day write my book. It is published for the first time on page xi.

Last, but by no means least, my sincere thanks to my agent John Pawsey and to Rod Green, my editor, and the gang at Deutsch Publishing.

I hope I've done her proud.

Sharon Davis
2008

ESSAY

The trouble with "history" is that when you live through it, it is "now", and it is only after it has been distanced by time that you see it against a broader backdrop. I mention this because reflecting on Dusty Springfield today, I get all sorts of thoughts and perspectives which perhaps would not have occurred to me when she was at the height of her stardom. For not only was Dusty a vocalist and personality that people loved and admired, she was also a cultural icon in much the same way as Jean Harlow, Jane Russell, Rita Hayworth or Marilyn Monroe. Of course, her stature didn't perhaps equal the heights achieved by some of those but her image and persona, like theirs, fulfilled a deep cultural need.

Collectively, we seem to crave access to certain images and icons at any given time, and these vary according to our needs, fashions, and the collective mind-set of the times. Dusty managed to become much more than just a vocalist who made hit records, she was an image, too, and one that harmonized with the spirit of the sixties and seventies. She was both the girl-next-door and the extraordinarily glamorous girl-next-door who was bound to "go places". She carried a degree of femininity that was so strongly etched that it seemed quite right and natural that her appeal should brim over to respond to the charms of both sexes.

In one sense, there was something kaleidoscopic about her: looked at this way she was every teenager's dream of sexual desirability, and yet, looked at another, her sexuality was so deliciously ambiguous that, like all true icons, she was way above considerations of conventional and narrow sexual morality. Maybe she appealed to the latent lesbian in all of us!

What I loved most about Dusty on the occasions I met her, was that there was nothing of the "star" about her. She radiated star quality for sure, but behind this she was charming, friendly and, amazingly for someone whom fame had touched, good mannered! I wish that as she got older she had been given the opportunity to perhaps move into acting because I feel sure her huge emotional reserves could have been successfully channelled in that direction but, alas, it was not to be.

Like all great stars she had ambiguity; she sang and radiated warmth and affection, and yet, a tiny element of sadness and loneliness was also visible; a paradox that was perhaps more universally recognized on a subconscious level by her public than she or her record companies ever realized. When you become a star or a celebrity it is sometimes difficult to know just why this has happened, and it's easy to fret that one day you'll be "found out" and everyone will realize you are just another human being who happens to have a special and unusual talent. But it is a paradox which makes such people all the more loveable.

Dusty did not always have confidence in herself. She did not always cherish herself. And she was troubled by the gulf between what she had been told life was all about, and what life demonstrated to her it was really all about... Anybody can be a star if they are determined or ruthless enough, but to be a human being requires skill, talent and artistry. Dusty managed to be both, and being the one never compromized being the other.

Dave Godin

Chapter One.

GOIN' BACK

"She was the very essence of fabness..."
– Neil Tennant

On Friday 12 March 1999, hundreds of mourners gathered in the rain to say farewell to Dusty Springfield. Emotional crowds lined Hart Street as Dusty's body was carried by a horse-drawn glass hearse for the funeral service at St Mary The Virgin Church in Henley-on-Thames. Resting against her coffin was a large pink and white floral arrangement spelling out "Dusty". To the sound of "You Don't Have To Say You Love Me" her coffin was carried into the twelfth-century church, her brother, Tom, leading 300 mourners, who included her secretary Pat Rhodes, devoted carer and friend Simon Bell, manager Vicki Wickham, Madeline Bell, Kiki Dee, Lulu, Elvis Costello, Neil Tennant and Chris Lowe, as well as legions of her devoted fans who had travelled considerable distances to pay their last respects.

Dusty Springfield was the heart and soul of British music.

Or, as Neil Tennant said, "She was the very essence of fabness..."

Mary Isabel Catherine O'Brien was born on 16 April 1939, five months before the start of the Second World War, in a nursing home at 87 Fordwych Road, West Hampstead, a middle-class area of London close to neighbouring Kilburn with its thriving Irish community. Her birth was registered in the Metropolitan Borough of Hampstead on 23 May by the deputy registrar Dr Boreham, and the certificate noted her father, Gerard Anthony O'Brien, was an accountant, and her mother, Catherine Anne, a housewife. The family home was 97 Lauderdale Mansions, London W2 – an imposing, five-storey building on a tree-lined street – before they moved to Sumatra Road in Maida Vale. In later years Dusty admitted memories of her birthplace and indeed her family addresses were sketchy and, unfortunately, she had little idea of time frames either!

Her mother, Catherine, or Kay to her friends, had moved from Ireland to London with early ambitions to be an entertainer. For a staunch Catholic girl in her twenties, the stage wasn't considered an appropriate working place because it was assumed that in the theatre she would face all manner of temptation. Instead, Kay contented herself with amateur dramatics which, to some extent, placated her free spirit. At the age of 31 she met a fellow music enthusiast, Gerard, whom she later married. Nicknamed OB, Gerard was an income tax consultant whose job included attending court and giving evidence at trials. Dusty's birth certificate showed that he was an accountant although, according to Dusty, he never took the examinations because he thought it was beneath him to do so.

Born in India, OB's childhood saw him travelling the world. As a youngster he journeyed to and from Britain to attend a public school in Derbyshire. "The boat went so slowly that he must have had time only for a plate of curry before it was time to turn round and go back to school again," Dusty joked, before adding that this probably contributed to his introvert manner which she later inherited. Although his childhood was unsettled, Dusty's father's family led a privileged life in India. They had servants and were highly respected. He nursed aspirations to become a concert pianist, but they were abandoned when he married and had a family to support. He did, however, teach his children to play and introduced them to classical music, which Dusty loved until she discovered jazz and, later, pop music. When she was older, she recalled her musical upbringing by saying, "a good burst of Mozart can restore one's faith in the entire world!" OB would also devise quizzes by tapping out notations on the back of her hand, or playing pieces of music for her to identify. But there was also a dark side to OB and, from time to time, Dusty suffered the wrath of her father's temper. When she later questioned him about why he had hit her, he denied doing so.

Kay was of a different temperament altogether. Impulsive and quick-witted, she was born in Dublin, Ireland, and raised in Tralee, coming from a large family. Her father, parliamentary correspondent for the *Irish Independent* and editor of the *Kerryman*, the County Kerry newspaper, would regularly take his daughter to London to sit in the House of Commons. Looking at pictures of her mother as a young, blue-eyed, black-haired girl, Dusty remarked, "People always think of the Irish as red-haired but they forget that when the Spanish hit Ireland they had a good time!"

It wasn't until four years after their marriage that the O'Briens started their family, their son, Dion, being born on 2 July 1934. Five years later his sister, Mary, arrived and together they were raised by their seemingly mismatched parents. Their reserved and awkward father must have struggled to relate to their volatile, restless mother who, believing she was trapped into marriage to escape spinsterhood, adopted the role of wife and mother according to her Catholic upbringing and her family's expectations. In the ensuing years it became apparent that Mary (who in future will be known as Dusty, her adopted professional name) had taken on her mother's attitude to life, while Dion (who in future will be referred to as Tom, the name he adopted as an entertainer) inherited their father's personality. The O'Brien's marriage appears to have been far from what one might view as conventionally happy but, being Catholics, divorce was never an option. They muddled through their life together, with their children privy to their regular arguments and tensions, making the most of the moments they shared as a loving family between spats. Dusty remembered that "They had a lousy marriage. They tried hard but never got along. My mother always discouraged me from thinking about marriage."

It wasn't unusual for her parents to stay up most of the night, retiring at four in the morning, or throwing food around their kitchen. Once, when a fed-up Kay was cutting bread and butter, she decided to lob a piece of chocolate Swiss roll against the wall. There was a pause before the rest of the family joined in. At other times she would make a trifle, get bored with it, and whack it with an enormous spoon. Little spots of custard and cream exploded around the kitchen and went undetected for weeks.

Dusty also recollected being "a large child for a small child" about whom people could think of nothing to say, except that her hair colouring was lovely. She found this amusing because it was extremely red and styled in what she called "those awful corkscrews which I could sit on, which was most uncomfortable." Her memories of childhood were patchy and often contradictory, but being envious of her brother, who excelled in everything he did, while being lectured by her parents to watch and learn from him, was something that stayed with her for life. Dusty also remembered taking a nose dive from the kitchen table onto the stone floor, hitting her head, as well as falling from her pram onto the pavement, again injuring herself; the sort of mishaps, in fact, that befall most lively children.

Dusty also had childhood memories of happier times, playing with boats in her bath; eating peppermints, humbugs and ice lollies; playing on the playground swings until she felt sick; and holidaying in Bognor, a seaside resort on the South coast. She loved escaping from reality with her mother to the local cinema, where they often stayed all afternoon, watching the main and B-movies, totally immersed in the gaudy technicolor world of glitz and glamour. The slash of red scarlet that was Betty Grable's lips hypnotized Dusty from an early age, and the images from the era stayed with her, later influencing her own style and appearance. Dusty's introduction to the big screen, however, was not a romantic epic or costume drama, but the sci-fi cult classic *The Invasion Of The Body Snatchers* – "I don't know how my mother allowed me to see it!"

In stark contrast, another early movie memory was *When Irish Eyes Are Smiling*, the gentle story of a songwriter who travelled to New York to sell his songs and search for his girlfriend.

Dusty adored the 20th Century Fox musicals, June Haver becoming one of her idols as she sang and danced her way through technicolor melodramas, yet she was equally enamoured with the wackiness of The Marx Brothers and the extrovert jazz performances of Jelly Roll Morton. Although Dusty couldn't dance, she could absorb. Occasionally, when her mother was elsewhere, she swapped her two-shilling-a-day lunch money for a nine penny bag of broken biscuits, using the change to creep into the Curzon cinema in Mayfair to watch sexy foreign movies. Later on, she saw countless plays at The Old Vic, soaking up the performing arts, feeding her desire to be an actress or, at the very least, to be noticed. Dusty craved attention. Living in her brother's shadow left her lacking in self-confidence. Outward displays of affection had no place in the household, which further alienated the young girl desperate to be loved. In a desperate cry of attention, she once held her hands on the radiator in their front room until her palms became bright red. But nobody noticed. Isolation led to resentment which, in turn, put a strain on what she called her "raging ambivalent" relationship with Tom. But whatever adverse feelings she had towards him would turn to gratitude when he unwittingly encouraged her to start singing.

Prior to the outbreak of war in 1939, the family moved from Lauderdale Mansions to Sumatra Road in Hampstead, before relocating to the market town of High Wycombe, Buckinghamshire, but they failed to settle and marked time until they could return to London. For the first three months they lived in the basement flat of The Red Cow public house, before moving into a flat over a coal shop, and later to 2 Hylton Road, an area known as The Sands. Neighbour Doreen Bates told journalist Stan Alexander that her mother used to baby-sit six-year-old Dusty when Kay worked, adding "My mum used to sit us on the kitchen table and give us a cup of tea and a biscuit while we waited for her mum to collect her. She was a lovely young girl and she used to laugh all the time. I remember her striking red hair the most."

Kay O'Brien kept a spotless house, notwithstanding the occasional trifle explosion, but not so the garden. It was overgrown because her husband believed the plants would eat him; even the constant complaints from their neighbours made no impression on him. Probably more disconcerting, Dusty remembered that the neighbours' chickens would lose their way in the jungle that was their garden, never to be seen again!

With the war as the backdrop to her early years, Dusty was drawn to the music of the day – the swing of the Glen Miller Band, the chirpy Andrew Sisters, and the patriotic musical sentiments of Vera Lynn and Anne Shelton. Up to the age of eight, she remembered being a nice girl – "quite pretty, dressed in pretty frocks, and I wasn't fat. Then I caught measles and got fat and horrible." She threw terrible tantrums and her favourite whine was "it's not fair". Two years on and she was the rebel from St Trinians, convincing herself she was the worst kid in the world. She also developed an adolescent crush on a German prisoner of war from a nearby prison camp. Prisoners were regularly sent out to work in the fields as well as in the parks and gardens of the local community. She admitted being drawn to his blonde Nordic look, but, much to her dismay, he paid little attention to her. "I suppose it was the pebble glasses I wore!"

Listening to the radio, like the cinema, was another reality escape and often a lifeline during the war years. One of the biggest attractions during the mid-fifties was *The Goon Show*, one of the most popular and influential British radio shows of all time. Starring Spike Milligan, Harry Secombe and Peter Sellers as the principal voices, playing dozens of characters, Milligan's scripts mixed ludicrous plots with surreal humour, catchphrases and outrageous sound effects. It became Dusty's favourite show as she memorised key phrases, mimicking the voices into adulthood. With television still in its infancy, like many other children around that time, Dusty and Tom created much of their own entertainment – music – and to this end rifled their mother's kitchen for saucepans and spoons to pound a crude beat for their quavering voices. They sang for their neighbours and presented their own radio broadcasts. In fact, their father rigged up a microphone in one room, enabling them to "broadcast" their performance to the next room. That was, Dusty said, the nearest they came to feeding their musical ambitions as children. OB also taped his children singing, although the meanings of some of the songs were lost on the young Dusty. At the age of 12, however, she said that she recorded a ragtime selection on a Philips reel-to-reel in their garage. Tracks included a rousing version of "When The Midnight Choo Choo Leaves For Alabam", "I Love A Piano" and "Pretty Baby". In a later interview she was to contradict that version of events, claiming that it was at her first appearance in a talent show in Ealing where she first sang the songs. Whatever their origin, her fans were thrilled to hear the whole medley, probably dating back to 1953, on the *Simply Dusty* Earbook CD release in 2000. Kay O'Brien said "…When they were young, they always made music. Mary didn't have any music lessons but she sang in the school choir. There were always musical instruments lying around. I remember I would push open doors of the rooms and instruments of all sorts would fall over."

When the children were older, Tom played piano accompanied by Dusty on a cracked second-hand pair of maracas, or on an old cigar box filled with marbles. He shared his passion for Latin American/Brazilian music with her, until she too was pretending to be Carmen Miranda and her band, The Banda de Lua. This fuelled her determination to visit Rio de Janeiro at carnival time, an ambition she was later to fulfil.

Tom attended the Royal Grammar School, while Dusty started school life at The Sands County Primary, later St Augustine's Catholic Primary School, where she stayed until passing her 11-plus examination (on the second attempt). She then progressed to St Bernard's Convent, run by the Daughters of Jesus, an order founded in the Diocese of Vannes, France, in 1834 to care for the sick and poor and to educate girls. Indeed, part of Dusty's education was caring for the sick in her neighbourhood.

During the early fifties, the family returned to London, making their home in Kent Gardens, a respectable Ealing suburb. Dusty attended St Anne's Convent School, Little Ealing Lane, Northfields, opposite The Dick Turpin public house. The thriving, fee-paying school was the heart of the community and run by the dedicated Sisters of Charity of St Jeanne-Antide Thouret, an international community in the Vincentian tradition, founded in 1799 by Joan Antide Thouret in Bencanson. (In 1986 the convent became the King Fahad Academy which relocated in 2005, leaving the once-proud buildings to stand empty.) Uniforms were compulsory, right down to the design of the passion-killer knickers, while the standard of education was high. Dusty was one of 500 who were indoctrinated into Catholicism with its fire-and-brimstone teachings, the daily regime of studying the Catechism, and the weekly attendance at mass and confession. During confession, Dusty said, she made up sins to ensure she was spiritually cleansed for those she had yet to commit.

The school's teachings demanded that the girls were modest in dress and manner. Sex before marriage was regarded as an outrage ranking at the forefront of the countless other regulations designed to ensure an acceptable Catholic way of life which was intended to be just that – for life.

The pressure on the young girls to adhere to the rules was overwhelming and, when rules were broken, the punishments meted out by the nuns were severe. Keen to be regarded as a model student, Dusty followed the religion's teachings to the letter although in later life she dropped Catholicism and, despite reports to the contrary, did not return to it for comfort when she discovered she was dying from cancer. Strict Catholicism and the way of life of the modern, newly liberated teenagers were bound to clash. While

some were to reject the religious element of their education completely, others among Dusty's school chums decided to follow the
calling to become nuns, a thought that also passed through Dusty's
mind. She went on a novitiate (a probationary period) for spiritual guidance, but discovered she lacked the strength of character
needed to lead the restrictive life of a religious order. As an adult,
Dusty admitted that it took her years to dismiss what she called
the stupidity of the religion's morals and its inability to answer her
questions, although she also acknowledged that Catholicism had
worked for many, including her mother.

Dusty had few fond memories of her school days because she felt
they were her hard times, particularly the physical activities. She
claimed that, while out riding, she was dragged upside down by a
horse along Greenford Avenue in front of a 97 bus. Then, in her
fourth year, and against her better judgment, she was persuaded to
join the hockey team. She loathed the game, yet was photographed
with them, sitting in the front row with her hair short, wearing
glasses and a big smile. As an adult, she became addicted to football
– watching not playing – and joined the tennis circuit as a spectator,
befriending Wimbledon winners like Billie Jean King and Rosie
Casals. Her most abiding memory of school, however, was of her
craving to be an entertainer; it was her music that she remembered
with a loving enthusiasm. She formed her own group with two
friends, Jean and Angela, but was disappointed when their commitment fell short of her own ambitious standard. Nonetheless, they
were chosen to perform on feast days and in the annual convent's
concert. On the eve of one such concert, the Geography mistress
attended their dress rehearsal and banned them, claiming the use of
deep purple lighting during the "St Louis Blues" created an erotic
effect. The song was one of the first to cross over into mainstream
music, with the most popular version being Bessie Smith's 1925
interpretation. With Dusty strumming her acoustic guitar, the girls'
harmonies were tight and some of the songs corny, but she was lapping it up, learning her future trade.

Telling the nuns she wanted to be a blues singer caused a few problems in the sisterhood, where becoming a nurse or a secretary was far more acceptable. To be fair, Dusty had no idea what a blues singer was, but to her young mind it sounded exotic and fed her fascination with black voices and black faces. Dusty had a fierce crush on Peggy Lee and later credited her as the reason she turned to singing. By copying her vocal style, and that of Ella Fitzgerald, Dusty was ridding herself of her own "funny little voice". The result was the first whisperings of a voice that would grace millions of records.

As well as sports, Dusty hated most of her lessons, but didn't have the courage to cheat to guarantee high grades. She sat six O levels and passed four – Geography, French, History and English Grammar – failing Maths and English Literature. The latter she blamed on Jane Austin's *Mansfield Park* which she loathed, preferring the American author Bud Shulberg, who wrote about Hollywood. Dusty left the convent aged 16, harbouring disturbing feelings of inadequacy, yet fired with a determination to succeed. She had been a respectable, but not outstanding, student while her brother, who spoke nine languages, left school with numerous academic honours, enabling him to move through several jobs in banking and stockbroking, before joining the Royal Artillery. He later switched to the Intelligence Corps as a Russian translator until 1958.

With her education behind her, Dusty courted the idea of becoming an actress. She had already been a regular visitor to The Old Vic, which in turn probably inspired her to attend The Jane Campbell Acting Class in Ealing. Her first stab at serious acting was brief and she recalled that her attempts at mime were pathetic. Within a year, she was to take a giant step to change her appearance, creating a glamorous new image to help launch her musical career. She changed from a "librarian-looking schoolgirl" into a young lady dressed in a black sheath which she'd purchased in Harrods. It was the glamorous style that had ignited her imagination, and she believed that it was at this point she determined to shed the persona that was Mary O'Brien.

Behind her closed bedroom door she experimented with clothes and make-up, coaxing her hair with backcombing. She practised movement and dance in front of her mirror where, in her mind's eye, a picture of one of her Hollywood icons smiled back. Dusty's ambition came at a high price, her later teenage years being subsumed by her determination to recreate herself. She had no steady boyfriend like other girls of her age, claiming her passions for music and the cinema were far more important, and the boys she did date were fed up with her because she talked only of her herself and her future. Parental influence and the school system which segregated the sexes had, in any case, left Dusty terrified of boys. "To us," she said, "men were mysterious objects rather than people you love and with whom you feel comfortable." When she mixed with them in later life, she enjoyed crushes rather than involvement, citing drummers as her weakness "because the image of a powerful, hard-driving man behind the equipment was a strong one."

While the O'Briens happily blundered through life, the outside world of the late fifties moved on in great strides. Newspaper headlines told of guided missiles, atomic bombs and nuclear power plants. The USSR launched Sputniks 1 and 2, the latter carrying a dog, the first creature from Earth to go into outer space. Queen Elizabeth II opened Gatwick Airport while her eldest son, Charles, became the Prince of Wales. The film world and music industry were diversifying. Musicals like *South Pacific* and *Gigi* were released alongside musiflicks *Jailhouse Rock* and *The Tommy Steele Story*. Music appeared to be in utter turmoil. Bill Haley had been welcomed as a divine decadent saviour in 1955, but was ostracized two years later in the face of intense competition from the likes of The Everly Brothers, whose extraordinary career that was to span nine hit singles, kicked off with "Bye Bye Love" in July 1957. They reinforced the American stranglehold on British record buyers imposed by artists like Bing Crosby, Nat "King" Cole, Little Richard, Andy Williams and, of course, Elvis Presley. Home-grown talent eventually retaliated with Tommy Steele, Lonnie Donegan and Frankie Vaughan soon joined by Cliff Richard, a superstar in the making. Shirley Bassey and Petula Clark were also beginning to make their mark. Television was starting to take over the world and 1957 saw the birth of the first British television pop series *6.5 Special*, where viewers regularly watched rockers such as Marty Wilde and Terry Dene.

While pop music was making its presence felt, the O'Brien children began performing as amateurs. Dusty was taken by her parents to a small club near Sloane Square to watch Tom play. He introduced her to the manager, telling him that she could sing, too. "He looked at me disbelievingly," Dusty recalled. "I suppose he'd never seen such an awkward-looking teenager before." Nonetheless, he agreed to audition her, and as she strummed on her brother's guitar, the audience stopped talking and turned to listen. When she'd finished, the applause was encouraging; so much so, she was offered a job at 17s 6d a night. Mary O'Brien was in showbusiness. As time passed, the pair sang and played their way through 100 songs a night, often in despair when some audiences appeared uninterested in their material, particularly when Dusty was performing a plaintive Neapolitan song. "Maybe I should have sung to sad Neopolitans!" she later laughed. Through tears of frustration one night, she sobbed to her mother that she was quitting singing. Kay agreed, saying perhaps she wasn't cut out for the job after all. Dusty believed her and got a job – albeit short-lived – demonstrating toy trains in a department store. One day she fused the entire lighting system while showing the workings of an electric train to a young customer whom it later transpired had no money to buy the train anyway!

Working in the department store was one of several jobs through which Dusty breezed while considering her future. By now her brother was making inroads on the club circuit and encouraged Dusty to do the same. Deciding to give singing another try, one of her first engagements was in the smart Belgravia supper club, The Montrose. Sylvia Jones, who owned the club, told the *Mirror*'s Anton Antonowicz she had to obtain Dusty's parents' permission to allow her to perform, adding, "She was terribly young, but extremely good. Of course, she didn't have the black eyes and the beehive then. She was 16, self-possessed and had lovely auburn hair. With Tom, she'd play at debutante parties in Eaton Square, for example, which she loathed because although the mothers were friendly, the daughters were vile!" Dusty's memory of being supported by her parents at this stage in her life was confused, but it is evident that they did support her, particularly her father, who, after travelling home from work in the rush hour, would journey back from Ealing into central London to dig his daughter out of a drinking club where she was being paid one guinea for a four-hour performance.

While new British acts struggled for record sales in mainstream music, others without recording contracts remained at the heart of the business, working night after night in club and theatre land. Of the many acts in this category were Riss Chantelle and Lynne Abrams, known as The Lana Sisters, a duo formed in 1958. With their tulle skirts, held together by a drawstring that was whisked away to reveal lamé pants, this attractive couple performed a diluted but cheerful brand of British rock 'n' roll on the theatre circuit. In time, they decided to revamp their act by adding a third member who would not only add another vocal dimension but round off the line-up on stage. Riss placed an advertisement in *The Stage* and from the numerous replies they chose Dusty who, at the time, said she was performing in a bar in Victoria in the evenings while working part-time during the day at Bentalls department store on Ealing Broadway "doing something with dustbins".

The extended Lana Sisters rehearsed in the mornings in an old Metropolitan theatre along London's busy Edgware Road, and it was here that the young Dusty learned her craft, practising close harmonies in the style of The Chordettes and The Beverley Sisters but not, as it transpired, as successfully. While instructing her eager 18-year-old protégé on showbusiness etiquette, Riss omitted to mention some of the pitfalls of working in a theatre. Subsequently, Dusty stumbled from one incident to another, breaking years-old theatre traditions as she went – like whistling in the dressing room, regarded as being disastrously unlucky. To break the spell the offender had to go outside the door, turn round three times and swear! Dusty refused to do this, dismissing the tradition as rubbish. She later tripped and tumbled down a narrow staircase on her way to the stage, splitting her tight, pale blue, lamé trousers. With her knee hanging out of the material, Riss dragged her on stage in time for the opening bars of their performance. Riss said, "She ruined the act, and that particular promoter gave us no more bookings."

Dusty's comedy of errors would continue to plague The Lana Sisters even after she'd left them to join her brother's group The Springfields. The two groups were appearing on the same bill and, just as Riss announced their second number, there was a dreadful clatter of cups and saucers backstage. Dusty had been walking behind the backcloth with a tin tray full of crockery which she accidentally dropped, sending cups rolling across the stage.

Evelyn Taylor part-managed The Lana Sisters and fully-managed the emerging British star Adam Faith who made his debut hit with "What Do You Want" in 1959, singing in his distinctive, shaky voice. Working in an office run by Joe Collins (father to Joan and Jackie), which Dusty remembered as being a sleazy little place where the main business appeared to be booking dates at US airbases – of which the trio did their fair share. Dusty's first appearance as a Lana Sister was at the Savoy Cinema in Clacton, where they wore blue silver lamé Capri pants with tulle skirts over them. From then on they performed where they could – supporting acts like Nat "King" Cole, Tommy Steele and, of course, Adam Faith, appearing twice at the Royal Albert Hall's Festival of Music, touring Ireland, and performing free at countless charity functions.

Among the few vocal groups to top the British singles chart in the 1950s were The Stargazers and The Johnston Brothers, and both achieved this before the culture shock of the devil's music – rock 'n' roll. During the mid-fifties, along with the new skiffle groups, The King Brothers were among Britain's leading bands, notching up eight Top 30 hits between 1957 and 1961. They were still hailed as one of the country's top groups when The Beatles crashed into the music business. Other vocal acts who enjoyed hits during the fifties included The Beverley Sisters, The Mudlarks, The Southlanders and The Kaye Sisters. Popular music fans were generally ignored by the BBC's radio programmes, which catered for the middle-aged, but by early 1960, programmes like *Saturday Club*, *Pick Of The Pops* and *Easy Beat* were scheduled to attract younger listeners. Thankfully, Radio Luxembourg revolutionized entertainment by broadcasting non-stop rock and pop music across the channel every evening, whereupon thousands listened to groundbreaking sounds on their tinny transistor radios, usually within the sanctity of their bedrooms. Television was a new medium when rock music hit Britain, but by 1957 *Cool For Cats* and Jack Good's *6.5 Special* became compulsory viewing for the youngsters. After leaving *6.5 Special*, Jack Good launched *Oh Boy* which ran until 1959, the same year that *Juke Box Jury* hit the small screen. Two years later, *Thank Your Lucky Stars* was the best of the bunch that included *The Billy Cotton Band Show* and *Sunday Night At The London Palladium*. However, it was *Ready, Steady, Go!* in 1963 that snatched the musical crown. These were the shows that Dusty watched, longing to be able to take her place in front of the studio cameras. She would not have long to wait.

The Lana Sisters were briefly signed to Fontana, a subsidiary label of Philips Records (which, ironically, would be The Springfields' record company) where their 1958 debut single, "Chimes Of Arcady", was a version of the 1930s original by The Frank Luther Trio, and was an interesting insight into the Lanas' harmonizing skills. Another lightweight rocker, "Buzzin'", followed five weeks later, which they promoted on the *6.5 Special*, appearing along with Don Lang and his Frantic Five, and Joe Brown and the Bruvvers. Author Paul Howes noted that their third single "Tell Him No" carried "a slight Springfields' flavour", but despite appearances on television shows like BBC's *Drumbeat*, the single sold poorly. One that could so easily have given the ladies their first hit was "(Seven Little Girls) Sitting On The Back Seat" which Al Saxon released in October 1959. Unfortunately, they lost the sales battle against hit versions by Paul Evans and the Curls, and The Avons. Into the sixties, The Lana Sisters' "You've Got What It Takes" swapped their fragile rock for a Latin tempo, while "Someone Loves You, Joe" and "Two-Some" followed.

While Dusty was learning her trade, she had moved to London, her parents to Hove, and her brother had hooked up with Tim Feild (the odd spelling inherited from his American father) who was an old Etonian and world traveller, with a flair for music. After his demobilization from the navy, Feild had hitched his way across America, Europe and the Far East with only his guitar for company. Upon his return to Britain, he sang in clubs and entered a television talent show, *Bid For Fame*, losing in the semi-finals. He was later to meet and begin working with Tom, their musical ambitions based solely on what Feild called an "inborn feeling for harmony". The aspiring duo dragged their act through any club that would book them but, like The Lana Sisters before them, realized they would probably work better as a trio. And Tom knew just who to recruit.

With a year's experience behind her, Dusty was ready to move on. She admitted that she felt musically claustrophobic and was impatient to try other ideas. She wanted to offer suggestions about changing The Lana Sisters' material and stage presence, but held back because of her inexperience, adding "I was only 18 years old and my life was so busy, and in a way, so narrow." She could not, however, hide her restlessness from Riss and Lynne who, as early as 1960, noted their new recruit wasn't as enthusiastic as she once had been. They also came to the conclusion that Dusty's intention had always been to use them as a stepping stone on her way to a professional solo career.

Meanwhile, with her working life a whirlwind of commitments, Dusty realized that her teenage years were passing her by at an alarming rate. She had never dated; she had never had time to fool around with friends on a Saturday night, or even made excuses to her parents and stayed over with friends. She hadn't got drunk or lost her virginity. She lived her teenage life through others, and later mourned her lost years, saying "I look back and regret that I didn't have a silly youth. Sometimes I think there's something sick in not having those years of popcorn and fun." As an adult she did claw back some of her lost youth by throwing tantrums, playing tricks on her friends, and lobbing food at unsuspecting victims in restaurants or at her private parties, in much the same way as her mother had done years earlier. (The *Sunday Mirror*'s Dr Catherine Hood theorized that the attraction in throwing food around was not only that it was naughty and forbidden, but that it also raised adrenaline levels making a person feel more invigorated.)

Of course, Dusty could have changed her lifestyle by abandoning her singing ambitions to return to everyday life; but she didn't. Instead, she decided to press on until a successful solo career was within her grasp. What she lacked now was the courage and confidence on which ambitious people thrive, and all the time Mary O'Brien was lurking within as the shy, awkward, unattractive schoolgirl. A new identity was necessary, an alter ego who possessed all the qualities that the schoolgirl lacked but who, at the same time, was an extension of her own personality. The process was slow, but the effect was devastating.

In 1960, when readers of the *Melody Maker* music paper voted The Lana Sisters seventh Favourite British Vocal Group, Dusty's brother put a plan in place to include her in his future. The Lana Sisters were performing in Taunton and, as he and Tim Feild were singing nearby, he visited Dusty before showtime. They hadn't seen each other for some weeks but, as it was clear to her he was anxious and excited about something, they arranged to meet after the performance. The offer was exactly what she wanted – "two men and a girl would make a novel group" was her thinking. The remainder of the week at Taunton was a nightmare as she mulled over her future. On the one hand she was desperate to move on, but on the other was terrified of leaving the security of the trio. Each morning she'd rehearse with Tom and Tim in a nearby field, returning to the theatre in the evening in time to perform with Riss and Lynne. "I was so nervous about the whole thing, not only about the new group but leaving the sisters, that I could hardly sing at all. I felt awful about leaving them. I kept thinking that they thought I had only used them for experience. Maybe I had... Sometimes you have to let people down in order to get on... this was a lesson in life I had to learn, but I won't pretend it was easy."

From the outset, it was apparent that Dusty's voice would be the new trio's big selling point. But they needed a catchy name. Many stories have circulated in the media about the origin of the name The Springfields, and one of Dusty's favourites was that they were sitting in a field and it was spring! More likely, it was while they were looking at a map of North America, the birthplace of their favourite music, that they spotted several areas called Springfield. As for the name "Dusty", well, the singer also had great fun with this over the years, saying on one occasion that it was from "messing about with dustbins in Bentalls" and on another that it was a convent nickname. Years later, when pressed on the point, she insisted she was "still looking for the bugger who gave her the name."

The Lana Sisters went on to become The Chantelles, with Riss leading Jay Adams and Sandra Orr through a career that began with "I Want You" on EMI Records' Parlophone label in 1965. Three others followed – "Sticks And Stones", "Gonna Get Burned" and "I Think Of You". Switching to Polydor Records, "There's Something About You", a one-off 1966 release, was accepted as a fringe Northern Soul classic. A year later, CBS Records issued

"The Man I Love", with their final outing "Out Of My Mind" issued in America only under the name The Chantelles Of London, to avoid confusion with the US group of the same name. When the trio disbanded in the late sixties, Riss opened Chantelle Music and managed Nola York, singer, writer and one-time Chantelle.

With their plans more or less in place, The Springfields needed work, and because of their chosen style of music – a cross between The Kingston Trio and The Weavers – they had little choice but to hit the folk clubs. Their agent was Emlyn Griffiths, a Welshman with a monocle, who looked more like a British butler than a music agent. Pat Barnett, who was to become Dusty's personal secretary, worked for him after leaving Kavanaghs, the literary agents. She remembered he did little in the office, saying "He used to go out and have his pink gin and come back to sleep it off. So that left me to manage the office alone."

The Springfields were booked, sight unseen, into Butlins Holiday Camps, travelling for 16 weeks around the country in an old, and often unreliable, Volkswagen Camper. They covered 1,200 miles and earned £55 per week, out of which they paid their expenses and their agent's commission. Tim Feild told the *Sunday People* in 1963, "Just try travelling that far in that time with your dearest friend and see how dear that friend is to you at the end of it!" The holiday makers made large and noisy audiences, but Tom used them to iron out weaknesses and build on strengths in their routine so that when the red coat season ended, they were ready for the London stage at The Churchill Club in Mayfair. They performed there for 19 consecutive weeks and it left them utterly exhausted. Finishing at 4 am, they caught the all-night bus in Oxford Street back to Ealing Broadway, then walked the last mile home. Dusty later recalled dreary backstage conditions where hostesses sat chain-smoking night after night as they waited to be called to the tables; the grey-faced people who spent huge amounts on the evening's entertainment, and their cramped little dressing room.

From London's Mayfair, the trio switched to the variety theatres, often playing to half-full houses. This time they shared their dressing room with 30 people or more. Dusty said they were joined by five Czech tumblers, a magician with his doves, a Spanish dancer, a female fire-eater who used petrol, a teenage singing group, and a pianist and piano! She didn't know whether to laugh or cry! She also recalled this time in her life as one of misery and boredom; petty jealousies, tired jokes and hatred of the treatment afforded them by other artists. While lesser groups would have abandoned the business, The Springfields did the opposite – they worked harder to perfect their act. It paid off. As their popularity grew, so did their audience pulling power and it was this that prompted Philips Records' Johnny Franz to invite them for an informal audition in April 1961. The cockney producer, with a pencil slim moustache, was also head of A&R, possessing a unique talent for spotting potential recording artists. He had flexed his musical muscle playing piano in London clubs, had worked for the BBC after the Second World War and as Anne Shelton's pianist. He joined Philips Records in 1954, beginning a career that was to span 20 years and over 70 British hit singles. The Springfields sat on his desk, playing guitars and messing around with a version of "Dear John". "By the end of the first chorus it was obvious that here was a fresh, new sound which had a folksy quality," Franz said. "In no time at all we got them into the studio to record this title for their first single."

Telling the tale of soldier John Maguire's love exploits, the cheeky "Dear John", recorded at Philips' studios in Stanhope Place and released in April 1961, was a re-working of the American Civil War song "Marching Through Georgia". Advertised in the media "as recorded by Britain's most popular new singing group", promotional photos showed a short-haired Dusty, standing slightly behind and between Tom and Tim with her hands resting on their shoulders. The group looked strangely vulnerable with their clean-cut image. The single sold steadily but it wasn't enough to hit the charts. Instead, "Dear John" became a turntable hit although radio programmers were unsure how to categorize the musical style. In fact, during a BBC programme, Tom Springfield was told by its producer that he must decide whether they were a folk or a pop group because they could not be both and be successful. Dusty felt they lacked the class necessary for a folk group, but as yet hadn't developed a sufficient pop background to be a rock band. Successful folk groups were few, but The Springfields' happy-go-lucky attitude towards the music would, she hoped, help them create a more distinctive, recognizable sound that would attract mainstream record buyers. She was proven right.

Chapter Two

ISLAND OF DREAMS

"We'd had such fun being The Springfields, ever since that idyllic sunny day when it all began."

The sixties opened with a whisper rather than a scream with number one singles from two crooners Emile Ford ("What Do You Want To Make Those Eyes At Me For?") and Anthony Newley ("Why?"). More dynamic competition was on its way, however, from the new breed of rising stars like Craig Douglas, John Leyton and Billy Fury who, along with the already established Adam Faith and Cliff Richard, were to revitalize pop music. Female singers were rare, with only Shirley Bassey, Marion Ryan, Joan Regan and Anne Shelton making irregular chart inroads, but that was set to change.

American artists were no longer guaranteed British hits. Indeed, of the 40 or so singles which soared into the US Top Five, only seven achieved the same position in Britain. Six of them were chart-toppers on both sides of the Atlantic, namely Elvis Presley's "Are You Lonesome Tonight" and "Surrender", Del Shannon's "Runaway", The Highwaymen's "Michael Row The Boat", Bobby Vee's "Take Good Care Of My Baby" and The Marcels' "Blue Moon". Included in the singles that bombed in Britain were those by artists Dusty grew to love, like The Shirelles, Ben E King and The Marvelettes. Her unashamed passion for these and other soul acts would later be reflected in her own recordings when she happily acknowledged she "had swiped ideas left, right and centre".

The Marvelettes' US success spearheaded the first rumblings of a new, exciting sound from Detroit, Michigan, being created by a young, ambitious black man, Berry Gordy Jr. Known for its lucrative motor vehicle industry, Detroit would soon boast a new export – Motown Records. From humble beginnings, Gordy and his handful of staff forced the industry, and later the world, to accept a raw, earthy music which was to become lovingly known as The Sound Of Motown. Little did he realize that his shaky start in 1959 would not only introduce a distinctive multi-million selling trend that would successfully span 30 years, but also spawn many international artists as well – Martha and the Vandellas, Diana Ross, Marvin Gaye, Stevie Wonder, The Supremes, The Temptations and the Four Tops among them. Based on a simple beat, complemented by a handful of repetitive arrangements and verses against a tight, disciplined sound, Motown music would become recognizable from each song's opening bars thanks to the dedication and inspiration of the company's in-house musicians, the Funk Brothers. When The Marvelettes' "Please Mr Postman" was released in Britain on the Fontana label in November 1961, it failed to attract high-profile promotion, remaining a cult sound, alongside hundreds of other American R&B classics which, although released, didn't attract mainstream record buyers at this time.

As a member of The Springfields, singing cute folksy, country and western music, Dusty's love of Motown and R&B was all-consuming; she played the records relentlessly, digesting notes and phrases, memorizing the feel and emotion of the songs until the time arrived for her to record her own versions. Of all the Motown acts with which she later worked, Dusty enjoyed a lifelong special friendship Martha Reeves, who fronted the Vandellas. Meanwhile, she chirped away on lightweight songs, smiling as she did.

This was the musical environment into which The Springfields ventured when their name appeared on the Philips label. Recorded on 18 July 1961, and released ten days later, "Breakaway", the follow-up to "Dear John", was their first hit single. Written by Tom, the energetic, brisk song with a memorable chorus heralded the start of the trio's career in a minefield of heavy competition.

John Leyton's "Johnny Remember Me" had just replaced Shirley Bassey's "Reach For The Stars" at the top of the singles chart, and for the three folksy newcomers, the top 40 hit was an incredible achievement. Their third release, "Bambino", was chosen by Tom during a sun-drenched holiday on the Italian Riveria. An ancient Neopolitan children's carol ("Tu scendi della stella"), the sad song in waltz time, with lyrics re-written by Tom, was perfect for the 1961 Christmas market and easily shot into the top 20. The Springfields now meant serious business. "We were terribly cheerful," Dusty laughed. "We were also very loud and we jumped up and down a lot, and that seemed to impress people!" When not jumping about, they were frequently heard on the radio with regular slots on *Saturday Club* and *Easy Beat*, and on family entertainment television shows like *Thank Your Lucky Stars* and *The Benny Hill Show*. Only Dusty was experienced in the machinations of television, but even she now found it hard going. "Everything is rushed and we were never satisfied with our performance. My hair caused awful problems too. My natural red came out black and I looked as if I was wearing a giant busby!" Becoming a blonde solved the problem. As for Tom, who never liked performing before an audience, he admitted they used to fool around on the set and, quite regularly, mimed the wrong words to their songs. This was a blessing for Dusty, he quipped, because she never remembered the lyrics anyway! When miming on television was banned and performers sang live, Dusty struggled on, with her audiences willing her to get the lyrics right. When she didn't, they sang them for her.

Dusty quickly had to lose the feeling of being rushed and dissatisfied by television shows as she was about to be thrown into the whirlwind that was Association Rediffusion's *Ready, Steady, Go!* one of the most significant music programmes of the decade. Dusty met the show's editor Vicki Wickham on the pilot show in 1962 who said, "... We started being silly and chatting, and Dusty started playing me black music and we became friends." They were both gay but not lovers, and for a time they shared a flat in Westbourne

Grove, London. When Vicki left the programme in 1966, she moved to New York where she later worked with Marsha Hunt and Jimi Hendrix before managing Patti LaBelle and the Bluebelles, among others. Nona Hendryx, a member of Patti's group, became Vicki's partner. Vicki would also later manage Dusty. The pilot was successful, so the show was fully launched a year later, when Vicki wrote the scripts, booked the artists and acted as producer. Regular presenters were Cathy McGowan and Keith Fordyce, and Dusty was happy to contribute towards the general chaos that made the programme extra special to music fans.

The Springfields' various talents were one of their strongpoints. They not only sang but played guitars, banjos and conga drums, and were composers and arrangers. At a push they could sing in nine languages including Hebrew, Russian and Greek. And, of course, they had Dusty, who was emerging as a glamorous, powerful singer, but who, when the spotlights were turned off, had the less attractive job of being keeper of their instruments. She told DJ Roger Scott in 1989, "I was the one who sat on Crewe station guarding the guitars in case they got stolen, while the boys went and had sandwiches in the buffet." She was also responsible for their strange double-headed microphone which Tom had designed. On the other hand, the boys had to carry her stage clothes, which irritated Tim Feild beyond words. "She goes for the exotic creations which require at least 14 petticoats. And Dusty, in true grande dame fashion, flatly refused to transport her own clothes. Tom and I had to carry her petticoats in and out of theatres. A chore which roused my temper."

Dusty said "Yes, he did complain. He had this canvas bag contraption. It looked rather like those recovering pods from the ocean after a space shot. They were triangular and landed with a splash. I always used to think they looked just like my skirts bagged up. I was constantly saying 'don't drag them on the floor'."

Tim came from a wealthy family and was used to a household that included a chauffeur and servants. So, he was taken aback by some of the antics Dusty and Tom got up to, and cited the following,

"On a journey (they) were quite happy to pull into a transport café for a plate of steak and kidney pudding. I had been used to – and preferred – something a little more elaborate."

Journalists speculated about a possible relationship between Tim and Dusty, but to no avail. Tim was married and Dusty was gay, although at this time the media suspected nothing. However, top London DJ Norman Scott recalled the first time he'd met Dusty as a Springfield. He was waiting outside the theatre's stage door with other fans following their performance. "It stuck in my mind as the two guys were screaming from their dressing room – 'Dusty's a lesbian! Dusty's a lesbian!' which she appeared to take in good humour. This was the first time I'd thought about her being gay and thought it was really a strange way for the guys to behave. Especially in front of us fans." When the media later discovered Dusty's sexuality, unlike her performing partners, they kept her secret.

With two consecutive hits to their credit and being voted Britain's top group in the weekly music papers *New Musical Express* and *Melody Maker*, The Springfields were disappointed when their fourth outing "Goodnight Irene" in February 1962 bombed. It was, perhaps, not a wise choice because it was a cacophony of muddled music which one reviewer claimed "sounded like a back street market in Cairo." A month later their first album *Kinda Folksy* was released and, with no hit to ride on, potential sales were lost. Those listeners who did buy it enjoyed genuine folk songs like the beautiful, warm, whispery harmonizing on "Two Brothers" and "The Green Leaves Of Summer" or the tongue-in-cheek "They Took John Away This Morning", where a twangy-vocalled Dusty teased and weaved through the melody. The O'Brien siblings' love of the complicated vocals and excitable musicianship of Latin American material shone loudly and frenetically through tracks like "Tzena Tzena Tzena", while the singalong, melodic "The Black Hills Of Dakota" returned the pace to normal. "The album is energetic, tuneful, imaginative" one critic glowed, while another wrote "... they belt through a song with all the lusty enthusiasm and spirit necessary to hold the listener's attention and approval." Also this year, the trio embarked upon their first major tour, as support act to Bobby Vee.

In April 1962, their version of the folk song "Silver Threads And Golden Needles" was another poor seller but, when issued in America by Mercury Records, it hit the top 20 in September, selling one million copies on the way and earning them the distinction of being the first British sixties' group to crash into the American chart. It was also an unexpected hit in other countries, including Australia where it soared to the top of the charts. "It's surprising how an American hit can set the wheels turning," Tom Springfield said. "People have been very good to us in Britain and we've got on tremendously since we started. But these US offers have started coming in like a whirlwind..."

When Mercury Records' Shelby Singleton heard the single he issued an immediate invitation for them to record in Nashville, but that wasn't possible due to their commitments on the home front. Dusty had also been in hospital, suffering from acute throat strain, resulting from, she said, the way she produced her voice to fit in with the group's vocal styling. "Seems I do everything all wrong when it comes to singing. Experts have told me that I'm straining this and fracturing that, but I can't help it ... If I tried to do it all the right way round, I'd probably end up sounding like some coloratura soprano." She was fit enough to perform at The Pavilion Theatre in Weymouth, although four shows were later cancelled because Tim Feild had a stomach illness.

For their next outing, Tom chose "Swahili Papa", recorded at Philips' Stanhope Place studio. Released in August 1962, it was a novelty, with a cheeky lyric over an African war chant, including a "whoops" from Dusty which she hated. So did the public. And it was the last recording to feature Tim Feild, who had decided to leave the line-up due to his wife's ill health, although he later admitted artistic differences was the real reason. He never shared the O'Brien siblings' driving ambition and disliked the bickering within the group. "We'd row over this, row over how a song should be sung, what engagements should be accepted and innumerable other details of the act. Finally, I decided to chuck it all in."

Feild's successor, Mike Longhurst-Pickworth, later known as Mike Hurst, was quietly spoken, tall and slim, and, with his clean image, he was the perfect replacement. "I had known Tom for some time and we moved roughly in the same circles. We both played guitars and both went to the same parties. As our paths crossed we struck up a friendship. But he was the professional entertainer and I worked in insurance!" Nonetheless, he was asked to audition in Coventry where The Springfields were appearing. "I was a Springfield before I knew it." In fact, it was some time before the public realized that Tim had been replaced.

It was December 1962 when the trio made the trip to Nashville to record, and Dusty wasn't sure who got the worse shock, her or the studio musicians. "It was a disastrous experience for us. They didn't realize it took us three weeks to rehearse one verse (at home). In Nashville, they'd write a song in the morning and we'd go in and start recording it in the afternoon!" Tom believed they acted and sounded like characters from *The Beverly Hillbillies*, while Dusty felt they were out of their depth, adding "Here we are in Tennessee singing country music that the people there were born to ... we had to work out every note." As if that wasn't bad enough, she developed laryngitis. "It wasn't a particularly happy experience!"

Despite the traumas of their recording sessions, Dusty found other consolations in America. Their recording commitments fulfilled, they hit New York with the idea of grabbing quality relaxation time. Dusty said, "The first thing I did was put on the TV because I'd heard they had all-night TV. Then Tom, Mike and I went down Broadway and ate shortcake. We finally got to bed at seven, and at nine I was awake to watch one of my favourite programmes with a hand puppet called Lamb Chop."

They then headed for Carnegie Hall to see Earl Scruggs where, Tom in particular, raved over the popularity of Blue Grass music. His sister, meantime, sucked in R&B in its purest form. "I remember walking through Times Square, where all the record shops were, and the music was blaring out. There were records like "Tell Him" from The Exciters, which we had never been exposed to in England. We were still with Patti Page and Theresa Brewer, both fine singers, but not exactly my cup of tea… And this to me, being a little white, convent-educated Irish teenager, was an amazing thing." The Exciters' single was particularly important to Dusty because she could approximate the voices – something not done in British studios – while the actual excitement of the song's "feel" left her breathless. More importantly, it would change the way she treated music. She also became acquainted with Dionne Warwick's "Don't Make Me Over", an overwhelming experience as she recalled – "I actually had to sit down because it was different to anything I'd ever heard before." The two singers would eventually cross paths and establish a great friendly rivalry.

"Island Of Dreams", another traditional Irish number where Dusty enjoyed a solo spot, sung this time with a slight American twang, was released as a single in November 1962. It was the first to feature Mike Hurst. When they returned to London, the single had dropped from the chart. That was a mere hiccup because The Springfields' promotional machine was quickly cranked up, including television spots where, during one performance, Dusty was clearly agitated by novice Mike Hurst who was happily singing to the camera lense. She tried to make eye contact with him several times, before moving sideways towards Tom. One hazards a guess that he was either standing on her foot or prodding her with his guitar! They also promoted the single nightly on the Del Shannon tour, whereupon it took on a renewed lease of life. The song wasn't one of Dusty's favourites – "I wince every time I hear it. I loved the song but didn't think we did it justice. I had a sore throat when we recorded it and I knew I sang out of tune. I don't want to sound ungrateful to everyone who bought it, but I never thought it was any good at all." Bum notes or not, the single had chart-topping potential in Britain, but unfortunately Elvis Presley and "Return to Sender" pushed it down the rankings. The Springfields, however, weren't disappointed – they had their first top five hit.

Recorded at the same session as "Island Of Dreams" was a track scheduled for March 1963 release. Titled "Little Boat", and written by Tom and Clive Westlake, it was featured in the film *Just For Fun*. Advertised as "a big teen musical" with Mark Wynter, Bobby Vee, Ketty Lester, The Crickets and Freddie Cannon, among its list of artists, the film was the follow-up to *It's Trad Dad*. The Springfields made a cameo appearance, singing the song which was initially the flipside to their March 1963 single "Say I Won't Be There", and later included on *The Springfields' Story* double album in March 1964.

Before long, groups like The Springfields were being challenged by the mighty musical force that would revolutionize modern music – The Beatles. Spearheading what was to become The Merseyside Invasion, the quartet began making their presence felt in 1963 with "From Me To You", the first in a raft of multi-million selling singles. In London, The Rolling Stones heralded a boom in British R&B that included likeminded groups such as The Animals from Manchester, and Spencer Davis from Birmingham. British artists were taking over, although many still relied heavily on American music. For the time being though, The Springfields decided to take the challenge by sticking to their winning formula with "Say I Won't Be There". It was one of several Tom had penned pre-Springfields and was adapted from the traditional French song "Au Claire De La Lune". His initial attempts to get it published were rejected. He said "It's slightly different from the version I first wrote but I changed the lyrics after we decided to take it out of storage." Once again, Dusty was prominently featured, and it was their second single to soar into the Top Five. The Springfields promoted the song across the media, including Alan Freeman's *Here Comes The Girls* television show, where the trio was featured in a mock recording session. One memorable moment was that of Dusty standing on a pile of telephone directories to enable her to reach the microphone! Dusty had first met Alan Freeman when The Lana Sisters were performing in a Midlands club. He was part of the touring show with organist Cherry Wainer. This particular night the organ had broken down and, with no act prepared, Freeman was forced to keep the audience entertained. He delivered a stream of gibberish until a replacement organ was brought to the stage. A relieved Freeman raced off and bumped headlong into Dusty. She asked if he was hungry and shared her chips with him. The two remained buddies and when Alan became top BBC DJ "Fluff" Freeman he regularly played her material.

The album *Folk Songs From The Hills* was released in April 1963. Arranged by Bill Justis, it featured Neal Matthews from The Jordonaires and was, one critic raved, "an absolute knockout. The threesome attack these songs with a vigorous spirit and enjoyment." One of the most commercial tracks was the album's opener "Settle Down" where Dusty led the catchy melody. A cover version of Faron Young's 1958 original "Alone With You" features a sax break, a first in their recordings, while the appealing "Cottonfields (The Cotton Song)" was later covered by The Beach Boys, and "Foggy Mountain Top", featuring a scratchy violin arrangement, highlighted Dusty and Tom's shared vocals. Happily for all, *Folk Songs From The Hills* was a well-balanced, extremely enjoyable release. Meanwhile, the entertainment world continued to fete them. So far they had starred in their own BBC TV music specials where Dusty was hostess. They combined her solo spots with group songs, but failed to show the fun side of their personalities. Her stage-wear had changed; she had abandoned her bright coloured, stiff-petticoated skirts for hip-hugging outfits. Her hair was more maturely styled, often loose-waved, and she began wearing sunglasses. Slowly, she was detaching herself from the guys, establishing her own identity. Dusty was getting bored, she wanted to move on.

Although her record sales had slumped in Britain in recent months, Connie Francis headlined the Scottish Royal Variety Show in July 1963. The Springfields were also on the star-studded bill and it was a timely performance to promote "Come On Home", released that month. It was the last hit from the extraordinary "folk trio" that never really was a folk trio. Following his instincts, Tom decided to move from commercial country music into a form of R&B which he considered suitable for the British public. "We've got our usual row on disc but this one's a little more split up into odd bits. For instance, instead of getting the middle eight, Dusty comes in all over the place. I play a 12-string guitar for the intro and Mike gets a guitar solo… People will say it's not us, but it is." His complacent attitude misread the fickleness of their fans because the single stalled at number 31 after a six-week stay in the chart. However, it did show for the first time the gritty edge to Dusty's voice, a taster of what was to come, although it was a singing style that would eventually ruin her voice.

While the punchy "Come On Home" battled for chart places, The Springfields were finalizing their plans to disband – a move they had planned for some time. Dusty claimed she had already signed a solo deal with Philips Records and had started recording, although there is no documentary evidence to support this. Tom, on the other hand, was experimenting with other acts. When the news broke, the producers of *Sunday Night At The London Palladium* booked them on 6 October 1963 for their final televised perform-ance together. Dusty agreed on the condition their last song was "So Long, It's Been Good To Know You". Tom disagreed, feeling it was too corny. After much haggling, his sister won. What Dusty didn't expect was her lack of control while singing the song before the Palladium audience. "In the middle of the song I started to cry. I remember Tom throwing me a look of complete amazement as I sniffed beside him. I knew what he was thinking, that I was weep-ing on purpose as a good piece of stagecraft." It wasn't; she was crying from fright. "I was scared of the way ahead, the way alone." Once the curtain hit the stage at the end of the performance, she broke down completely, crying "We'd had such fun being The Springfields ever since that idyllic sunny day when it all began."

Ex-Springfield Tim Feild wasn't surprised to hear the news. "I guessed (they) would be breaking up ten months ago, when I left... the truth of the matter is that I reckon (they've) reached the stage where they, like everyone who lives in close contact, are getting on each other's nerves... It happened to me. That's why I got out, even though at times we had lots of fun." In 1967, Mike Hurst told a *Disc & Music Echo* journalist that while a member of the trio he went mad "and spent every penny I had. I was broke for two years afterwards and I was petrified. I never want to go through that again." With business partner, Chris Brough, he opened a production company, was taught music production by Jim Economedies, and went on to manage Cat Stevens.

At the time of the break-up The Springfields were the top British vocal group of the pre-Beatle era, earning £1,200 a week. Dusty said "Everyone tells us we're mad. Well, we've always been mad. It's a big chance and we're taking it. It's better to gamble while we're at the top, rather than when we're on the way down." Tom added "We saw The Beatles coming and we weren't rock 'n' roll. Our group had gone about as far as it could. We were also quite fed up with each other. So it was the time to pursue solo careers."

Naturally, Dusty, with her burning solo ambitions, was blamed for the group break-up. She made no secret of the fact that she was tired of their happy, lively outlook and the cheery songs which meant little to her. Instead, she wanted to embrace black soul music, to emulate her Motown idols, and record her own music, so she let the rumours run their course. Besides, she had other things on her mind, like being voted eighth Top British Female Singer in *Melody Maker* readers' poll while still a member of The Springfields. "I have no regrets. Now is the time to look forward, not back. Even if we were asked to get together for some very special engagement I doubt if we would. Our decision is quite irrevocable."

Dusty had £100 in her bank account and several white shirts. Within two years her clothes were designed by Darnells of London, and she was feted as Britain's new singing sensation.

Chapter Three

WISHIN' & HOPIN'

"In all modesty, I am the only Dusty Springfield!"

With her lightly mascaraed eyes, discreet bouffant with curls teased behind each ear, pink lipstick and a pale complexion, Dusty Springfield was in demand – everyone wanted a piece of Britain's newest rising star. The instant fame, however enjoyable to her ego, exhausted the person. The more her alter ego was publicly exposed, the further Mary O'Brien slipped into the background to protect her growing fragility. Almost overnight, Dusty's life had been turned upside down, and there was still so much for her to learn about the business – and herself. Nobody had prepared her for the media's assault on her life. At first she laughed at the misquotes and fabricated incidents, but when the press began squeezing the very life out of her, she rebelled. In the meantime, she protected the Dusty Springfield image by being everyone's darling. "I was very sheltered and suddenly I was taken out to these little clubs off Sloane Street. I didn't know what people were talking about and I didn't know anything about the food they were serving. I was raised on potatoes. So I developed this front so they wouldn't know. Because if they knew the real me, they wouldn't like me."

For her first solo recordings Dusty intended to re-create the sounds that haunted her while keeping a commercial slant to convince record buyers she was a saleable commodity. Striving to achieve the American style, she became frustrated by the inability of studio musicians to reproduce the sound she wanted. Black musicians had the ability to feel and "emotionalize" their music, while the British tended to rely on a slap-on effect that was razor-edged rather than rounded, or a harsh sound instead of a lingering smoothness. Dusty persevered, pleaded with her musicians and, for the first time, began to doubt the viability of her solo career. Happily, for her fans, she gritted her teeth and trusted her soul.

Dusty seriously considered recording her version of Barrett Strong's hit "Money (That's What I Want)" composed by Motown boss, Berry Gordy Jr, and first released in March 1960. She may have changed her mind when The Beatles cut the song for their first album, knowing, however good she believed her own version to be, that she couldn't compete against their rapidly escalating popularity. Burt Bacharach and Hal David's "Wishin' & Hopin'" was another choice. This composing/producing duo played a major role in styling mainstream music during the sixties, and Bacharach in particular was responsible for revolutionizing the actual composition of a song, with his artistry apparent in every note. At this time he was working with Dionne Warwick and "Wishin' & Hopin'" was the B-side to her "This Empty Place". Dusty admitted she had chosen the single's flipside because "This Empty Place" was beyond her! She was also heavily into Phil Spector's "Wall Of Sound" productions, which provided the magnificent musical backdrops on tracks by The Crystals, The Ronettes and Tina Turner, among others. It was a combination of this and her beloved soul music that she prayed she could reproduce in London's Olympic Sound Studios. And she very nearly made it with "I Only Want To Be With You". The song was produced by Johnny Franz and written by Ivor Raymonde (who had worked with The Springfields and was now her musical director) with Mike Hawker, lyricist for Helen Shapiro. There was only one possible criticism – her voice was practically buried by the music, and this would continue to irritate her public in some later releases. ("I Wish I'd Never Loved You" in 1964 or "Your Hurtin' Kinda Love" a year later, are good examples). Nevertheless, "I Only Want To Be With You" was a superb solo debut, released on 8 November 1963, less than five weeks after The Springfields' performance at The London

Palladium. Carrying the fullness of a synthetic gospel punch with an indelible hookline, and support vocals from Mike Hawker's wife Jean Ryder, it was awash with movement and raced into the British chart to peak at number four passing silver status on the way.

Prior to its release, the singer was tormented by huge bouts of anxiety, noting "I suffered agonies of doubt. I didn't think I had the right image and I didn't think I had the face of a pop singer. I waited in agony for six weeks, hardly daring to appear in public in case people asked me about the record. I just didn't want to talk about it." By her very nature, Dusty ignored the good reviews to mull over less flattering ones, which moaned her voice was submerged in the music and blamed her for the distortion. She immediately defended her work, saying that nobody in Britain had yet been able to catch the Phil Spector sound – where one microphone is placed in the middle of a studio, with the musicians, backing singers and lead vocalists playing into it – but she had tried, adding she had actually spoken to Spector who loved the single's sound. "We talked for a long time. He said he thought [it] would do well in the States because it had a good 'white' sound. He knows; he's heard the real thing, and he said there was always room for good white sounds in America."

The single's flipside, "Once Upon A Time", also carried the Spector flavour, but more interestingly it was her second composition. (The first was "Something Special", the B-side of her second single.) Lack of concentration was the reason she gave for not pursuing songwriting; she would start a song from a melody that bugged her or from a phrase she liked, by plucking away on her guitar which, she said, was rather a haphazard way of working but was the only method she knew. "It just doesn't flow that easily though. I just wish I was one of those people who got inspirations in the back of a car, or travelling on a train. But I'm not." As her voice spread across the world, she was inundated by composers wanting her to record their material. The only downside, of course, was that somebody else got the composer's royalties!

To ensure "I Only Want To Be With You" charted, Dusty was put to work by her personally chosen manager, Vic Billings. In a way, they learned their trade together after first meeting when he worked for Tito Burns, one of The Springfields' agents. He was a novice in managerial skills but worked his way through the system until he opened an office in London's South Molton Street. By 1963 he was an established manager with clients who included new singing idol Eden Kane. To be fair, Dusty had already laid some ground work around the release of the single by performing for British troops stationed in West Germany, and co-hosting the 4 October 1963 edition of *Ready, Steady, Go!* By coincidence, it was The Beatles' first appearance on the programme and during Dusty's interview with them, John Lennon made her blush.

"Is it true that when you were a kid you were shot for stealing apples?" Dusty asked him. "Yeh," he replied.

Pointing to the side of his face, she said "Is that what these beautiful marks are?"

"No," answered John, "They're scabs!"

Backing off, Dusty quickly added "There's nothing there at all really..." but John immediately joked back, "Let me see your scabs!" with the other Beatles egging him on. Dusty made a hasty retreat.

She later said, "... I'm not a natural interviewer but I just sort of hid behind my beehive and read things off little cards. Actually, I much prefer singing to interviewing but it was a nice way to fill in three weeks between the end of The Springfields and the time my first record was out."

When the single hit the shops, Dusty was on the road, touring the country with Freddie and the Dreamers, Dave Berry, Brian Poole and the Tremeloes, and The Searchers. Tito Burns asked Fred Perry to be Dusty's lighting and stage manager. They first met briefly when she was a Lana Sister, and later when he was working with Frank Ifield and she was with The Springfields. By this time Dusty was a blonde and Fred failed immediately to recognize her. "Dusty was very glamorous with her hair teased within an inch of its life!" he recalled. They met again in Jaegers, a small café in London's Bond Street; Dusty, wearing a turban and a genuine snakeskin coat, bantered with him awhile before giving him the job – and paying 3s 3d for his cheese salad lunch. He stayed with her for 25 years as her lighting and stage designer.

Opening in Halifax, Dusty was forced to use Dave Berry's Crusaders as her backing group. They performed admirably with him, of course, but were unsuited to working with her. She went "ballistic"; it was her debut solo tour, her future rode on this and she was hampered by not having a dedicated backing band, resulting in what she regarded as an abysmal performance. It was, incidentally, during this tour that Fred Perry coined the phrase "the woman wants to make an album every time she steps on stage." Maybe Dusty had a point this time! It was a one-off lesson learnt, Dusty took matters into her own hands and hired her own group, The Echoes. An established group, The Echoes had toured Britain supporting named acts like Gene Vincent and, thanks to group member Doug Reece's mum who spotted Dusty's advertisement for a backing group, they contacted the singer. She gave them some Ray Charles' material to play and, out of the several bands she auditioned, The Echoes got the job, beginning a journey many musicians would sorely envy.

As her public appearances intensified to cover radio and television, Dusty felt the strain of being without Tom and Mike. There was nobody to bounce ideas off, to support her, or even to carry her clothes. It was lonely being alone. She had always suffered from stage fright and that was, she said, now magnified, as she flashbacked to her first solo performance at The London Palladium. While waiting in the wings to go on stage, a lock of hair fell across her forehead. She asked a nearby make-up artist for some lacquer, took the offered spray can with a hand that shook uncontrollably, squirting sprays of sticky lacquer all over the place. "I realized this was no ordinary stage fright, it was a feeling of… they're waiting for the big mistake." In time, her stage fright would become manageable, but it never disappeared entirely. On the upside, however, singing "I Only Want To Be With You" she was the very first solo artist to be featured on BBC TV's brand new music show *Top Of The Pops* on 1 January 1964, broadcast live from their Northern Studios in a converted church in Manchester. Until the Musicians Union banned it in 1966, artists mimed to their singles; in fact, the show's hosting DJ was clearly seen placing the stylus on the disc as the act was introduced. The single burst into the American Top 20, earning her the distinction of being the second British artist to do so after The Beatles. Dusty said "I was very lucky. I had no trouble establishing myself as a solo artist because, unlike so many groups, The Springfields broke up while we were still immensely popular. And my solo career came hard on the heels of the break up."

Alongside Fred Perry, Dusty also relied on Pat Barnett who had worked for The Springfields' agent Emlyn Griffiths. "Dusty asked me to work for her when she went solo. I never expected her to remember that, but she did. It was a 24/7 job and lasted nearly 40 years. But I never regretted one second... even though it involved buying eyelashes, tights ... doing anything and everything. Going to programmes with her to make sure she was looked after. You really needed another woman around for things like helping her dress. So I was a personal assistant really, not strictly secretarial." Pat travelled around Britain with the singer and in between times operated her fan club from her apartment in Hornsey, London.

While "I Only Want To Be With You" ruled the airwaves, The Springfields were seen making a cameo appearance singing "Maracabamba" and "If I Was Down And Out" in the British lightweight music movie *It's All Over Town*. They shared the billing with artists like The Hollies, Frankie Vaughan, The Bachelors and Clodagh Rogers. When The Springfields' contribution was released as a single, Dusty's publicist, Keith Goodwin, who had worked with the trio, quipped the single posed a potential problem, explaining "Dusty's high in the charts and if (The Springfields') record gets plugged, she could easily find herself fighting herself!" The situation didn't arise because the Springfields' single was definitely down and out – and gone. Not so "I Only Want To Be With You", which grew legs. During November 1987 it was the musical backdrop for the Britvic 55 television advertisement which also featured the singer herself. And cover versions were rife, including hits by The Bay City Rollers in 1976 and The Tourists, with lead singer Annie Lennox, three years later. Ex-page 3 model Samantha Fox also recorded the song during the eighties which peaked in the British Top 20. These re-recordings prompted Dusty to say she wished she'd composed "the bloody thing".

While Dusty looked down on audiences from the cinema screen, she kept her feet firmly on the ground by keeping a watchful eye on the immediate competition like Cilla Black and Kathy Kirby. Enjoying one hit so far with "Love Of The Loved", Cilla was destined to have a string of hit singles throughout the sixties, including a British chart topper that Dusty should have had. Meantime, Kathy Kirby was on her second hit "Secret Love" which, like Dusty's debut, peaked at number four.

Before 1963 closed, Dusty performed in Dublin and Belfast before treating herself to a trip to Paris to see Motown artist Little Stevie Wonder perform at the Olympia Theatre. She then spent Christmas with her parents in their Sussex home. In 1964, the workaholic singer continued to fulfil British dates but took time out for herself to see Phil Spector's group, The Ronettes, at the Granada Theatre in Harrow on their opening night as support act to The Rolling Stones. She then recorded her second single, before travelling to Holland to perform on the television show *Ontmoetingen met Russ*, but due to her sore throat she limited her performance to miming two songs. Her poor health had been exacerbated when, on the way to London airport, her minicab was involved in an accident, which had left her badly shaken up. A bad bout of flu and nervous exhaustion followed, leading to recording sessions being postponed, and dates in Liverpool, Lowestoft and Blackburn cancelled. It was clear that the strain of her heavy work schedules was taking its toll. As she said at the time, "I was completely rundown. I was so fatigued that I was able to catch anything, and I did. I don't like backing out of work, especially when fans are expecting to see me, but I'm afraid it had to be done. I'll have to learn to take things at a less hectic pace in future."

Dusty's earning power had, of course, increased enormously since The Springfields. As their expenses were usually so high, Dusty hadn't earned what she called "real money". Now that had changed dramatically. From the initial world sales of her first single alone she had earned £20,000, and when she toured her fee was £1,500 a week. This was, of course, offset against the unpaid time she spent promoting her career; still, she grinned, "That's better than splitting it three ways!"

In early February 1964 she had recovered sufficiently to appear at a charity gala staged at The Royal Albert Hall with The Rolling Stones, the Swinging Blue Jeans, and Brian Poole and the Tremeloes, before supporting the release of her second single "Stay Awhile" with a handful of one-night performances. Again penned by the Raymonde/Hawker team, it was a hasty choice but a pretty safe sound with its dual tracking over a plethora of overpowering orchestration. The mood was muddled. "The business of finding records is tricky," Dusty told journalists. "One of my weaknesses has always been that I don't have the courage of my convictions. If I think something is right for me and everyone else says I'm wrong, I end up with their line of thought." She did admit that the single's release was too rushed, particularly as "I Only Want To Be With You" was still in the chart, but she'd had no choice. "If the record had been delayed I'd have missed all those plugs like doing the Palladium TV show, and that's an ideal programme on which to introduce the new single. Artists like myself are dependant upon radio and TV exposure ... I want to fit in as many as I can before I go out on tour at the end of the month."

With a slightly larger beehive and a more liberal use of the spit mascara, Dusty hit the promotional trail, ultimately pushing the single to number 13. While it climbed, Dusty and Vic Billings flew to New York. "I didn't get a second to myself," she sighed. "The minute I got in my hotel room – pounce – business, agents, publishers. There was no time to get out." She did manage to escape to meet Burt Bacharach at his apartment. Apparently, he'd already heard tracks from her forthcoming debut album, including her workings of his compositions "Wishin' & Hopin'" and "Twenty Four Hours From Tulsa" which had delighted him, and thought she could be interested in other tracks. He played her the former Flamingos' member Tommy Hunt's version of "I Just Don't Know What To Do With Myself", released in May 1962. Dusty was mesmerized – "He sang it slowly and with a terrible sort of yearning," she recalled. "Suddenly I felt a lump in my throat." Sobbing, she ran into the bathroom to compose herself before re-applying her make-up and brushing her hair. Without thinking, she put Burt's hairbrush into her handbag, and only discovered it when she returned to her hotel. During her phoned apology he told her to keep it as a memento of their meeting.

On future trips, Dusty spent time with the quietly spoken composer, fuelling rumours they were lovers. When the media actually found the guts to print this, Dusty furiously retaliated – "Burt is a great talent and is one of the most attractive men in the business, but to say we were in love was just sheer nonsense." However, Pat Barnett believed if the timing had been better, Dusty would certainly have had a relationship with him.

Leaving Vic Billings to cement business deals for her future promotional visit, a tired but excited Dusty returned to London on the morning of her opening night at the Fairfield Halls, Croydon. Eden Kane was there to greet her at the theatre. And once again, the media speculated a relationship had grown from their six-month friendship, and their affectionate way of greeting each other. Eden Kane told reporters they dare not mention the word 'marriage'; that they enjoyed each other's company and saw each other when they could. Dusty also played the game by insisting to the *Daily Mirror* that, "he's the nicest boy I've met and I've taken him home to meet my parents." Yet, she told the *Daily Express*, "What really makes me sad about it is that people sneer and say 'oh, she needs the publicity.' It makes me feel so tatty. That's the trouble with this business."

Within two weeks she hit the headlines again, this time in a body hug with Dave Clark (drummer with the Dave Clark Five). They both denied they were lovers at the time to prevent rumours circulating. By August 1964, pictures of her kissing The Searchers' Frank Allen were splashed across pages in the music press. An obvious straightforward publicity shot to promote their tour, this was far from a private embrace as the other Searchers were pictured looking on.

Four days following her Croydon date, Dusty and the Echoes embarked upon a spring tour with The Searchers, Bobby Vee, Big Dee Irwin, taking in 29 dates, with twice-nightly shows, kicking off in Slough on 29 February and closing in Liverpool's Empire, where The Searchers' drummer Chris Curtis remembered Dusty was peeved with her road manager. He told *Record Collector*'s Spencer Leigh, "She rang up George Henry Lee's and asked for some cheap crockery and they sent it round to her dressing room at the Empire. One by one, she threw every piece of crockery down the corridor, and the road manager never did anything wrong again." Dusty recalled, "I was terrified audiences would be unsympathetic, but from the second I stepped on stage they were with me. The act went pretty well, but it was a bit nerve-racking, especially the opening night. I know I was raw as a solo artist but it was a great experience." Even at this early stage in her career, she admitted she didn't intend to sing pop songs for the rest of her life because her real ambitions lay in America. For the time being, though, she followed the advice of the people around her.

"I Only Want To Be With You" was also the title of her first EP (an extended play disc of four tracks) in early March, the same month as she left London for a 21-day tour of Australia and New Zealand with Gene Pitney, Brian Poole and the Tremeloes, and Gerry and the Pacemakers. "There were 6,000 fans waiting at Sydney airport, and 8,000 at Adelaide. They climbed fences, ran across fields, even got out on the tarmac. They rocked the bus laid on for us so much I thought it would overturn." The artists stayed at the Southern Cross Hotel in Melbourne which became besieged by over-enthusiastic fans. Dusty added "I went out for a stroll and got myself surrounded and ended up in the very wet fountain outside the hotel." Needless to say, the tour was a great success.

Once again, journalists tried to forge a relationship for Dusty, this time between her and the good-looking American singer Gene Pitney, but discovered Gene wouldn't play the game. "She wasn't my type," he told author David McGrath after her death. "Too much make-up, too much hair. I like (women) to be very natural. Dusty was over the top." As a performer, Gene was more upbeat about Dusty. "The fear and insecurity racked her body at every show I did with her. I felt so bad for her, but there was nothing to be done. Somehow, she would get over it and go out and do a show that was always a winner. I never saw her do a bad show." Dusty believed Gene to be an overwhelming neurotic, and confessed she did him a great disservice in New Zealand, when he was on stage. She nipped into the lighting booth when the engineer turned his back, and turned the green spot onto Gene. She then left the booth, locking the door behind her. Gene Pitney finished the remainder of his act, lasting 20 minutes, resembling the Incredible Hulk!

By the end of the tour, Dusty had been given enough woolly koala bears to start a zoo and among her personal purchases were three kangaroo skins which she intended having made into a fur coat. There was, she noted, a bullet hole right in the middle of one. "I'm leaving it in, it'll be right in the middle of my back. I shall call it my 'James Bond Model'!" Her excess baggage cost a fortune.

She then flew to Honolulu for a short holiday, where she said the music inspired her so much that she wanted to record an album featuring Hawaiian or Maori melodies against English lyrics. It was an idea that failed to materialize. From her paradise island, she flew to Los Angeles as part of a 16-date tour that included performing on Dick Clark's American Bandstand, before flying to New York for a spot on the prestigious Ed Sullivan Show. The entertainment programme was televised each Sunday and artists fought to bask in its high profile. Actually, Dusty nearly didn't appear because, under the American Labour Department's exchange agreement with Britain, Dusty wasn't considered "famous" enough to appear. In typical fashion she fired back, "In all modesty, I am the only Dusty Springfield!" She used the spot to promote her first two singles. Among the many acts on his show, Ed Sullivan will probably be most remembered for the young, gyrating Elvis Presley, when the studio cameras were forced to concentrate on his face and upper torso only. And for introducing The Beatles to America. While in New York she intended to record with Burt Bacharach, but that fell through, so she spent time listening to his unreleased material. "I was falling off my stool in ecstasy," she enthused to *Melody Maker's* Bob Dawbarn. "He gave me four nice songs and now I'm thoroughly concussed. For once I've got too much good material." She also saw Peggy Lee perform at New York's Americana, where she sat in awe in the packed audience, lapping up every note her idol sang.

Dusty had travelled 50,000 miles by the time she returned to London, where her immediate concern was to promote her first solo album. Titled "A Girl Called Dusty", the cover showed her dressed in a denim shirt and jeans against a blue backdrop. Her image was casual, and deliberately aimed at the young buying market. Her two singles had raised doubts about her range of material but the album completely dispelled those, as it attracted both soul fans and mainstream record buyers. The cross worked perfectly; the album was a credit to her, and deserved its Top Six placing in the chart. No singles or B-sides were included, but she chose wisely from her R&B and Motown collection, selecting Lee Dorsey's bouncy "Do Re Mi", The Supremes' raw-sounding "When The Lovelight Starts Shining Through His Eyes", the syncopated "Mockingbird" from Inez and Charlie Foxx (during which Dusty herself sang) and two from The Shirelles – "Mama Said" and "Will You Love Me Tomorrow", both classic R&B titles. "I knew exactly how to sound like a Shirelle, and can go off into my Shirley Alston impression quite easily. I slavishly copied the originals because we hadn't caught on to them in this country, so I could get away with it." Ray Charles' 1954 hit, "Don't You Know", proved a strange yet adventurous choice. The remaining tracks were "Nothing" (originally recorded by Marie Knight in 1961 when it was tagged "Nothing In The World"), while "My Colouring Book", a showbiz standard, Dusty soul-ized, and with Lesley Gore's "You Don't Own Me" she took her first step towards feminism.

From the Bacharach/David stable she included "Anyone Who Had A Heart", "Wishin' & Hopin'" and "Twenty Four Hours From Tulsa". Although not issued as a single, her version was as popular as Gene Pitney's hit. "That was one of the first times that a woman took a song that was essentially male, and by singing virtually the same words, it became a different song," Dusty explained at the time. "Driving off into the night, being picked up at some gas station and this, that and the other, it was quite outré." In October 1964, *Ready, Steady, Go!* ran a competition where viewers guessed who was singing the speeded up version of the song. Dusty wasn't advertised to appear on the following week's show but Gene Pitney was. A foregone conclusion from the viewers' viewpoint – but not so! Dusty's version had been played, and she joined Gene on the programme as a surprise guest.

"A pot pourri of British soul" one critic wrote, while journalist Peter Jones went one step further, aguing "Dusty is a unique talent, full of expression, fluidity, emotion. She can match the Americans on their own terms for 'feel'. She is a perfectionist. Her album is slightly marred for the strength of some of her backing sounds, but it's still a great album." The singer happily admitted she was guided by Johnny Franz because, "If I'd had my way completely the album would never have sold a copy because I came up with some pretty obscure stuff." That "obscure stuff" included a pair of Mary Wells' songs, and paying homage to other Motown acts but, taking wise counsel, Dusty chose to leave them out.

Not wise counsel but a lack of courage stopped Dusty releasing her version of "Anyone Who Had A Heart" as a single, so when Cilla Black enjoyed a British number one with her interpretation in February 1964, Dusty was in absolute despair – "I had heard the song before Cilla did... Dionne Warwick sang this number at the Olympia Theatre in Paris. It had such depth of feeling, such pathos. Nothing against Cilla, but I'd take Dionne's version all the time ... I just didn't dare record it (as a single) in case it was a flop, and in the end I plumped for something safe – 'Stay Awhile'."

And Ms Warwick's version? She struggled into the British top 50, with her sales attributed to diehard soul fans. Born in New Jersey, Dionne Warwick first sang in Newark's New Hope Baptist church. She played piano with The Drinkard Singers, a gospel unit managed by her mother, before studying at Connecticut's Hart School of Music. Around this time, young Dionne formed The Gospelaires with her sister Dee Dee, and their aunt Cissy Houston, mother of Whitney. As backing vocalists, they worked for Garnett Mimms and The Drifters, and it was through them that Dionne later met Burt Bacharach and Hal David. Their first joint release, "Don't Make Me Over", set the blueprint for further classic collaborations, where the exquisite interpretation of their finely sculptured compositions soon earned the title "uptown soul".

To prevent Dionne Warwick missing out on another chart-topping single, Burt Bacharach kept her next single under wraps and released it simultaneously on both sides of the Atlantic. The ploy worked. Titled "Walk On By", Dionne flew to London to promote it, guaranteeing a place in the British top ten hit in April 1964. During this trip she met Dusty, who took her sightseeing around London. They drank bitter on draught at The City Arms in the East End while listening to the piano being played in a hearty fashion. "Dionne just had to get up there and sing along and as her hostess I had to join her. So we sang a couple of good old standards." After eating cockles at Tubby Isaac's stall, they wandered around Petticoat Lane, where Dionne bantered and argued with stall holders. The two had great fun in public. However, behind the scenes, Dusty confessed "I feel Dionne did resent me because she felt I'd stolen a couple of hits from her like 'Wishin' & Hopin'... and I tried to get along with her but I always found her a little cool." Indeed, two decades later, Dionne moaned that she still hadn't forgiven Dusty or Cilla, and felt that she had recorded very expensive demos for them to copy and enjoy. "If I had, during the course of the recording, coughed or sneezed, that would have been an intricate part of what they recorded."

Dusty may have got the last word. In 1993 she introduced Dionne to Vidal Sassoon, who decided her hair needed re-styling and colouring. When the public next saw her she was a blonde!

Following selected British dates, Dusty returned to St Anne's Convent in Ealing on 6 June 1964, to be guest of honour at a fete organized by some of her former teachers to raise funds for a new chapel. The media carried a picture of the smiling star surrounded by grinning nuns under the caption "Dusty and her swinging nuns!" She then returned to her own world to appear in Brian Epstein's production *Pops Alive* at London's Prince of Wales theatre, before flying to Paris with Johnny Franz and Vic Billings to play a handful of new songs to her record company's European representatives. Dusty then grabbed a week's holiday in Rome before returning to London to support the release of her third single, Tommy Hunt's "I Just Don't Know What To Do With Myself". Although she had been ecstatic over the song when she first heard it, now she wasn't so sure, and even tried to stop its release. Thankfully, she failed. The song shot into the British Top Three, denied the top spot by The Beatles' "A Hard Day's Night" and

The Rolling Stones' "It's All Over Now". The gorgeous melody was expressive in the extreme, and the emotion Dusty injected into every syllable of the lyrics was draining and yet wonderfully addictive. In complete contrast to her previous singles, she threw her heart and soul into this powerhouse of a ballad. This was the first of several ballsy ballads, and gave birth to the dramatic arm waving, hand gesticulations and body language that lived the very tragedy of the song. Dusty dug deep and delivered. It was scheduled for American release a year later with "Your Hurtin' Kinda Love" on the flip, but was pulled at the last minute. Instead, it turned up as the B-side of "Some Of Your Loving".

The next two months were chaotic for the 25-year-old as she performed, recorded and prepared for her forthcoming American concerts which were part of Murray The K's Rock 'n' Roll Extravaganza at New York's Fox Theatre, the heartbeat of black music and sister theatre to the Apollo. Before she could plan her act, however, she honoured dates in Britain, including a week's stint in Coventry during August with The Searchers and Eden Kane. All did not go entirely according to plan as she was forced to drop songs from her act due to phlaryngitis. Meanwhile, "All Cried Out" was released Stateside in May to coincide with her pending visit. The single was a follow-up to "Wishin' & Hopin'", and once again highlighted her beloved Spector sound, where her double-tracked vocals, supported by The Breakaways, fought against the overpowering and often distorted musical backdrop. Hand wringing and tearful, it was powerful in the extreme and possibly one of the best releases from her early career. It was issued in Britain as a track on the EP *Dusty*, with her version of Marvin Gaye's frenetic Motown classic "Can I Get A Witness"; a heartbreaking interpretation of Raymonde/Hawker's composition "I Wish I'd Never Loved You" and "Wishin' & Hopin'". Released in September 1964, *Dusty* was her first serious stab at the wounding, emotive black/soul music she adored, where she transformed the songs into personal issues that were her secrets.

"She rang up one night and said 'Daddy and you must come to America with me'. And we did, it was marvellous," recalled Kay O'Brien in 1964. Dusty had planned to spend time with her parents between performances at Brooklyn's Fox. But it was wishful thinking. "When I discovered we were starting at ten in the morning and finishing at one the next morning, there was no time between shows to get a meal and the temperature was 90 degrees." After a while, her brother, Tom, flew over to be with them, leaving Dusty to meet them for a meal at 2 am after the show finished. She'd then visit an all-night hairdresser or shop for essentials.

The 10-day engagement left an indelible memory; it was a dream come true. "It was the era of Beatlemania and Murray the K liked to consider himself as the fifth Beatle. He thought I was from Liverpool and decided he'd got to have me! There were a couple of other white acts on the show, The Searchers were there but they weren't on it constantly like I was. And other white acts would come in for three days, like Jay and the Americans. Murray hedged his bets with a few white acts." Motown's The Temptations, The Supremes, The Miracles, Marvin Gaye, The Contours, Martha Reeves and the Vandellas were also on the bill, alongside Phil Spector's Ronettes. No-one was allowed to leave the theatre during the day, so the acts were confined to tiny dressing rooms and the hallways for 12 hours at a stretch. Card games were rife, but the most popular pastimes were talking, eating and drinking. "I mostly hung out with The Ronettes because I shared a dressing room with them which was an extraordinary experience. It was like 104 degrees in this very, very small dressing room, and all our beehives were in there – three black beehives and one white one! It was collisions constantly!" Ronnie Spector, on the other hand, thought Dusty was nuts, as she wrote in her autobiography *Be My Baby*. "When Dusty got upset, she would go out to the hallway and throw cups and saucers at the stage door. After a throwing session lasting only a few minutes Dusty, with a grin on her face, returned to her dressing room. By the second show you had to step over piles of broken china just to get to the stage... I never could understand the craziness of some performers."

Dusty said "Next door to us were Martha and the Vandellas, and on the other side were The Supremes. I remember Mary Wilson was always reading Latin books and Diana's mum helped me turn up my hems because I was always buying things that were too long." Her act was "I Only Want To Be With You" and "Wishin' & Hopin'", with Martha, Rosalind and Betty providing backing vocals. Dusty often returned the favour because there was usually a Vandella missing when Martha was due on stage. "I never actually got to go on stage with them but I knew all the routines and knew exactly how to sound like a Vandella. And since they were also singing back-ups for Marvin Gaye from the wings, I used to do that as well.

"I had a lot of good times, very heady times being involved in this show. After all, what could be more stimulating than listening to the brass arrangements of The Temptations from the side of the stage. That was heaven to me. I didn't like performing there, but I wanted to stand there and soak it all up so that I could use it. But I could never get anyone to do it. And this is where I got this priceless reputation of being difficult in the studios because I was always asking the musicians to do things they couldn't understand."

Martha Reeves first met Dusty when Murray the K pulled her aside, asking her to help the British singer who was extremely distressed. Knowing how loneliness can become unbearable, Martha agreed, only to be met by the sound of breaking crockery from inside the dressing room. She waited outside for the noise to stop and persuaded Dusty to open the door. "I could see that she had been crying and her make-up was a mess, with black streams of mascara running down both her cheeks." She noted the dressing room resembled a war zone with a cardboard box crammed with broken china on the floor. Dusty started chatting, became calmer and with Martha's help cleared up the debris. She then fixed her make-up to join the show's finale, holding Martha's hand. "She was lonely and

I realized then how sensitive she was behind that tough barrier she put on." Each day when the Motown star arrived at the theatre, her first task was to check up on her new friend and, if she was out of sorts, she would stay with her until the mood lifted. One evening when Martha was ordering a takeaway, she asked Dusty for her order – it was a bottle of vodka which Dusty later drank alone.

Years later when Dusty admitted she had an alcohol and drug problem, Lesley Gore told Martha that she was to blame. "I was horrified," she wrote in her autobiography *Dancing In The Street*. "I prayed immediately that if I was guilty of turning her into an alcoholic, it was not my design." Martha was wrongly blamed because Dusty herself confessed how her drinking got out of hand. "We had six shows a day and I got laryngitis and thought I can't face it. Then one of The Temptations gave me a cup of vodka. I drank the whole bloody thing, and felt better." She hated the taste but loved the effect. "Everyone was partying. I was always very well treated. I was essentially the token white and I was very protected. Just generally when I used to hang out with the Motown people and with the Wilson Picketts of the world, and things like that. Nobody ever laid a finger on me. It was 'don't lean on her, she's with me'. Nobody would dare, so I would blindly blunder through all sorts of situations which when I analysed them, were really rather tacky. Y'know, hotels with no windows in them, Malcolm X and so on. Perhaps not tacky, but quite dangerous environments to be in for a very naïve white singer." Before long, she was experimenting with cocaine which pumped her with short-lived confidence. Then pills, starting with downers, later a handful of reds. "I drank them down with two bottles of bad pink Portuguese wine and fell down the stairs. I was covered in bruises but thought everybody did this. But not everybody did." For the time being though, in 1964, Dusty lived the life.

Without any respite, the singer followed her heady 10-day experience with a short tour across America with The Searchers and Eden Kane who had flown in when the Fox commitment was finished. However, the strain was far too much for Dusty who collapsed in Tulsa. "Every song I sang was an effort but somehow I managed to get to the end of the act. But my voice was terrible." She stumbled off the stage, not knowing where she was, but knowing she wanted to lie down and sleep for ever. She was ordered to take three weeks' complete rest, and remembered boarding a plane at Idlewild airport, wondering what her destination was – but not really caring. After 10 warm and relaxing days in the Caribbean, her health and spirits were slowly restored, so she persuaded Vic Billings to accompany her to New York to spend time visiting friends, catching concerts and recording a selection of titles with producer Shelby S Singleton. "I believe Tulsa taught me a lesson. I don't think I'll ever work at the same pressure again… Some people said I had a nervous breakdown but it wasn't that bad. I was just totally exhausted." She failed to listen to herself. This was the second time her career had been put on hold through illness and within a short time it was to happen again.

Upon her return to London "Losing You" was released on 16 October. Recorded in London during June, the slow, sweeping ballad, unlike the drama attached to "I Just Don't Know What To Do With Myself", with its infectious sloping melody, was easy and comfortable, allowing the strings to caress her voice rather than battle with it. And it reunited her with her brother, Tom, who co-wrote it with Clive Westlake. Dusty was unsure the smooth melody would work for her, so when it peaked at number nine she sighed with relief, while Tom had fulfilled his ambition to compose a hit for his sister.

It was also this month that she met up with Martha Reeves again. The trio was in London on a seven-day promotional trip, and despite a gruelling workload, the girls shopped together in London's Bond Street, dined together and were invited to Dusty's Guy Fawkes party. The Motown group's television spots included *Thank Your Lucky Stars* and *Ready, Steady, Go!* where Dusty was spotted out of camera range in a corner watching her friends' act before performing "Losing You", with the hem of her skirt held up by sticky tape.

While plans were being made for the New Year's Eve edition of *Ready, Steady, Go!* which would include Dusty, she was on the road with Brian Poole and the Tremeloes, Herman's Hermits and Dave Berry. With The Echoes behind her, she burst on stage at the Edmonton Granada wearing a white blouse, emerald green skirt and matching high heeled shoes, to the strains of Martha Reeves and the Vandellas' "Dancing In The Street". She sang her hits, plus a medley of songs she wished she'd recorded – "Secret Love", "My Boy Lollipop" and "There's Always Something There To Remind Me" before "I Can't Hear You No More" closed the show.

The London Centenary Committee of the Dr Barnardo's Homes was one of many charities to approach Dusty during the year. They asked her to help raise £250,000 to build a new home for physically handicapped children. She agreed and recorded "O Holy Child" on 27 November 1964, written by Tom and family friend Peppi Borza. All royalties and Philips Records' profits went to the charity.

A further British six-day tour early in December kicked off in Doncaster and closed at the Gaumont in Hanley on the 6th. Another successful trek, but it ended in disaster for Dusty when she was given a bill for £10 to pay for the theatre cleaners' overtime after a backstage bun fight. She was in her dressing room, she said, recording a spot for a local hospital. Other artists in an adjoining room started making raucous sounds so she told them to keep the noise down. Within minutes, cakes, swiped from a buffet laid on by the theatre manager, started flying through the air. "I've never seen anything like it," manager Gerry Bennett told the *Daily Mirror*. "The dressing room was a shambles!" In response, Dusty, who was preparing for her South African trip, moaned the incident had been exaggerated. "I admit I threw some sugar, but if two cleaners earn £10 for two hours overtime, then I'll be a cleaner!"

Within a week the singer hit the headlines again. This time it was the international press, with not a flying cake in sight. Three days after the Hanley incident, Dusty and the Echoes flew to South Africa and into a political incident involving the governments of the two countries, when Dusty made a stand against apartheid. Vic Billings, who travelled ahead of her and the group, was given an ultimatum soon after arriving in the country, warning that Dusty must not perform for multi-racial audiences. This completely contradicted her contract, which had made it quite clear she wouldn't appear in segregated theatres. Vic Billings also stated it was because of this condition that he had agreed to the visit. Dusty explained, "What we'd done was to find a loophole in the South African law that I didn't know existed, that the promoter knew existed, that I could play to mixed audiences so long as I played in a cinema with a live show." The South African government was so incensed the loophole had been discovered that they made Dusty the scapegoat.

With dates lined up in Johannesburgh, Cape Town and Port Elizabeth, Dusty was excited about the whole experience of visiting South Africa but, following their concert before a multi-racial audience in Cape Town, which was the fifth of seven dates, Dusty returned to her hotel to be served with a written notice ordering her to quit the country within 24 hours. The Echoes' Doug Reece recalled that "We were picked up at the hotel and taken to the airport under armed guard. At the airport our luggage was taken to the plane and we had to walk across the tarmac to the DC10. All the blacks wore dark blue boiler suits and red berets and formed two lines for us to walk between to board the plane. As we passed they all took off their berets, smiled and nodded. It was one of those moments you never forget." Dusty thought, "Oh, you did notice, even though I fucked it up!"

A government representative told the South African media that Dusty had been warned on two occasions to observe the country's way of life regarding entertainment, and that if she failed to do so, she'd be asked to leave the country. She chose to defy the government. "Miss Springfield was not arrested," a British Home Office spokesman reported. "On a strictly legal view the South Africans appear to have acted within their rights." He then concluded that Harold Wilson's government had no grounds to intervene on Dusty's behalf because "she failed to comply with the requirements of local law and custom."

Naturally, it was open season on her when she returned to London airport. With a straight face, feeling emotionally drained and completely exhausted, she sat in a chair, hands clasped on her lap, journalists firing questions at her from all angles. Dusty told the truth about "the very unpleasant experience" insisting that she was not a political creature but had taken a stand against apartheid, before adding "I may sue the South African government ... if they want to sling mud around they've picked the wrong person because I have a far more deadly aim." Celebrities like Max Bygraves and Derek Nimmo openly criticized her for making the situation harder for them to work in South Africa, insisting her trip was nothing more than a publicity stunt. "That was the biggest hurt," she told *Record Mirror*, "I cried for days." On the other hand, she was supported by 15 Members of Parliament who signed a Commons motion applauding her action in standing against "the obnoxious doctrine of apartheid." The Beatles' Ringo Starr was one of many to rush to her defence, saying "Good for Dusty. I would have done the same thing. It's stupid to have segregated audiences, especially as the music came from the Negroes in the first place."

"I know nothing whatsoever about politics," she told *Melody Maker*. "I have done no wrong... I have no political views. But if anyone pays me the compliment of wanting to watch me on the stage, then they should be allowed to buy a ticket, irrespective of colour, creed or religion. And that is all there is to it." She added that she would never return to the country until the whole apartheid situation was sorted out "which I don't think will be in my lifetime." Sadly she was right. The fact that Dusty had donated her £2,000 fee to black orphans was not made public at the time.

Dusty's agent, Tito Burns, later cancelled South African dates for The Searchers, The Zombies and Eden Kane. When Adam Faith was asked to leave South Africa for refusing to perform to segregated audiences, the Foreign Office stated that, like Miss Springfield before him, he only had himself to blame. A short time later, both Dusty and Adam were verbally attacked by the singing duo Peter & Gordon when they stopped off in London from South Africa. "Our tour went very well but there has been considerable reaction to what Dusty and Adam did," Peter Asher told the music press. "Theatres which had, up until then, been multi-racial are now segregated. The trouble has started the government being interested in the theatres... we decided to say nothing to anybody and, as a result, we played to multi-racial audiences." He concluded by saying that black people now resented the stand Dusty took, and believe it may have been good for her conscience but was bad for them. Dusty responded with "... if you are capable of wearing blinkers it's a very good country to be in."

Her music was banned in South Africa, but it continued to dominate the world's charts, securing her international popularity. On the home front, she was now a much-loved household name, and when the *New Musical Express* readers voted her the top British Female Vocalist, and second to Brenda Lee in the World section, she knew she had made the right decision to go it alone.

Chapter Four

IN THE MIDDLE
OF NOWHERE

"I have tried sex with both men and women.
I found I liked it."

It was an exciting time to be in the record business. Although The Beatles and The Rolling Stones continued to dominate the British charts, more groups had broken through to claim chart action of their own. The Animals, with gritty-voiced Eric Burdon on vocals, and the sweet-sounding Hollies from Manchester led the way, while emerging London groups continued to fill the capital's nightclubs. Some new names to 1965's Top 20 were The Yardbirds, The Who, The Moody Blues, The Seekers and The Walker Brothers. Dusty, Petula Clark, Sandie Shaw, Marianne Faithfull and Cilla Black continued to grow in popularity. They weren't in competition with each other, but rather showed a combined, determined feminine front to grab their slice of the music business.

Thanks to Dusty, The Beatles and The Rolling Stones in particular, Motown music was gaining momentum with hits from Mary Wells ("My Guy") and The Supremes ("Where Did Our Love Go"). When the Tamla Motown label was launched in Britain in March 1965, via a deal with EMI Records, the profile was much higher but, generally speaking, R&B or Negro music as it was called, still had a long haul before it claimed its rightful place in British music. Fans of the music had no option but to frequent underground nightclubs or tune their transistor radios into Radio Luxemburg's often distorted transmission from the continent. But help was coming – in the shape of pirate radio stations with sharper reception and hip DJs. The most famous of all was Radio Caroline which started transmission on Easter Saturday, 28 March 1964, on 199 metres (1520 kHz) with a power of 10 kilowatts from a ship off the coast of Felixstowe, Suffolk. DJ Simon Dee made the first announcement and all-day music was brought to Britain for the first time, breaking the BBC radio monopoly. Shortly after this, other offshore stations were set up. Not everyone was delighted by this new development. Some suspected that a plethora of free music on the radio meant that people did not feel it necessary to go out and buy records. Dusty said "They certainly hit my sales. It's a bit of a vicious circle though, because if they're not around, you won't get the plugging and if they are around you don't sell so many records."

Overall, however, there is little doubt that Caroline and her offshore sisters helped fuel the pop music explosion of the sixties; all stations gave airtime to new groups and record labels which sprang up during this time, and all were instrumental in promoting American black music. Without their existence, black acts would have taken longer to chart in Britain. It seems ironic, however, that while black music was fighting for British recognition, American blacks were fighting for their lives in what was to become known as "the long hot summer". Riots flared up within three weeks of President Johnson signing the Civil Rights Bill which was designed, among other things, to protect black constitutional rights. Not all American states agreed with this and black segregation continued. Dusty had taken her own stand against discrimination in South Africa, which could have easily damaged her career beyond repair, but all she could do now was bring the American plight to the media's attention with her continued promotion of black music.

In January 1965 Dusty performed in the San Remo Song Festival, staged on the Italian Riviera. She was eliminated in the semi-finals and stood by as Kiki Dee and Petula Clark made it through to the finals. "... I watched (Kiki) from the wings... she did very well in front of a good, emotional Italian audience. There was me, just snivelling in the wings as she sang... She's got fantastic control for a girl of her age, I can't get that sort of voice control..." While there, Dusty was also reunited with American soul singer Timi Yuro, whom she had first met on the set of *Ready, Steady, Go!* in 1963. Timi Yuro had been touring the country with Dion, Brook Benton and Lesley Gore. She was unknown in Britain (although soul fans raved over "Hurt" in 1961) but, thanks to Dusty's intervention, she was given a spot on *Ready, Steady, Go!* to promote her current single "Down In The Valley". Dusty was so in awe of the American that she fluffed her lines during the short interview that accompanied her television appearance. It's thought the next time they met was at London's Finsbury Park where Timi was appearing. Dusty fan Steve Dodd remembered he was waiting outside the theatre when he was distracted by somebody making an enormous production of parking a car outside the stage door. "It developed into a Buster Keaton-style silent comedy as more and more passers-by and a policeman or two became involved in helping the struggling driver manoeuvre their (small) car into the (quite large) parking place. Eventually it was accomplished and out stepped – Dusty! Curtseying to the cheering crowd she slipped into the theatre." Timi Yuro died at the age of 63 in March 2004.

"Your Hurtin' Kinda Love", Dusty's next single, was released to mixed reviews. She was supported in its ambivalent lyrics by The Breakaways but fought against the blanketing, suffocating, musical backdrop on a complex tune she loathed to perform live. Her anger and frustration roared through the dramatic storyline of hurt and, thanks to Mike Hawker's lyrics, she told the world. Dusty admitted it was recorded in a rush (on one version you can hear her cough) and that she had, over the years, grown to hate it. "If you do a rotten performance, you can try to forget and hope some others will forget, but if you make a bad record it's there forever. There's something terribly final about them." The single struggled before peaking in the Top 40 and, irrespective of what she said, the song was recognized by purists as an anthem for the broken hearted.

While Dusty struggled for a chart placing, her brother Tom's group, The Seekers, sat at number one with his composition "I'll Never Find Another You". It was the top-selling British single of 1965, with its follow-up, "A World Of Our Own", at number four. Since becoming a full-time writer, Tom's work was much in demand as artists like Frank Ifield, Matt Monro and Kathy Kirby recorded his work. Tom headed his own publishing company, Springfield Music, an affiliate of Chappells, for his own work and some of Dusty's, such as "I Only Want To Be With You". He later expanded his portfolio by penning television themes for programmes like *George & The Dragon* and writing songs for comedian Charlie Drake to include in one of his Christmas shows at the London Palladium. Tom also managed dancer/actor/composer Peppi Borza, who would often be seen in Dusty's company; accompanying her on tour, on holidays, or hanging out with her in nightclubs. Pictures of them together would hit the headlines, with the usual romantic suggestions that, of course, came to nothing. Dusty did have strong feelings for him – but as a friend. During the eighties, when he was dying from AIDS in the Lighthouse hospice, she was a frequent visitor to his bedside. She either travelled alone, or singer and friend Simon Bell would drive her.

Dusty also passionately cared for another male presence in her life. A small and older male named Einstein. He travelled with her, listened without comment and allowed her to dress him. She had found Einstein, pinned up by one ear in a shop window along London's Oxford Street. His resilient smile and dingy appearance won her over, and to the day she died the little teddy bear was her constant companion.

During February "Losing You" was released in America and, prior to flying to New York to promote it, Dusty appeared on the peak-time entertainment show *Sunday Night At The London Palladium* as well as touring Ireland with a launch date in Dublin. As "Dancing In The Street" climbed the American chart, Dusty phoned Martha Reeves to invite her to the annual carnival in Rio de Janeiro. As she had no dates booked, Martha met Dusty, Tom and Madeline Bell at New York City's La Guardia Airport. "We flew together on three different planes and boarded, slept, disembarked, filled out papers, showed our passports and ignored the stares as we enjoyed each other's company," Martha wrote in *Dancing In The Street*, recalling that only hours before she had been freezing in a mid-winter storm, while now she was being sun kissed in the tropics. They walked from Ipanema to Copacabana, and from every point could see the large statue of Christ on Corcovado with His arms outstretched. In 1990 Dusty recalled the trip, laughing at the funny time she had, "I've still got the picture of Martha standing at the statue, she's got gold lamé on, and we're wearing head scarves to protect our wigs. Madeline's there, too, and this boy, who's gorgeous... what a bizarre lot we were. I could never forget Rio, it was the craziest five days in my life. We danced non-stop for five days which takes some doing. I think it was something to do with the fact a lot of ether was sprayed into the air. It's permanently there and has a paradoxical effect. We keep going, you go right through it... it's actually a stimulant." Martha added "I was thrilled to be there, a dream come true, and we did dance everywhere we ventured because there were samba bands on every street, in every establishment we visited. Tom didn't attend very many places with us, we mostly saw him at the hotel. It was very exciting to see the elaborate costumes and the men in drag, portraying all of our historical women figures."

But Dusty's dancing days were cut short. "I trod on a broken bottle and it went through my foot. It stopped me in my tracks. They sewed it without any anaesthetic because they see a lot of broken bodies in carnival and they were not impressed by this white woman treading on a broken bottle, then screaming the place down. It's all part of the rich tapestry of life I suppose." Martha said "The reason for the stomping on the broken bottle was never explained to me. However, it was after a heated argument."

Years later Dusty remarked the trip was a spontaneous decision which had cost her dearly. Her problem was, she explained, that many of her friends didn't have her spending power and if she wanted to be with them, she had no choice but to cover the whole cost. "… It seems so mean not to. In the past I had many friends but there is no way of knowing for sure whether you are liked for yourself. So now I have few really true friends." Another instance of extravagance came when she was in Cardiff for a concert. She became bored and hired a car to return to London, only to return on the train the next day to perform. And again, climbing into a cab parked along London's Baker Street she said to the driver, "Blackpool!" On the other hand, Pat Rhodes (née Barnett) laughed when she recalled Dusty's attempt at cost cutting. "She thought she'd better not take me on a cabaret date as it would cost £10. Of course that was ridiculous; that £10 wouldn't have made a bit of difference. It's just that sometimes she gets guilty at the way she splashed money around."

Upon her hobbling return from Rio de Janeiro, Dusty cancelled engagements due to her badly cut foot, but was well enough at the end of March 1965 to start a three-week tour with The Searchers, Heinz and The Zombies, and the occasional guesting by Bobby Vee. While on the road, the *Dusty In New York* EP was released with tracks "Live It Up", "I Want Your Love Tonight", "I Wanna Make You Happy" and "Now That You're My Baby". It reached the Top 13 which thrilled Dusty because she loved the songs, saying they represented her introduction to American music. But, more importantly, she flirted musically with writers and producers who would feature heavily in her future career. Before she had time to draw breath, Dusty joined the select few to appear at the NME Poll Winners Concert at (the then) Empire Pool, Wembley. With The Echoes she sang her pet love "Dancing In The Street", "Mockingbird" with Doug Reece, and "I Can't Hear You No More."

With her career regularly documented in the media, journalists longed for insights into Dusty's personal life. Her name became linked to several men (all in the music business) but most were later dismissed as publicity opportunities to promote a tour or new release. The most persistent of them was Eden Kane, real name Richard Starstedt, whose brothers Peter and Clive were also in the music business. Eden had been a major artist since 1961, following his debut hit "Well I Ask You" but by now he was struggling, and this prompted reporters to ask Dusty whether she was paid to provide him with a publicity service. Naturally, questions of a presumed affair abounded – "I was supposed to be engaged to him ... but I can honestly say there was never anything serious between us." Eden Kane later admitted on a BBC4 documentary *Girls And Boys: Sex & British Pop*, "At the time insiders knew Dusty was gay. We had the same manager and he decided to link us romantically. So, on the front page of the *Daily Mirror* was a picture of myself and Dusty captioned, "Are they engaged?", which was ridiculous. But at the time it was a way for the publicity machine to give *her* some promotion." Yet when Dusty was later questioned about the romance, she said there was no substance to the story, which, Paul Howes later wrote, was "very puzzling if the whole episode was contrived to mislead the public about Dusty's sexual preferences." If the truth be told, Dusty much preferred Eden's brother, Peter, although it appeared she never pursued him.

Burt Bacharach and Gene Pitney continued to be linked with her, as journalists became more determined to match her with someone... anyone. Mirror-imaged pictures in the press prompted all manner of rumours because a ring on a right-hand finger would be seen to be on the left. Television appearances were the worst as she laughingly explained that "They often reverse the cameras. I actually sang half a song with a ring on my wedding finger and the other half with it on my right hand. I'm thinking of wearing one through my nose next!"

While the mainstream media puzzled on, Dusty enjoyed herself on London's gay club scene. The most famous venue for lesbians was The Gateways Club, off King's Road, which became internationally famous when it was used as a backdrop for the 1968 film *The Killing Of Sister George*. Dusty was a regular guest; wearing dark trousers and blouses, she wore her hair short and relaxed in the company of others, who enjoyed her friendliness, her wicked sense of humour and her parties. One of the regulars, Archie, told Jill Gardiner, author of *From The Closet To The Screen,* that Dusty was open with The Gateways' crowd – "But you never pushed things too far, not when somebody's in the limelight. A lot of us knew that Dusty was gay but we didn't say it to anybody else." While another regular said that "She was very fanciable." Another of her favourite haunts was a cellar club under The Sombrero restaurant along Kensington High Street. Nicknamed "Yours And Mine", music business people and artists were regular visitors because they preferred the atmosphere and, of course, the music, which was predominately American dance or unreleased British cuts.

Dusty's secret was kept despite rumours dogging her throughout her life and, as her future manager Vicki Wickham told the *Sunday Express* in 2000, "Dusty knew people realized she was gay. What good would it have done to make a big public announcement... I always felt it was nobody's business." However, quite unexpectedly, in 1970 Dusty went public about her attraction for women in an interview with the *Evening Standard*'s Ray Coleman, saying she was "perfectly capable of being swayed by a girl as by a boy..." Later, she told the *News Of The World,* "I have tried sex with both men and women. I found I liked it." For now though, in 1965, Dusty was the straight gal about town, enjoying a lifestyle ordinary folk only dreamt about.

When 20-year-old Dusty first moved to London she lived in Baker Street with a Scottish couple who, she said, became substitute parents, before sharing future homes with girlfriends. Invariably these situations ended in separation because "...we would eventually get on each others' nerves."

At Dusty's invitation, Martha Reeves & the Vandellas were to be special guests on her forthcoming television special, but with Berry Gordy planning to send the first Motown Revue to tour Britain to celebrate the opening of the Tamla Motown record label during

March 1965, Dusty's plan was changed. Following a licensing deal with EMI Records, it seemed logical to include all the touring acts with Martha, Betty and Rosalind. So now Dusty was joined by The Miracles, Stevie Wonder, The Supremes and The Earl Van Dyke Sextet. (The Temptations, who weren't on the tour, flew in for the television show.) With her now hosting, the' programme was originally called *Dusty Springfield Presents The Sound Of Motown*, but somewhere during production the title was reduced to *The Sound Of Motown* and as such was taped on 18 March for screening on 28 April at 9.40 pm. Berry Gordy flew his parents and his three young children from Detroit to be in the audience. When filming *The Sound Of Motown* was finished, a "Welcome to Britain" party was hosted by singer Dana Valery in Holland Park. Mixing with the Motown stars were Rolling Stones Brian Jones and Bill Wyman, The Seekers, Eric Burdon, Sandie Shaw and Madeline Bell. The celebrations lasted all night.

Two days later, the Motown show kicked off at London's Finsbury Park with Dusty in the audience. She sat with friends, but instead of thoroughly enjoying the show became annoyed when she was constantly asked for her autograph, saying "I'm here as a fan as well, you know." When her work commitments allowed, she followed the tour by car, driving her 1964 Buick Riviera with right-hand steering. When Martha wasn't working, the two shopped and went on sightseeing trips; they hung out with mutual friends in London, like John Reid (then Motown's product manager and later Elton John's manager), Michael Aldred and others inside the music business. Martha always treasured her time with Dusty because they were fun and unpredictable. Once during the Motown tour, Dusty gave her cause for concern when she kept crying because of problems in her personal life. They chatted long and hard but she refused fully to confide in Martha and, as Dusty had been sleeping badly, it was decided she should stay the night. Next morning, however, when Mickey Stevenson (Motown's R&B director) popped by to tell Martha about changes in that evening's scheduling, he spotted the sleeping Dusty. Martha said "… She lay there with one of her big legs stuck out from under the comforter – fishnet stockings and all. For the rest of the day, all the men on the show kidded and teased me, as though something odd had transpired." She was amazed how others saw their friendship but she cared little.

Before *The Sound Of Motown* hit the small screen on 28 April, the Motown artists had returned to Detroit and Dusty had flown to New York to record a spot on NBC's *Hullabaloo*, hosted by Sammy Davis Jr. Like other fans, she watched the show that Rediffusion's Elkan Allan described as "One of the greatest hours in the history of television." Not only was it the first of its kind to be screened on British television, but it was also the only show devoted to a particular style of music or record company. The stage was designed to show all the artists at once, with the cameras shifting from one to another with ease. It was fast-moving, non-stop Motown music which encompassed versions of other acts' songs, like Dusty's version of Betty Everett's "I Can't Hear You No More" backed by Martha and the girls. The acts sang live against Motown's own pre-recorded tapes, and among the musicians present were members of the company's Funk Brothers, Jack Ashford, Eli Fontaine and Earl Van Dyke who boosted the sound by playing alongside the taped music. With the concept changed, Martha Reeves failed to realize that The Supremes, who didn't know Dusty, would steal her group's limelight, as she noted "At first I didn't mind that my label mates joined me as well … but as the show progressed Berry took command and some of the shots displeased me. I took offence when Berry began moving acts around until The Supremes were in a co-starring position." Fans later agreed, however, that "Wishin' & Hopin'", Martha's duet with Dusty, accompanied by the Vandellas' support vocals, was the show's highlight. Dusty said of Martha – "I absolutely idolized her. I loved to listen to that voice... she sort of lost control in the upper registers at one point, but (then) so did I."

The Sound Of Motown was an unqualified success in entertainment, a monumental moment in time; Tamla Motown was launched in great style. With the demise of Rediffusion, the show's tape was thought destroyed but, when Dave Clark purchased the *Ready, Steady, Go!* footage, he also acquired the rights to the Motown show which he later marketed as a commercial video titled *The Sounds Of Motown*. It included footage of Marvin Gaye, who wasn't in the original 1965 show and tour. "I think I unofficially helped push Motown an awful lot because... I made people listen to it," Dusty once said. She also admitted she had a dog called Motown although she didn't see that much of him. Certainly, the artists welcomed the chance to work with her again after their great time together at the Fox Theater, New York, the preceding September. "When the acts returned to Hitsville, one of The Supremes, I believe it was Diana, stopped in my office and told me that Dusty had named her dog Motown," recalled Al Abrams, Public Relations Director 1964–66. "So I decided we would buy a fancy bejewelled collar for our namesake and send it to Dusty as a gift from everyone at Motown. Shortly afterward, we received a gracious handwritten note from Dusty on her personalized blue stationery expressing her delight for the gift. It was a truly wonderful touch of class from a great performer, who actually took the time to pen a personal note of thanks on behalf of Motown – the dog."

Throughout May 1965 Dusty threw herself into a club tour that included Stockton, Newcastle, Manchester, Bradford and Rotherham; the work was concentrated and exhausting, but necessary because her next single "In The Middle Of Nowhere" was due for release on 11 June. Recorded a month earlier, using The Echoes, Madeline Bell, Doris Troy and Lesley Duncan as backing vocalists with Alan Price on piano, Dusty had a lot riding on this single because her last, "Your Hurtin' Kinda Love", failed by her standards. She openly admitted that the lack of chart action had worried her and this time she didn't want to let down anyone involved in the recording, which she described as "a family thing".

This had, she said, relieved tension in the studio and made her less inclined to lose her temper when she felt things went wrong. Reviewers zoomed in on the fact that Alan Price played a rolling piano, and that Doris Troy's spirited chanting contributed to this bright and breezy tune, where Dusty bounced her way through a snapping showcase of British Americanism written by Bea Verdi and Buddy Kaye. The song was loud and noisy, and once more the singer grew to loathe it, claiming it made no contribution whatsoever to her career. How wrong she was; the single peaked at number eight and reached the American Top 100.

This was the first single to feature Madeline Bell and Doris Troy as support vocalists. Already part of Dusty's life, Madeline hadn't been acknowledged as her backing singer until now. Born in Newark, New Jersey, she was 16 when she joined her first gospel group The Glovertones, where she stayed for nearly two years. Upon leaving school, Madeline worked as a meat packer in a supermarket before joining the Alex Bradford Singers who were, at the time, the most popular gospel group in America. Regular touring work led to them appearing in *Black Nativity*, a huge success that later went European. When the show returned to New York, Madeline stayed one more season before returning to London. She knew no-one except record producer Norman Newell who produced her first solo recording. It bombed, but it enabled her to find work on the cabaret circuit. After months of touring, making little money, she decided to swap the stage for the screen and accepted a job as an usherette earning £7 a week in Westbourne Grove's cinema, just off Bayswater Road. The very day she started, fate intervened. "Dusty had heard about me somehow," she explained to Chris Williams, editor of *Ladies Of Soul* magazine. "I'd gained something of a reputation as a gospel singer and at the time she was looking for a new sound for her records. Dusty rang me up and offered me my first session singing engagement. I got £7 for working just three hours." Madeline and the cinema parted company, and within a short time she was turning down work. "I was lucky though. I just happened to be in the right place at the right time. I did a lot of early sessions with Kiki Dee and Lesley Duncan, and people in the business said we had a 'different sound' on record, which at the time everybody wanted." In time, Madeline worked three sessions a day, seven days a week, earning herself the reputation as Britain's top session singer.

Thanks to Madeline Bell, Doris Troy also joined the Springfield club. They were buddies in New York and, when Doris visited London for the first time in 1965, she looked up her friend. Like Madeline, New Yorker Doris started singing in gospel groups from a young age. During the fifties she joined The Halos and began writing her own material, like "How About That", for Dee Clark. To soul fans, Doris was a rare commodity because she recorded her own work, including the immortal "Just One Look", "Whatcha Gonna Do About It" and the Northern Soul classic "I'll Do Anything (He Wants Me To Do)". Dusty loved her songs, so it was pure fate when Madeline invited her to the recording session for "In The Middle Of Nowhere". Doris Troy's warm, vibrant voice could later be heard on countless recordings by The Rolling Stones, The Beatles, Billy Preston and Pink Floyd.

By July, work had taken its toll again, and following a visit to a Harley Street specialist where she had x-rays taken, Dusty was ordered by her doctor to rest for at least a month. Her last collapse had been in Tulsa the preceding September but it seemed this breakdown in health was far more serious. Doris Troy said "Dusty pushes herself all the time and singing is her whole life. With her, it's a physical thing as well as mental. She doesn't just stand there and remember the words, she puts personal bits in – she puts her whole physical being into a song." Ex-Springfield, Mike Hurst, added that it actually wasn't her work that made her ill as much as the worry that went with it. "I've never known anyone like her in my life. She's the greatest perfectionist I've ever met... one little slip to her is like the end of the world, whereas other people wouldn't even notice." He first became aware of this when The

Springfields recorded their biggest hit "Island Of Dreams". Dusty insisted Mike and Tom were singing flat (but omitted to say she was too) so they recorded nine takes of the song, released the last take – and she still wasn't happy.

From Harley Street Dusty went to Cornwall before heading for the Virgin Islands where she stayed a while before flying to Arizona to meet Peppi Borza. "We thought we'd drive to the Wild West," Dusty said at the time. "We ran out of petrol and the journey took 15 hours even in a Thunderbird." Apart from this moment of madness, she watched television and listened to music before moving to New York and back to London. Whenever she returned from the States, Dusty would be loaded with records. She had an envious collection of imported soul discs which were invariably piled up without sleeves in various parts of her flat. She would also meet with American music publishers, searching out music for herself, not wanting to wait for a British record company or publishing house to bring them to her attention. She needed to be one step ahead, with her finger on the American pulse. Any thoughts relating to recording American originals, Dusty discussed with Doug Reece at her home as he remembered, "She would point out things that caught her ear, and I'd try to remember what she liked so that it could be put into practice with The Echoes ... After most of these sessions, which could go on for most of the night, we would go to The Golden Egg in Oxford Street, or drive out to the airport to watch the planes, have scrambled eggs, crunchy bacon, toast with butter and tea."

In early September, Dusty returned to London to promote her third single of the year, "Some Of Your Lovin'", a gloriously constructed ballad penned by Gerry Goffin and Carole King. It was originally earmarked as a track for her second album but the result was so stunning, she wanted it issued as a single. During her last trip to New York, the writers gave her a demo recording of the song with the instruction that if she didn't like it she could dump it. Quite the reverse, Dusty loved it – "I'm embarrassed to say, I feel almost conceited, but I'm very proud of that record." She was relaxed; no vocal straining or catching, just a potent performance from a girl who could transform notes into dreams. With Madeline, Lesley and Kiki Dee backing her, the single shot into the Top Ten, and was the only song she took home and played.

Born Pauline Matthews in Bradford in 1947, Kiki Dee was spotted by Dusty's manager in a Newcastle television studio. She signed a deal with Fontana Records where she released a handful of singles which were later included on the *I'm Kiki Dee* album in 1968. After working with Dusty, Kiki was the first and only British female singer to join Motown Records where she recorded the critically acclaimed *Great Expectations* album in 1970. In time, she was destined for greater stardom. Lesley Duncan, on the other hand, became an in-demand singer/songwriter. Following a string of unsuccessful singles like "I Want A Steady Guy" in 1963 recorded as Lesley Duncan and The Jokers, to the magnificent "Sing Children Sing" from the album of the same name in 1969, Lesley eventually came to the attention of Elton John who recorded her composition "Love Song" on his *Tumbleweed Connection* album. Until this time, she worked as a session singer for the Dave Clark 5, T-Rex, Pink Floyd and, of course, Dusty. From working with Elton John, Lesley never looked back.

Session singers were usually nameless, receiving little or no recognition on record labels, and earned a living supporting someone else's career. The most notable included the Mike Sammes Singers or The Breakaways whose shrill voices could be heard on many a hit single. Dusty was probably one of the first to publicize her support by crediting Madeline, Doris, Kiki and Lesley. Future sessioners included the multi-talented Kay Garner, and Simon Bell whom Dusty acknowledged was one of the finest singers she'd heard. "Simon can stand and sing an entire show in my key so I can actually do a soundcheck from out front."

By way of thanks to her support singers, Dusty lent her vocals to their own recordings, and Madeline Bell probably benefited the most. Using the name Gladys Thong, Dusty can be heard on her first album *Bell's A Poppin'* in 1967 where Madeline looks like she's wrapped up in silver paper on the album's front cover. It didn't need Keith Altham's sleeve notes to tell listeners that Dusty was included because she was easily recognizable. Dusty also featured on Madeline's second album *Doin' Things*, another remarkable release from this much-underrated singer. Happily, her time would come when Dusty's career was at its lowest. Meantime, the two voices blended perfectly, as they wove through the strong melodies on two highly acclaimed releases. Mary O'Brien's second alter ego was also heard on a pair of Lesley Duncan tracks, and a year later on The Echoes' single "Got To Run" on which she also played the ashtray, and on Kiki Dee tracks like "Why Don't I Run Away From You" in 1966. Contractually, Dusty wasn't allowed to advertise the fact that she was performing elsewhere but one assumed Philips Records turned a blind eye, or rather, ear. "I'm very strong willed and I do [it] for the fun of it, so why shouldn't I? … They sing on my records and we're all friends." Miss Thong also contributed to Wee Willie Harris's single "Someone's In The Kitchen With Dinah", a twee, novelty outing. It was hardly an artistic achievement but certainly indicated Dusty was willing to try anything. This she did quite literally when she added her vocals to Doris Troy's dynamic R&B single "I'll Do Anything (He Wants Me To Do)" in 1968, a powerhouse of a performance that has stood the test of time in soul quarters.

Meanwhile, back in September 1965, "I Just Don't Know What To Do With Myself" was scheduled for American release. Copies were pressed, but for some reason withdrawn. It was said that Dusty was responsible because she firmly believed the single was unsuitable for the US market. And she didn't hide the fact that she was angry at the sloppy way her career was being handled there, fearing she was losing her grip on the music scene. There was little she could do about that while she remained based in London, and when she did eventually move Stateside it was for different reasons entirely.

Ev'rything's Coming Up Dusty, her second solo album, was issued in October 1965, and was a musical masterpiece from start to finish. The opener "Won't Be Long" was one of several tracks Dusty wanted to re-record, but was persuaded otherwise. "I'd loved to have heard more of the piano," she reasoned at the time. "There's a note there, 'E', I think that I hit for the first time ever." Of the Goffin & King composition, "Oh No! Not My Baby", she noted, "I had difficulty reaching those high notes. Doris Troy, Mad and I worked on the same mike. Every time I got to a high note, they forced me up to it. It ends up like the Madeline Bell Show. Not her fault." Dusty adored Maxine Brown's original and loathed Manfred Mann's cover version, so wanted this to be a single to mark the difference between the two. She was over ruled again, which probably lost her a serious number one single contender.

Jimmy Radcliffe's "Long After Tonight Is All Over" was as near to a Burt Bacharach sound that could be achieved in a British studio. "My favourite song for tempo, sort of Drifter-ish. People ask me who I think I sound like. Well, it's Baby Washington here." Dusty's brother played Latin piano on "La Bamba", almost reminiscent of The Springfields way of having musical fun. She said there were fond memories of her standing in the middle of the studio conducting the orchestra through the unfamiliar tempo. And this was also the case during the powerful ballad "Who Can I Turn To?" because Dusty insisted the song carry a Latin beat, which was slightly alien to the styling of the song. Ivor Raymonde added the strings and supervised the magnificent trombone solo. Baby Washington's influence was also heard on "Doodlin'", where Dusty took hours to unravel the lyrics before admitting "I've a feeling I did it in a key too high," and on "That's How Heartaches Are Made", which allowed Dusty to wander through her emotions against a fiery arrangement. As she described it in her own words, "the drunken woodpecker [sound], or constipated woodpecker, with a 'cinema' organ approach which was deliberate. That's the rhythm sound I like." Some time previously Dusty had asked The Zombies' Rod Argent to write a song for her and "If It Don't Work Out" was it. With him on piano and Dusty with a sob in her voice, the song began slowly to build into a musical explosion of guitar, brass and drums. Another possible single that was overlooked. Once again, Doris Troy and Madeline Bell shared support vocals on Garnett Mimms' "It Was Easier To Hurt Him", of which Dusty said "It's really the only one where I get a bit drowned [because] I was running from mike to mike on this one." With Ronnie Price on piano, Dusty felt the beat was much heavier on her version than on Cilla Black's single "I've Been Wrong Before". "Ronnie (Verrell) is such a sympathetic drummer; hear the way it swells, then goes down. Brother Tom calls it Horseguards' drumming." Again, the three ladies sang their way through "I Can't Hear You" and "Packin' Up". The Echoes' contribution was heavy and exactly what Dusty wanted to achieve with guitars, brass and Doug Reece's bass. But it was "I Had A Talk With My Man" that was her overall favourite. Selected at the last minute, Dusty admitted "It's such a lovely song but I was hoarse and I'm still amazed that it came out." Other tracks recorded for the album included her version of The Velvelettes' timeless classic "Needle In A Haystack", a hard-hitting, typical Motown song originally released in 1964. Dusty was unhappy with the result and intended to work further on it for possible future release.

The album caused a sensation. Although it could easily have been titled *Ev'rything's Coming Up Dusty, Madeline and Doris*, it was an innovative, overwhelmingly addictive release which presented Dusty as an international singer in a league of her own making. To mark the occasion, the disc was marketed in the most ambitious package ever issued in Britain for a pop singer. The cover was in book form, 12 pages of colour and black-and-white photos, while full colour pictures were featured on the thick card sleeve. It was the first time a record company had used such a lavish production and even The Beatles' *Beatles For Sale* album wasn't as elaborate. And the critics? This was typical – "She's now completely absorbed the Negro influence she's dabbled with and the result is a soul-packed set full of drama and captivating Springfield magic." *Ev'rything's Coming Up Dusty* sold £5,000-worth of records per day to reach number six in the chart in October 1965. For its short-lived American release, copies of the British cover were imported to package the American pressings.

The album displayed Dusty's determination to utilize the best she heard in American music. But the more she stood her ground, the more she was branded as a troublemaker by those who worked with her. "I was swiping things left, right and centre to record. It was pretty phenomenal to get that sound because the guys I had to work with – they were all sweethearts – but they were all playing standard basses. I was actually the first person to ask them to play a Fender bass. I really was a stickler for just getting there, just as close as I could, and that's where my reputation came from because I kept saying 'no, that's not it' and so on." R&B musician Dave Randle elaborated further: "What Dusty heard and saw of Motown, say, was very influential in her Philips' recordings. She insisted they got a bass player who could play fingerstyle instead of the then ubiquitous Bert Kamphaert-type of plectrum bass. She was unusual in making demands on the tracks and arrangements. Maybe Motown was doing just what she wanted but the result of those Philips records was unique. A big sound that transferred to other artists once Dusty and Franz had set the pace. Johnny Franz is the unsung hero of British pop thanks to his work with Dusty and the Walker Brothers."

Pat Rhodes was present during the recording sessions, and perhaps balanced the tension between singer and musicians. She recalled that when Dusty first became a soloist there was a lot of leg-pulling between her and Johnny Franz, but also serious discussions before a track was actually recorded. "And a bit of a temper when musicians wouldn't then give her the sound she wanted. She always struggled to get the right sound and because she's female, she always had this constant fight. Like 'what does she know, she's a woman.' And that's when we used to have some of what they called the foot-stamping episodes." Dave Randle added "She had a rare vision of what she was creating, and like many such geniuses, she had little in common with many of the people around her. Any shared understanding had to be on their, rather than her level, so she was cut off, despite her success."

Generally speaking, Dusty recorded in stocking feet, wearing a headscarf and glasses. With a hand cupped over one ear, she would sing a line or verse over several times before being satisfied, then rush to the control box for the play back, where she turned knobs until the drums sounded like the Household Cavalry had just marched by to drown any mistakes she felt were there. More often or not, the Cavalry would drown her voice too. If she was unsure of a song, she'd re-record it until she was exhausted or the song was completed – then worry about it until it was released. She regularly used Philips' recording studios at Marble Arch in London, despite hating its modest equipment. "The acoustics made the recordings sound bland and it was like singing in a padded cell."

Dusty never denied the way she blatantly emulated her American idols, and when Cliff Richard publicly nicknamed her "the white negress" she wasn't offended. "In fact, I don't think it had any impact on me at all." The title did, however, cause resentment among the black fraternity, as she explained: "It's not much fun having a glass of whisky thrown in your face by Nina Simone, who called me a honky and resented me being alive. She was having a few problems which I thought I could solve by being nice. Huh, I was still as naïve as ever! I was on my crusade of being helpful to people who had problems and I was warned not to approach her but... I knew better, didn't I?"

As 1965 ended, Dusty crammed in a 10-day trip to New York and Hollywood where Vic Billings had arranged spots on every major television show he could. Upon her return, she rehearsed for her first and only appearance on The Royal Variety Performance, staged at the London Palladium before the Queen on 8 November. She had been due to perform a year earlier but to her great distress was dropped from the line-up. "I was very hurt by being left out [in] '64, particularly as I was told I was in it. It seems that the Powers-That-Be have a 'Let's Punish Dusty-Springfield-Period' every now and then. Probably because I won't do my sentence at Blackpool!" Whatever the reason, Dusty, wearing a stunning blue and green sequinned gown, sang a mighty version of "I Just Don't Know What To Do With Myself" in the show's 'discotheque segment'. It was considered one of the highlights in the evening's show that included Frank Ifield, Shirley Bassey and Tony Bennett. From the Royal spotlight, Dusty returned to the Northern club circuit where she stayed until the middle of December.

In his autobiography, *Red Rose Blues*, published in 2002, Labour veteran Joe Ashton remembered with a smile the night Dusty performed at Yorkshire's Greaseborough Working Men's Club. "The chairman introduced her with the words 'Before the show starts, I 'ave an important announcement. Would the man who urinated against the front wall pack it in. Now 'ere's Dusty Springfield!' Dusty creased up, unable to sing. Only to be told by the grumpy host – "Get on with it luv, or I'll cut your fee!"

Chapter Five

YOU DON'T HAVE TO SAY YOU LOVE ME

"I think the original Italian version of the song was far superior to mine."

For the second year running, Dusty celebrated the New Year by appearing in the mayhem that was *Ready, Steady, Go!* She battled through hanging balloons and streamers, and Dusty clones ("these little domed creatures with beehives and black eyes") to present some type of solid performance for television viewers as she kissed goodbye to 1965 singing "Some Of Your Lovin'", "In The Middle Of Nowhere" and "Let's Hang On" with Lulu and Madeline Bell. "Everyone was blotto and they were constantly being pulled off stands or down stairs. I mean, half of it didn't get on camera, it was chaos," remembered a laughing Dusty. "It was brilliantly funny trying to actually do any of the shows. I cared and thought I could do things right but that clashed horribly with the whole attitude of the shows. But it worked because they had an immediacy which other shows didn't have. You did wonder what was going to go wrong and that gave it attention." Very much an integral part of the programme, many people credited its success to Dusty because of her immense impact on British music. People took note when she was on the television and listened when she raved about her passion for soul music. The fact that she had appeared singing the wrong lyrics, with her hem hanging down, or with her hair sticky-taped to her cheeks, mattered not one bit. In fact, it probably added to the viewing excitement.

The music Dusty played at home was American R&B, spearheaded by Motown, Stax, Atlantic, and several independent labels like Wand, Savoy and Parkway. Deep soul, smatterings of jazz and a few classical discs could also be found. Visitors to her Baker Street flat were sucked into her personal music world. Vicki Wickham was initiated in this way, which in turn led to her opening the *Ready, Steady, Go!* doors to welcome American acts previously only known to a cult following in Britain. The show also broke uncharted territory by turning the studio dancers into stars as well, in much the same way as the later American television sensation *Soul Train*.

Dusty burst into 1966 with an upbeat, bouncy single penned by Bea Verdi and Buddy Kaye, composers of "In The Middle Of Nowhere." Titled "Little By Little" it carried a similar format, with Dusty bashing her way through inane lyrics against a thrashing pseudo-gospel musical backdrop, interspliced with shrill support vocals from Madeline, Kiki and Lesley. Reviewers loved this rousing song, but not all fell under its spell, as one moaned, "It's a spinning example of expert professional minds over mediocre material." Needless to say, it wasn't one of Dusty's favourites either, as she said, "It isn't meant to be a great number. It's a sustainer … Everybody wanted something lively after 'Some Of Your Lovin" so this is it. It's to keep things ticking over." Naturally, she promoted the release with numerous British dates, while Philips Records' marketing people saturated the music papers with advertisements including the *NME*'s front cover where The Rolling Stones' "19th Nervous Breakdown" took up most of the page, with "Little By Little" and Barbra Streisand's "Second Hand Rose" squashed at the top, on the right-hand side of the page. Despite being an also-ran, "Little By Little" hit the Top 20.

Now earning £1,000 a week, and considerably more in America, Dusty kept her accounts on tape and at the end of every month sent the tape to her accountant. To ensure her moments of extravagance were kept under control, Vic Billings paid her a weekly allowance of £40 for living expenses. Much of her money was spent on clothes which she often purchased from the continent because the public wouldn't have seen them before. If shopping in London, Dusty frequented Neatawear, C&A, Woolands 21 and Wallis, spending up to £40 a dress. Her stage gowns were, of course, more expensive – "I can usually only wear them once. I had a lovely dress made for the Palladium show that cost £300, and a year later I wore it for something else and people moaned what was I wearing an old dress for!" Eric Plant, from the Darnell of London fashion house, regularly clothed her. "Dusty wasn't very busty," he recalled, "and had a tiny waist, but God cursed her when it came to her thighs." She was an unpredictable shopper and although Pat Rhodes generally accompanied her, it was more for her company than for her advice, and to keep fans at bay. She wasn't a follower of fashion, preferring to choose styles that suited her 5 feet 2 inches, and she didn't have a favourite boutique or fashion designer. "It's only after I've bought the dress that I'll look at the label. And as for boutiques, I'm rarely in the same place long enough to make a particular one my favourite." When she tired of her clothes, fans who were close to her had first pickings. During the seventies, Dusty destroyed a lot of her stage dresses and reputedly burned some of her wigs. Following her death in 1999, Pat Rhodes found several of the singer's outfits in the back of a wardrobe. "Dusty would have dresses dry cleaned, then give them to me because she hadn't room for them all... They could fetch thousands at auction, but I'll never part with them. They bring back all the glamour of that wonderful age." Her shoes, size 5, usually cost about £10 a pair, and she bought in quantity, fearing heels could break and she'd be stranded somewhere with nothing on her feet. Her favourite perfume was Joy or Chanel No 5, and she kept her nail varnish to a minimum, usually clear or pearl.

But it was Dusty's hair and eyes that attracted most attention. Her hair pieces cost 30 guineas, her wigs double that amount, and were bought from London's two main sources, Wig Creations and Wig Artists. When not working, she wore her own hair which she back-combed at the crown to give her height. She admitted that, over the years, she made a huge contribution to the hole in the ozone layer, spraying gallons of lacquer on her hair, and had developed special muscles from years of teasing her hair. In 1988 she told Brant Mewborn, "To this day, I can hold my hands in the air longer than anyone I know. I can also sit bolt upright in a plane for hours. I didn't get to sleep because once you dented all that spray, you'd need all sorts of wrenches and things to get it out again."

She added "If you have to take off your glasses to put your eyes on, then you can't really see what you're doing, so you put too much on!" That was the reason Dusty gave for her jet black eye lids and eye liner, her trademark. She smothered her eye lids with kohl before putting mascara on her eye lashes and there it stayed for five to six days because it took so long to remove it. "Every night I wash carefully round the paint", she told journalist Maureen Cleave. "Then I sprinkle talcum powder over it before I go to bed ... One day I'm going to scrape it off and find no eye lids underneath!" What's more "It bothers me that this panda-eyed, immovable beehive image has stuck with me from the beginning!" Television make-up artists turned away when they saw her coming, and hotel maids raised their eyes when Dusty was in town. "I tried to sleep on my back, but inevitably when asleep went back to the baby position. I got it all over the pillow, but... now I put towels on the pillows." Often told is the story of her deciding to make up her eyes on a short flight. When the plane landed, she hadn't finished. She told Penny Valentine, "I came out wearing huge dark glasses and there were photographers everywhere and they kept asking me to take the glasses off. Little did they know that I had one entirely naked eye underneath!"

Being a star was an expensive business which was, she confessed, another reason why she worked herself ragged. Her financial worth was to rise dramatically with her next single, her first and only British chart-topper.

Dusty first heard the song "Io Che Non Vivo (Senza Te)" at the 1965 San Remo Song Festival performed by its composer

Pino Donaggio, and although it didn't win the Festival it made a huge impression upon her. She loved the sweeping melody flowing against the dramatic delivery of the lyrics; it was Springfield material for sure. It took Dusty a year to record the song because she needed to find a new set of lyrics, or at the very least an English translation. She tried and failed, as did her brother. She said she'd pull out the sheet music in the recording studio, flap it around as she asked for help, but nothing worked. In the end, Vicki Wickham heard herself agreeing to write the words; she was backed into a corner because Dusty wanted to record the song the next day. That evening, Vicki was dining with Simon Napier-Bell (then manager of The Yardbirds) and together they wrote what were probably the corniest of lyrics known to the world. Even Dusty was horrified to read them the next day, but could do nothing due to the recording schedule, and the fact that she'd sing anything just to get the melody on record. The backing track was already in place, the musicians were primed, but during the actual session Dusty complained there was too much echo on her voice. After much deliberation, the engineer recommended that the nearby stairwell would solve the problem. So Dusty stood halfway up the stairs, leaning over the banister to sing into a microphone hanging from the ceiling in front of her.

History dictates it took 59 takes (with take 53 being released) until she was happy with the result, later known as "You Don't Have To Say You Love Me". Commercially speaking it was her finest recording to date. From the big, blousy introduction, a desperately impassioned singer swept her broken heart through lyrics that really didn't warrant such passion. Projected by Ivor Raymonde's panache for plush and extravagant orchestrations that verged upon suffocation, the powerhouse of emotion was a milestone in popular music's history. It was a typical Dusty who said, "I think the original Italian version of the song was far superior to mine."

While the public flocked to purchase the single, reviewers were mixed in their opinions. One noted the song was recorded before feminists had started to be taken seriously. It was clear she was

attempting to stand her ground in pursuit of loveless sex by display-
ing an attitude of getting her own way without being emotionally
involved with a nameless partner. Another wrote: "It was damned
near perfect." It was also voted a 'miss' on the popular music panel
show *Juke Box Jury*.

"You Don't Have To Say You Love Me" was the number one
British single in April 1966, within days of Dusty's twenty-seventh
birthday. It passed silver status, later gold, based on international
sales, was nominated for a Grammy award, and was subsequently
re-recorded by many other artists, including Elvis Presley. Its popularity had its downside, as Dusty explained, "I dread [singing] it
live because of the key change. It's such a killer vocally. It's a sort of
a love/hate relationship. If everything else is going wrong, when I
get to that song, I know it's going to be all right. Besides, it gets me
off the stage." Forcing her voice to reach notes that weren't comfortably within her range had a devastating effect on it and would,
in time, affect her recording skills.

During her chart-topping month, Dusty was out and about in
Britain but still found time to rent a three-bedroomed house in
trendy Chelsea with a little garden and a roof that threatened to
blow off in a storm. She was in great demand on television, including appearances on her beloved *Ready, Steady, Go!* which had, earlier in the year, featured her as-yet-unreleased version of "Heartbeat" as its theme. Dusty had religiously copied the Gloria Jones'
original and Northern Soul classic for an EP intended for a February 1966 release. Due to technical reasons, the project was shelved,
but an edited and remixed version of the song was included in the
1994 compilation *The Legend Of Dusty Springfield*, and five years
later a newly mixed version of the complete recording was released
in America on the *Dusty* CD.

Back in 1966, Dusty spent time in Stockholm where, she told
Record Mirror, she wasn't very well known. "People are aware of
me, but more in the business than the general public. I don't think
I've had a big seller on the continent... they certainly don't like

me in Germany. They either like rock 'n' roll or country and western, and I don't fall anywhere near that." It was a different story in
Britain, where Dusty was recognized everywhere she went. It was
at this time that Dusty realized she could never lead an ordinary
life again. She enjoyed a life others envied; she was idolised by
millions, and had become a cultural icon as the face of the sixties
without being a dolly bird. But when an artist created a painting of
Dusty naked from the waist up, she was so incensed that her lawyers fought to have it banned from public viewing, prompting the
artist to complain"I wanted to immortalize the girl!"

While admitting that she enjoyed being recognized, there were
limits. She hated being photographed, a symptom of her need to
protect herself from undue invasion of her privacy. She was also very
guarded when it came to friendship. This stayed with her throughout her life. "I have very few friends. I like it better that way because
I've been let down by too many people to trust anyone."

Following Dusty's death in 1999, fans felt her memory was tarnished by comments in a book written by Vicki Wickham and
Penny Valentine. Pat Rhodes responded by telling Sarah Hook
in 2004, "Before Dusty died she said 'a lot of people are going to
say things about me you will find very hurtful'. Just remember this
– when I'm dead, Pat, they can't hurt me… Dusty named several
people and I'm sorry she did name Vicki. When she mentioned her
name, I honestly thought she was being paranoid because I never
thought Vicki would ever say anything to hurt Dusty."

"Thousands of fans converging on the massive Wembley Empire Pool for the biggest pop show in the world – the *New Musical
Express* Poll Winners concert with a dazzling host of stars – Beatles,
Stones, Walkers, Who, Dusty Springfield, Dave Dee, Roy Orbi-
son, Cliff, Shadows, and others. Where else would you find 10,000
pop fans? Where else would you see The Beatles and The Stones
on the same bill? Where else would you see 22 top stars in one
afternoon." So boasted the music paper's advertorial for the 1966
May Day gala, organized by staffer Maurice Kinn. Winning the top

spot in the World and British Female Singer categories, Dusty's act included "In The Middle Of Nowhere" and "You Don't Have To Say You Love Me".

As her career peaked, Dusty decided to address the problem with her American releases, and took the only course open – she threatened to go on strike with Philips Records unless the company released her from the American side of her contract, where she was represented by the Philips-owned Mercury subsidiary. The US label's president, Irving Green, flew to London for meetings with Vic Billings, but Dusty remained adamant – "I have no real quarrel with the company here, but in the US they have done virtually nothing to promote me or my records... I'm totally dissatisfied with the whole set up and I'm just not going to record again until something is done." Her strike lasted three hours, but resulted in her being signed to Atlantic Records in a £30,000 deal and in "You Don't Have To Say You Love Me" hitting the American Top Four. "Funny that!" she quipped.

Dusty's professional life became ever busier, but her greatest coup of all was to follow in Petula Clark's footsteps with a BBC1 television series of six 30-minute programmes. Titled *Dusty* it was screened from 18 August to 22 September 1966. She enjoyed herself on the shows but did not relish the hard work involved. She chose the music and used the programmes as a vehicle to sing material she couldn't record, from the likes of the Motown and Stax/Atlantic catalogues. The first show kicked off with a fast-moving version of the Four Tops' "Something About You", before calming down with "Chained To A Memory" and "I Believe In You". Her guests, the Dudley Moore Trio, jazzed their way through "I'm Old Fashioned" before she joined them to sing "Dat Dere". The American stand-up comic, Milt Kamen, guested on the second show which included Dusty's rousing interpretation of the Kim Weston/Isley Brothers' classic "Take Me In Your Arms (Rock Me A Little While)" and her two hits "I Just Don't Know What To Do With Myself" and "Goin' Back". "Some Of Your Lovin'" and

"Twenty Four Hours From Tulsa" were a couple of Springfield favourites in the third, where writer/comedian/actor Woody Allen was her guest. Dusty turned to jazz for the fourth programme's guests of The Four Freshman, and for herself, chose third-party repertoire like "Call Me Irresponsible" and "The Real Thing". One time comedy stooge to Dudley Moore, Peter Cook appeared on the fifth show, where Dusty opened with Dee Dee Warwick's "We're Doing Fine" and included her chart-topper "You Don't Have To Say You Love Me". Senor Wences, the prominent ventriloquist whose stable of characters included Johnny, a child-like face drawn on his hand, made a special appearance on the last show. Dusty started the show with Mary Wells' "You Lost The Sweetest Boy", and included "Losing You" among a handful of her favourite songs. The viewing average was 9.5 million for the series. Madeline Bell, Lesley Duncan, Barbara Moore and Maggie Stredder of The Ladybirds were her support vocalists, with a 32-piece orchestra under the leadership of Johnny Pearson. The series was held up for two weeks to allow the BBC to screen two half-hour shows recorded by Herb Alpert & his Tijuana Brass during their spring visit to Britain.

Following a number one single is always an awesome task for any artist, but in Dusty's case she'd already recorded it, such was her determination to re-associate herself with Gerry Goffin and Carole King. Originally planned as the follow-up to "Little By Little", "Goin' Back" was released in early July. Pat Rhodes said "Dusty had such a great peer respect for Carole King to the effect that when they once passed each other in a corridor, they both blushed and couldn't speak to each other." Dusty told Roger Scott in 1989, "There was something about her voice, it was like mine, very faulty... It can wobble sometimes and things might be a bit off, but there was something just wonderful about it." This time, though, Dusty appeared not to have exclusivity to a Carole King demo because Goldie and the Gingerbreads, who had lived in the same Bayswater block as Dusty, also recorded a version. There are varying stories surrounding Goldie and the girls' version, but the upshot was the composers did not like the alterations they made to the song and would not allow them to release it. Apparently, Dusty would often invite friends to her flat to hear demo recordings of songs she had under consideration. "Goin' Back" was one, but when she dithered for so long about recording it, Goldie swiped it without her knowing. Not being able to obtain the sheet music, Goldie was forced to adlib some of the lyrics during the recording. "When Goldie did it, I nearly committed suicide," she told *Melody Maker's* Mike Ledgewood. "I think this is the most adult song I have sung. And when Goldie's record was withdrawn, I breathed a sign of relief."

The song was a brave move, lacking as it did a strong commercial element and the huge, plush orchestration to which listeners had become accustomed. The song glowed with sensitivity as the lyrics sprang to life, Springfield-style, her husky voice accompanied by a single piano and flutes until the instrumental break where a previously hidden orchestra swelled to wash away the keyboards. Many predicted it to be her first major blunder, but the public showed that they admired her courage by pushing the single to number ten. Carole King said Dusty's version had reduced her to tears. "I knew as time went by that she was fiercely possessive of 'Goin' Back'," Dusty told Andy Peebles in 1989. "She wanted to do it herself... It was a very special song to her ... And she let me do it and to have that praise from her ... it was the ultimate accolade from someone who wanted to do it herself ... I'd never felt happier."

When her August promotional tour of America was postponed at the last minute due to an air strike, Dusty put the time to good use by holidaying in Carvajal, Spain, with Madeline Bell, Tom, Peppi Borza and Vic Billings. They rented a large apartment near the beach – "The weather wasn't all that fantastic but I've got some freckles which are pretty spectacular!" The holiday prepared her for the gruelling tours planned for the remainder of the year that included America, the continent and Britain. But first she had to promote "All I See Is You", her new single in September 1966. Clive Westlake, who first met Dusty as a Springfield, wrote the song with Ben Weisman. Clive was a struggling composer until he worked with Tom on "Pit-A-Pat" and "Little Boat" for The Springfields, and Dusty's "Summer Is Over". He then worked for Carlin Music Corp and, when Ben Weisman chanced to be in London following a trip from Italy, he gave Clive a half-written song in the vein of "You Don't Have To Say You Love Me" to work on. By chance, Clive had already composed another song with the title "All I See Is You" and simply transferred it to Ben's lyrics. He then played it to Vic Billings who instructed him to finish it because Dusty wanted to record it. "I loved this song," Clive said at the time, "and you can't imagine how proud I felt to hear 'the voice' of my life, singing it." Another intense, impassioned beauty, overflowing with warmth, "All I See Is You" had the same impact as her number one title. With its similar dramatic overtones and straining vocals, Dusty's neck muscles bulged as she wove her tale of a dying love. It gave her the chance to camp up the drama with outstretched arms, flicking hands and head flung back, bearing all the hallmarks of a twenty-first century diva as she promoted the song to enjoy a number nine British hit.

Dusty's headlining autumn tour opened on 27 September 1966 in London, and included the Alan Price Set, The Settlers and Episode Six. Dave Berry appeared for the first two dates only, but it was Dusty who stole the show. From the opening strains of "Take Me In Your Arms (Rock Me A Little While)" when Dusty, dressed in a sparkling blue, full-length gown danced on stage with her now characteristic dance movements learned from Martha Reeves, she had the audiences in her hand. "A singing powerhouse couldn't have come more beautifully packaged" one reviewer glowed.

As she celebrated the single's success, and being presented with her award for top British singer by *Melody Maker* at a function in the restaurant at the top of the GPO Tower, Dusty hit the tabloids once again. Needless to say, the headlines were not generated by her success, but by an "off duty" incident involving two cheese tarts. She was, apparently, infuriated when she saw the restaurant manager bullying a young waiter in front of her, so lobbed a tart at him. It missed and hit the barman. To ensure she was spot on next time, Dusty shook hands with the manager as she was leaving and pressed a slushy cheese tart into his palm. "Miss Springfield's a charming lady," was all he would say. Carole Gibson, a member of the highly acclaimed "Lets Talk Dusty" website, was in Madeline Bell's dressing room at the Cabaret Club in Manchester when she took a call from Dusty. She told her what had happened at the awards ceremony and said it was a bread roll, not a tart, and the incident would no doubt make the papers the next day. Which it did.

With no new album available, Philips Records issued a *Golden Hits* compilation during October in an attempt to bridge the growing gap between releases. A diamond of a record, rounding up all her hits to date – except "Stay Awhile" – it soared into the number two slot. Dusty then flew to New York for television spots, taking a couple of days out to rehearse a new act more suited to American audiences. More sophisticated, perhaps, she said, "but not in naughty tight dresses or anything like that", it was a set that would be suitable for her nightclub debut at Basin Street East, where some of the world's top jazz singers perform.

In her absence, an incident that had been haunting her finally reared its legal head when she was criticized by a high court judge for skipping the country when she knew a case against her was due to be heard. Dusty, who was wearing sunglasses while driving at night, knocked down 63-year-old Ida Metzger as she was crossing the road in London's Berkley Square. The accident was Dusty's fault through negligent driving, but neither she nor her passenger gave evidence. "I have no doubt that she was driving too fast and I don't suppose her ability to keep a proper look-out was enhanced by wearing dark glasses," the judge told the *Evening Standard*, before adding, "If my newspapers tell me rightly, she has recently gone to America. It seemed she knew the case was fixed and just went wandering off..." Dusty paid £1,900 in damages to Miss Metzger, with a first instalment of £500.

Neither was America a bundle of laughs as Dusty walked into another chaotic series of events. Buddy Rich, acknowledged as the greatest drummer of all time, and his band were her support act at Basin Street East. For various reasons, Buddy's band was not made available to rehearse with Dusty until the very day of her perform-ance, leaving her a measly two hours to work out 14 new arrange-ments. Dusty claimed that she "even heard him tell his band not to put too much effort into playing for me in case they tired them-selves!" She told Q magazine in 1988 that when she had first asked him if she could work with his band, his response wasn't what she had expected. "You fucking broad! Who do you think you fucking are, bitch?" Totally incensed, Dusty hit him and claimed to have knocked his toupee flying!

Vic Billings told author Lucy O'Brien that Buddy Rich invited his friends, such as Johnny Carson, to the opening night. "Rich did an hour-and-a-half. Carson about another three hours, and finally Dusty got on. She went down great, but there were big punch-ups going on. He'd announce her saying 'she's supposed to be a great singer, but I've seen better.' And she'd insult him." Certainly it helped sell tickets as the media printed every incident. Buddy Rich lost out because Dusty had the media on her side with com-ments like "...the spotlight should have been on Dusty Springfield, the British star" and "... what happened to Dusty shouldn't have happened to the British ambassador." Her performance included "Sunny", "England Swings", a Burt Bacharach medley and "You Don't Have To Say You Love Me". At the end of the season, members of Rich's band presented her with a pair of red boxing gloves, with a note reading "you were brave enough to do what we couldn't." The two again shared the British stage in March 1968 when they appeared on *Sunday Night At The London Palladium*. But this time they didn't talk. Three years later, they appeared on the same bill on *One Night Stand* – again there is no record of whether they spoke to each other, although Dusty did say they went on to become friends.

Before returning to London, Dusty spent some time in New York to record with Jerry Ragovoy and Herb Bernstein. "I'll Try Anything" was one of four titles recorded, and was scheduled to be a future single. Dusty intended to return in the New Year to complete this and record one further track, "The Look Of Love" earmarked for the forthcoming spoof James Bond movie *Casino Royale*. Meantime, she was committed to throwing herself into the British tradition of the pantomime, *Merry King Cole* being staged at the Liverpool Empire. At least, that's what the public expected. But Dusty didn't don a skimpy costume and fishnet tights, nor did she slap her thigh and court the principle girl. She wore a full-length, sparkling white gown with a red sash at the waist to perform a mini-concert of her own. During her act she did something slightly out of character from her normal performance when a large screen was lowered on to the stage. Using a long stick, Dusty pointed out the words to "Yellow Submarine" and "The More I See You", so the audience could sing along with her. She didn't hate pantomimes, she said, but couldn't have dressed up pretending to be someone she wasn't. "Luckily, Vic Billings nipped those kind of suggestions in the bud before they got to me... I just do my act at the end."

Unlike Dusty, other artists were revelling in the world of make-believe: Cliff Richard and The Shadows were in *Cinderella* at the London Palladium, Lulu starred in *Babes In The Wood* at the Wimbledon Theatre, and Eden Kane was in *Dick Whittington* at the Westcliff Pavilion. The first pantomime Dusty had ever seen had been the previous year when Britain's top female impersonator, Danny La Rue, played the starring role. "I went to see it because I was told he did a marvellous send-up of me. He did and I really enjoyed it... He was dressed up in a long gown, with sequins and he sang a couple of my hits... I was quite flattered." Danny La Rue, also an Irish Catholic, said "The people I impersonate are usually visually attractive and it's not a dig at them... a lot of them are my friends. Dusty Springfield is a great mover when she sings ... for her I have the dark lashes sweeping the floor!"

It was strange that Dusty felt the way she did about pantomimes given her love of drag artists, watching their acts in London pubs or catching Danny La Rue's shows whenever time allowed. The two became friends and socialized. At one of Danny's parties, however, held at his luxurious Hampstead home, the two clashed. Dusty was drunk and had left a ring in the bathroom after washing her hands. Some time later she noticed it was missing and, according to Barbara Windsor in her autobiography *All Of Me*, "[She] went into a drunken rage, screeching 'my ring, my ring, somebody's taken my ring!' Amid all the predictable jokes – 'who'd want your ring, dear?' and so on – Danny got very upset and ... [gave her] the most enormous diamond ring from his own collection... saying, 'There you are, darling. Have that. Nobody steals in my house.'" Her ring was later found.

Dusty also once said that she learned most of her make-up tricks from drag queens, adding "...what kind of mascara lasts longest, how to apply eye shadow, very serious decisions. If the truth were known, I think I'm basically a drag queen myself."

During a free Sunday in her *Merry King Cole* season, and against her manager's wishes, Dusty drove to London after the second show and flew to New York to do some more work on "I'll Try Anything". Composer Mark Barkan had met her during her Basin Street run, and played her the song at his home. "She was wearing this outrageous mini skirt with the name of my song 'Pretty Flamingo' on it," he recalled. (Manfred Mann had enjoyed a 1966 British number one with "Pretty Flamingo".) Playing the piano, Mark presented a rough version of the song, with Vic Millrose's lyrics, which she loved sufficiently to ask for a demo record. Composer/producer Ellie Greenwich recorded it because her vocal style was the closest to Dusty. Years later, Ellie explained that she had actually made demos of several titles for her, and that Dusty had kept them all. "She hired me to do background vocals on one of her sessions. So, there we were stood on mike, looking alike in our big blonde hair. She was one of my idols, so I tried desperately to sing exactly like her." Dusty returned to Liverpool with the demo that had been recorded and worked on in New York, but before she was satisfied with the result, she ended up recording the song at two different locations (the second in London) on three separate occasions. All that work gave her a number 13 British hit in February 1967, her first of the year.

With Madeline Bell and Lesley Duncan's prominent support vocals, Dusty transformed the simple song into an urgent, powerful performance. An unpretentious song, with bags of chorus, it was as punchy in style as its predecessor "All I See Is You" was dramatic. The single's sales were helped by concentrated promotion, including her appearance on *Sunday Night At The London Palladium*, her first for over a year. If "I'll Try Anything" had been issued a month earlier, the public would have seen a bruised and battered singer. During a weekend visit to Pat Rhodes' Hornsey home, Dusty had climbed the steps to the front door, slipped on an icy patch and fallen again into the dustbins on the pavement. When Pat opened the door to find out what the commotion was about, she too slipped with the same consequences. "And there we were both sitting on our bruised dignity for the world to see!"

With another hit single behind her – but still no new album – Dusty had reached a musical crossroads. Should she continue to compete for chart placings or concentrate more on the less stressful yet more lucrative cabaret circuit which had, to date, welcomed her warmly for her stylish presentations, goony humour and, of course, the voice? In three years she had carved herself a name in British music, inadvertently created a fashion explosion, and created an enigma – an alter ego that allowed the shy convent girl known as Mary O'Brien to blossom into an international artist. Yet the star still refused to accept just how talented she really was. Dusty would later face the dilemma of this enigma head on, but for now she had two great challenges – seasons in two top nightclubs: one in London, the other in Sydney, Australia.

Chapter Six

WHERE AM I GOING?

"If I have to go on Top Of The Pops *again, waving my arms about, I'll go potty!"*

M otown music continued to hit the British charts, and during January 1967 the Four Tops took London by storm with two shows before 14,000 people at the Royal Albert Hall. This was followed by dates throughout all the major cities. Madeline Bell was their support act and, with Lesley Duncan, also provided the Four Tops with back-up vocals. "It was the fanatical exultation of the Nuremburg Rallies, the incredible enthusiasm of a World Cup football crowd," enthused one reviewer, "and it was all there for the Four Tops before they even set foot on the stage." As for Madeline's performance: "She really won everyone's heart... A fine relaxed act, even though she was scared by the reaction of the crowd." And Dusty? She missed the show because she was in Liverpool. When the Four Tops' show hit Liverpool, she was recording in London.

Following dates in Manchester and Stockton, Dusty appeared once again at the *NME* Poll Winners concert at Wembley. She had also won four categories in the *Disc And Music Echo* readers' poll but was unable to accept the awards personally at a ceremony in London's Hilton Hotel because she was in America. She sent a telegram of thanks. The awards were presented to her by comedian Dave Allen during the *Sunday Night At The London Palladium* show on 19 February 1967.

On 8 May 1967, Dusty faced a huge challenge in opening a three-week run at London's top cabaret restaurant, The Talk Of the

Town, situated on the corner of Charing Cross Road and Leicester Square. When this type of venue eventually fell from favour, The Talk Of The Town closed, to be renovated and re-opened by nightclub tycoon Peter Stringfellow in 1983. He renamed it The Hippodrome, also the name of his record label to which Dusty signed two years later. Unfortunately, that would not prove to be an association made in heaven.

Returning to 1967, Dusty was earning £2,500 a week for her 45-minute nightly spot, backed by the club's resident Burt Rhodes orchestra, augmented by her own musicians. She also had Madeline Bell, Maggie Stredder and Lesley Duncan as backing singers. Her audience was mainstream music fans with a few bob to spend on a weekday evening. Younger fans inevitably found the ticket/meal prices too expensive. With a repertoire that included middle-of-the-road titles like "My Colouring Book", "I Only Wanna Laugh" and "If You Go Away", Dusty easily won over her audiences. She featured hits like "You Don't Have To Say You Love Me" and "I'll Try Anything", before diversifying with the Latin beat of "La Bamba". When the highly successful series of shows finished, Dusty always gave gifts to members of the orchestra, backstage staff and to her singers. This year she gave each of her singers a small, round, brass pillbox/locket with a white enamel face, set with rhinestones... and crammed with cannabis. On the back of each was a personal notation from her. Maggie believed the cannabis was a piece of topaz but when her husband explained what it really was, the hash was quickly flushed down the toilet! By all accounts, Madeline and Lesley were overjoyed with theirs.

While Dusty was wowing West End audiences, Sandie Shaw was representing Britain in the Eurovision Song Contest with "Puppet On A String". So nerve-racking did the young, barefooted singer find the ordeal that she decided she'd don a wig and assume a completely new identity as Dusty's kid sister. But, in the end, she swallowed her nerves and headed for Vienna in her pink, chiffon sequinned, frock to win the contest with a song she later grew to hate.

Dusty was never asked to represent her country in this contest.

"Give Me Time", another Italian ballad, was also issued in May. A gentle, poignant song, so typical of Dusty with its moving melody, the record started subtly, building steadily until the climax arrived to a chorus of cascading strings. Translated songs seldom work as well as they do in their original language, but this one was definitely an exception to the rule. Despite this, "Give Me Time", written by Melfa, Tommas and Morina, and recorded in London with Peter Callendar's English lyrics, struggled to reach number 24 in the chart. It was Dusty's lowest chart appearance since "Your Hurtin' Kinda Love" in 1965. It was a shame radio DJs didn't flip the disc over to discover the gloriously sensuous "The Look Of Love". This happened in America, and helped sales no end, pushing the single up to the number 22 spot. While Dusty's selling power may have seen some slight decline, her brother's career was in the ascendant, thanks to the continuing success of The Seekers enjoying their fourth million-seller with "Georgy Girl", from the movie of the same name. The film's original theme had been declined by Dusty and when The Seekers were approached, Tom felt it wasn't suitable for them either. He wrote the new song with Jim Dale and took it to number three in the British chart. Later on that year, Tom and The Seekers amicably split up, and a year later he released his *Sun Songs* album for Decca Records. Dusty wrote the sleeve notes. Singing was never his first love, he pointed out, and what he did as a Springfield was a specialized form of screeching. "If the audiences had heard me without the other two they would have taken to the hills!"

The year 1967 saw Britain fall under the influence of Flower Power and its associated drugs culture. The movement's philosophy was to do their own thing, abandon conventional society and blow the mind of everyone they met! Shops selling kaftans, bells and beads did a roaring trade, and 1967's music reflected this revolutionary lifestyle with songs like The Beatles' "All You Need Is Love", Scott McKenzie's "San Francisco (Flowers In Your Hair)" and The Move's "Flowers In The Rain". The ballads rose and fell, with Englebert Humperdink's "Release Me" and "The Last Waltz" the most successful while, on the other musical note, Motown was upbeat and happy thanks to The Supremes, Stevie Wonder and the Four Tops. Dusty fell somewhere in between.

Following the viewing success of her first television series, Dusty began rehearsals for her second – *Dusty* – to be screened in August. Another six shows were to be produced by Stanley Dorfman, with a formula that ran roughly as before, Dusty mixing soul with pop, ably supported by Madeline, Lesley and Maggie. She swung into the first show with "Live It Up", followed by her hit "I'll Try Anything". Warren Mitchell, star of the top-rated television sitcom *Till Death Us Do Part*, in which his character, Alf Garnett, amused and disgusted viewers to equal degrees, sang "Every Little While" with Dusty. American jazz singer and composer Mel Torme performed two songs on the second show before duetting with his hostess on "Can't We Be Friends", "Pick Yourself Up" and "Let's Get Away From It All". Dusty included her own 1966 hit "All I See Is You" and paid homage to Aretha Franklin. With openers "Come Back To Me" and "If I Lose This Dream", she introduced José Feliciano, the blind guitarist/singer who specialized in Latin Pop, on her third show. He performed "Goin' To Chicago" and, with Johnny Hawksworth on bass, "My Foolish Heart". Dusty closed with the Timi Yuro classic "You Can Have Him". Tom Jones, boasting a handful of hits that included two number ones, joined Dusty on the fourth show. They sang "Baby Baby Baby" together, following his solo spot which included "I'll Never Fall In Love Again". The Springfields' mournful "Two Brothers" was included in Dusty's repertoire much to the surprise of the audience. She chose Sam Cooke's "Good Times" to open the penultimate show, followed by a cheeky "If My Friends Could See Me Now", while Los Muchucambos, a family-orientated band specializing in Latin and Tefano, were her guests. She closed with Garnett Mimms' "It Was Easier To Hurt Him" and a hard-hitting version of "Heatwave" from Martha

Reeves and the girls. Ex-Walker Brother Scott guested on the last in the series singing "Mathilde" and "When Joanna Loved Me", while Dusty opened with the frenetic "Nowhere To Run" and closed with "You Don't Have To Say You Love Me", her ballsy ballad.

"I didn't like the first... show and I don't like the second... I don't much care for Dusty Springfield herself," one critic wrote, before adding, "Dusty's was a very noisy show. A Chicago machine-gunning immediately afterwards was like a patter of raindrops on roses." Another wrote, "Dusty was back last night... pop has changed and so has she. Now, it's mainly quiet and gentle. Flower Power and so on; but Dusty's impact seems to wilt as she becomes more muted. Come back noisy Dusty of 1965! We need you!" Dusty told *The Radio Times*, "It took me three or four shows before I felt I'd got the hang of this. With this new series I've got more confidence in handling television techniques."

She still, however, had one major problem due to her short sightedness. Unable to wear glasses because the effect would be wrong, and not able to wear contact lenses due to her heavy eye make-up ("and I always got cat hair in my eyes, so it didn't really work"), she had tremendous difficulty seeing the cameras. "They stick a piece of white cardboard underneath the lens to enable me to spot it. It's frightening that I can't read any kind of prompt card... I have great trouble remembering lyrics so I'm always prepared to invent suitable words to fill in."

From television she switched to the stage to complete dates around the country ending in Bournemouth, then grabbed a two-week holiday in California during August 1967. From there she flew direct to Tokyo for three weeks of promotion, having come second to Joan Baez in Japan in a poll for the world's best female singer. Leaving Heathrow, Dusty wore bells and beads over a multi-coloured striped trouser suit, with a huge hat hiding her hair. Photographers made much of her kissing Peppi Borza goodbye.

Dusty was out of the country when "What's It Gonna Be?", her fourteenth single, was released in September. The Jerry Ragovoy and Mort Shuman composition showed how adept Dusty was in bringing home a careless, almost throwaway number. She edged more forcefully towards her love of soul music by sounding more black than white. It was not as instantly commercial as some of her previous releases, but when Dusty was on her soul kick, her chart placings inevitably suffered. Susan Barrett also recorded the song and, as her version was also released late in 1967, it's not entirely clear who did it first. With Dusty not available to promote it, the single floundered and was her first not to chart. This was a great shame because it included some of the finest voices in soul music including Carole King, Nickolas Ashford and Valerie Simpson. Dusty had previously crossed paths with Ashford and Simpson in New York before they signed with Motown Records, as she told Andy Peebles on Radio 1 in 1989. "It was the week before they signed and they weren't sure ... they said 'we gotta play this for you ...we really want you to have it, but on the other hand we really need to sign with Motown. But if we don't, you can have it. And they played me the opening bars of 'Ain't No Mountain High Enough', and then the next week they signed with Motown. [The song] was everything that was stunning to me." Indeed, the song was tailor made for Dusty, but when Marvin Gaye and Tammi Terrell released their hit version in 1967 and Diana Ross her fireball interpretation three years later, she believed it was best left to the Motown artists. Susan Barrett, on the other hand, enjoyed an American hit. Dusty's version of the song was included on the Fab-U-Lus CD compilation *Wigan Casino Soul Club – 30 Years Of Northern Soul Memories* issued in 2003 because it was a popular play at the Casino and in Torch clubs. Joining her on this compilation were her personal favourites like Gloria Jones, Tommy Hunt, Nancy Wilson and Dobie Grey.

Heading for a three-week engagement at Chequers in Kings Cross, Sydney, within weeks of the single's release wasn't the wisest of moves. She needed to be seen by the British public, instead of performing on the other side of the world. The Australian gigs, however, were her second great challenge of the year, and she had little choice in the matter. But when she arrived in Sydney, she discovered there was no bass guitarist in her support group. So she flew in Doug Reece. "Australia was fun. I went prepared to hate it. Last time I was shoved from city to city and had a rotten time but this time the club in Sydney was good. The owners were nice and I enjoyed every minute of it." During her stay, she met hairdresser John Adams for the first time. He had his own salon and was hairdresser to most of the entertainers who performed at Chequers. "When I heard Dusty was there," he told *Disc and Music Echo* in 1968, "I phoned her continuously and finally, out of sheer exhaustion, she said 'OK'. It worked so well that she brought me back to England with her." Dusty also had time to hit the nightclubs and spend time shopping. The run was an overwhelming success, and when it finished Dusty headed for Los Angeles, checking into a hotel where she slept for four solid days. It's not clear whether it was the performing or shopping which tired her most.

Dusty then promoted the American release of "What's It Gonna Be?" before flying to New York, and later Bermuda where she fulfilled a ten-day club engagement. Thanks to her hands-on promotion, "What's It Gonna Be" reached the American top 40 and was her final hit under the Philips deal. While in California, she recorded the Lee Hazlewood song "Sweet Ride" for the teenage melodramatic movie of the same name. Darlene Love was among the support singers.

The failure of "What's It Gonna Be?" didn't prevent Philips Records releasing her third studio album, *Where Am I Going?*, in October 1967. It was aptly titled because it appeared that Dusty really didn't know, since a pot pourri of musical styles was on offer on the album. The cover, featuring a black-and-white picture of a smiling Dusty, knees together, wearing a mini dress and wide-brimmed hat, with a cartoon balloon in orange and off-pink asking "Where Am I Going?" was uninspiring to say the least. Nevertheless, *NME*'s Keith Altham wrote in the sleeve notes, "This is champagne Springfield with Dusty at her most sophisticated and dramatic" and to a certain extent he was spot on, especially with her cover versions. These included a take on the Cissy Houston original "Bring Him Back" which was almost identical to her peer's version, the uptempo beat and controlled vocals making for an exciting start. The album ranged from gospel to soul, playing to Dusty's growing obsession with Aretha Franklin along the way. She paid homage with "Don't Let Me Lose This Dream", followed by "I Can't Wait Until I See My Baby's Face", which she recorded after Baby Washington's original cut. The song was also recorded by Madeline Bell in 1965, Dusty providing support vocals. Dusty's version was a combination of all three, while her take on the Evie Sands' track "Take Me For A Little While" prompted Paul Howes to write, "The song is like a time bomb, waiting to go off. And it does. From cool supplication it gradually builds to frenzied demand."

Other noteworthy tracks included Betty Everett's "Chained To A Memory", a personal Dusty favourite, once again included as a tribute, this time to Betty's immense and often underrated talent. Earmarked as the follow-up to "I Just Don't Know What To Do With Myself", Dusty swiped "They Long To Be Close To You" from a Dionne Warwick album. Years later it became a hit for The Carpenters, featuring the awesome, yet tragic, voice of Karen. (Ironically, Dusty would record a duet with Richard during the mid-eighties.) Digging deep into her soul, Dusty delivered the perfect version of Chip Taylor's composition "Welcome Home", before changing musical direction with "Come Back To Me" from the musical *On A Clear Day You Can See Forever* and the album's title from *Sweet Charity*. The whole album was too mature and overpowering for Dusty's young audience. Apart from the handful of opening tracks, the album appeared to be aimed at the middle of the road market, hardly the direction for a successful pop singer. Peter Jones wrote, "This album is the centre piece of a tremendous lot of care and attention. Perfection has been aimed for and reached, almost without exception." Penny Valentine added, "With a perfect showcase for Dusty's talents such as this... it is easier to make a few minor complaints than to lavish... deserved praise on all concerned. So if there are a few niggly points then they are only things like the unevocative cover design, and the inclusion of a well worn song like 'Sunny'."

While Dusty was smarting over the fate of *What's It Gonna Be?* she also criticized the record company's handling of the album, as she told *Melody Maker* in 1968. "It really upset me because I'd worked hard on the [album]... One or two of the tracks were done a long time ago but hadn't been finished, the Bacharach track for one. Then I did a couple of standards as you're expected to progress in that way. A lot of the tracks though are semi-R&B which I picked myself because I liked them."

Dusty returned to Britain during January 1968 and launched into a week of engagements at The Castaways Club in Birmingham, followed by The Batley Variety Club in Yorkshire. She then took two days out to record in London where "Take Another Little Piece Of My Heart" was one of the tracks completed. It was a short stay because she returned to America in February to concentrate on television work before spending the remainder of the month recording in London. By now, certain journalists were berating her lack of commitment, causing her to retaliate hotly with comments like "I haven't been neglecting my fans. I'm the one who has been neglected in that nobody has given me any decent material to record." And the remark "If I have to go on *Top of the Pops* again, waving my arms about, I'll go potty," didn't help ingratiate herself with the public either.

When her planned cabaret engagements in America were cancelled, Dusty flew to Amsterdam to participate in the prestigious Grand Gala du Disque, sponsored by the Dutch record companies and staged in a giant exhibition hall with makeshift dance floors around the theatre for partying after the performances. Instead of joining in the fun, Dusty spent three days in her Amsterdam

Hilton hotel room claiming the rehearsal facilities were inadequate. The Grand Gala's organizer told the press that although Dusty was a wonderful artist she had made impossible rehearsal demands, while her manager (Vic Billings) had insulted everyone he met. "I had no option but to ask them to leave." Other participating artists included Nancy Wilson who said, "The orchestra doesn't thrill me... I realize that in an all-star show like this one, you must not expect the same treatment as in a show which you are the only star, but I have no complaints." The Four Tops and Vikki Carr were likewise satisfied with the facilities.

Also in March 1968, Dusty shared the same bill as the Buddy Rich Big Band on *Sunday Night At The London Palladium*. Despite viewers' hopes to the contrary, the two survived without a swear word being flung or a toupee taking flight. She then performed in Issi's Club in Vancouver, while behind-the-scenes discussions took place about her next single. Nearly nine months had passed since her last release, and Philips Records were panicking. Dusty, however, was adamant that she wouldn't approve anything until she was entirely satisfied with the result. The two titles under consideration were "Magic Garden", which she'd performed at the London Palladium show, and "It's Over", Dusty's personal favourite. The song's composer, Jimmie Rodgers, cut the original version but it was Terry Lindsay's interpretation which R&B connoisseurs considered to be a masterpiece because it was one of those awesome, personal, heart-wrenching experiences only a few could master. Dusty's version was an extremely poor attempt by comparison.

With Dusty's recording schedule taking precedence, she had no choice but to cancel performing "The Look Of Love" at the Academy Awards Ceremony in Los Angeles. The song had been nominated in the "Best Film Song Of The Year" category. Then, before she could draw breath, rehearsals for her third television series were underway. Titled *It Must Be Dusty*, she switched television stations to ATV – known as "the other side" – for transmission during May and June 1968. This time Dusty used Jack Parnell and his orchestra, with vocalists Lesley Duncan, Kay Garner and Maggie Stredder. Scott Walker guested on the first show which Dusty kicked off with "Come Back To Me". He sang "Let It Be" with his hostess, a solo "The Lady Came From Baltimore" and his hit "Joanna". Paying tribute to The Supremes, Dusty sang "You Keep Me Hanging On" in her varied repertoire. For show two, she included three of her own songs – "The Look Of Love", "Where Am I Going?" and "Sunny", and a duet with her guest, Mark Murphy, an American jazz singer of considerable note. Scottish singer/songwriter Donovan joined her for show three which included a soulful Dusty singing Wilson Pickett's "Don't Fight It" and Dionne Warwick's "Another Night", as well as her own hit "All I See Is You". For show four, she once again dipped into her beloved soul bag to deliver versions of Baby Washington's "I Can't Wait Until I See My Baby's Face", Arthur Conley's "Sweet Soul Music" and (with changed lyrics) "Hold On, I'm Comin'" from Sam & Dave. No hits this time, but an interesting duet with her guest British R&B singer and keyboardist, Georgie Fame, titled "This Could Be The Start Of Something Big". For the fifth show Dusty sang with both her guests, namely, her brother Tom and Julie Felix, after kicking off the show with Aretha Franklin's stormer "Think". Without question, it was Jimi Hendrix and "Mockingbird", his duet with Dusty, which were remembered and revered in coming years. On the penultimate show, the flamboyant guitarist, singer and composer had an attitude and a wildness about him that made compulsive viewing. He played his guitar with his teeth and set fire to his stage equipment. And there was petite Dusty, standing by him, totally unfazed and enjoying the musical moment. In the last programme, Dusty was joined by Don Partridge, a one man band and busker, as well as the British R&B/pop outfit, Manfred Mann. She opened with "Ain't No Sun Since You've Been Gone" and ended with "I Close My Eyes And Count To Ten", with a more mainstream selection in between.

Critics of the series had daggers drawn, citing it as poorly pre-

sented, unimaginative and certainly not entertaining. To a certain
degree, Dusty agreed with them, but pointed out "I didn't produce
it and all I can say is I tried my best and channelled as much energy
into it as the previous series. There was a total lack of imagination
about the whole series… and I hope to be doing the next series with
the old firm. I'll never work for that other one again."

While she was studio-bound, Dusty announced she had split
with Vic Billings, her manager since 1963. It was amicable, she
said, but she needed a manager who was capable of promoting her
internationally on a full-time basis, who wasn't hampered by British
business interests. On the agency side, she remained with impresa-
rio Harold Davidson. "I feel safe in that environment," she added,
while confirming she had a business manager/lawyer in the States
so felt a personal manager superfluous to her needs. She was committed to pay Vic Billings £20,000 in lieu of two years' work.

Meanwhile, it was work as usual, and once the ATV filming
was complete, Dusty, sporting a new, curly hairstyle and reduced
eye make-up, appeared on a *Special Royal Variety Performance* which
raised £40,000 for the British Olympics Appeal. Tom Jones,
Danny La Rue and Long John Baldry were among several of the
top names who joined her on this May gala. Following the show,
Dusty stood next to Tom Jones in the line waiting to be presented
to the Queen. Also this month, Dusty provided the cabaret at the
Alexandra Rose Ball at London's Grosvenor House Hotel, in Park
Lane. She captured the following day's newspaper headlines, not
for her performance but her arrival. Upset at the rising cost of living, spiralling petrol prices and the exorbitant price she paid for
her Kensington home, Dusty decided it was "economy week" and
bought a tandem which she and her chauffeur Alan Dunn pedalled
from her flat to the hotel. Wearing a trouser suit, she had a mishap
halfway round Hyde Park Corner when her bicycle clips fell off,
leaving her trousers billowing dangerously in the wind. With her
leg cocked in the air and a smile on her face, she dismounted with
the help of Dunn at the hotel's front steps. Princess Margaret also

attended, and was chauffeur driven but not, of course, on a bike.

One of the last jobs Vic Billings did for his client was to contact Clive Westlake for "any half-finished songs" he might have. With "Magic Garden" and "It's Over" now on the back-burner, he needed a tried-and-tested composer to win Dusty over. When she heard the demo recording of "I Close My Eyes And Count To Ten", she wanted it. "Please don't give it to anyone else," she pleaded in a phone call to its composer, when she discovered that Vic Billings had really intended it for Kiki Dee, whom he also managed. "I knew she'd like it because the lyrics are really a part of her... I think her past failure to do well in the chart was because she switched to uptempo. She can sing those numbers better than anyone else, but unfortunately the public won't accept her doing things like that. Her commercial field is with two-part ballads." Kay Garner and Lesley Duncan were the backing singers, and Clive Westlake's concerto piano introduction led to a plaintive Dusty weaving her soulful way through the tenderest of love songs, so suited to her styling. It was delicate and totally flawless, and when released on 28 June 1968, Dusty was pictured wearing beads and a waistcoat on the *NME*'s front cover, to advertise the fact that she was back. "I Close My Eyes And Count To Ten" returned her to her former glory as a top five singles artist. "The chart placing is good for my morale," she quipped, blaming her recording absence on inferior material and her absence from the country. One critic raved, "I will always remember the feeling, like an electric shock, I got when I heard this record" while another wrote, "A charming song, perhaps not instantly commercial, but that's not necessarily a failing." When the single peaked, Dusty announced she had signed a recording contract with Atlantic Records, home to Aretha Franklin, Eddie Floyd and a host of soul acts whom she idolized. Philips Records would, however, continue to represent her for the rest of the world. She planned to record in both countries, whereupon the two record companies could release each other's recordings. "The Atlantic deal is no reflection at all on Johnny Franz or anyone at

Philips in Britain," she was quick to point out. When "I Close My Eyes And Count To Ten" was released in America, the record was her last to carry the Philips label.

Meanwhile, Dusty was also making her debut in television advertising. Despite her previous reluctance to become involved with TV ads, she was persuaded by British Bakeries Ltd to appear in a Mother's Pride advertisement. The offer was attractively packaged at the record fee of £10,000 for a 30-second advertisement. "Great excitement rang through St Judes Church of England Secondary School, Old Bethnal Green, because word reached us that Dusty was down Norah Street filming," remembered fan Joan Gamble. "It was a very old, cobbled street with rows of terraced houses back to back. We gradually started to slip out from school, trying not to be too obvious, to go and see Dusty. We could see a fair crowd gathering, and there she was in the middle of Norah Street, amidst all the hustle and bustle of film crew, lights, wires and actors, splendid with the famous black eye make-up (why did it never look the same on us?) singing the praises of Mother's Pride. Fancy being stared at by a load of school kids? We had to eventually tear ourselves away and get back to boring lessons. After school it was toast for our afternoon snack – Mother's Pride of course. Well, if that's what Dusty ate, why not!"

Dressed in slacks, jumper and scarf, Dusty traipsed up the narrow Street with her cart, singing "I'm a happy knocker upper" with a light, whispery voice (and a hidden smile, no doubt) before balancing a loaf of bread on the end of a long pole for people hanging out of an upstairs bedroom window. No one ever asked why she didn't use the front door. The advertisement was screened during September. Norah Street was demolished in the seventies but, thankfully for fans, the advertisement survived.

With the words "The preparations are tearing me up in spite of the best laid plans," Dusty told journalists about her second Talk Of The Town season from 8 July to 3 August. "All has been left to the last minute and I'm in my usual panic." She intended to change the show's concept because, "having flung myself round the stage for 50 minutes last time and had the critics say 'she's too static', I shall probably nail both my feet to this floor this time... I do a little juggling and then there's the trampoline-leaping gnomes." More seriously, she broke all audience records by performing to over 15,000 people and was immediately approached for another month of engagements the following year – and there wasn't a gnome in sight! Instead, she overwhelmed her audiences from the start with her act, which included three costume changes and four male dancers. As journalist/author Penny Valentine, who sat next to Dusty's parents, wrote, "As the last bars of 'Satisfaction' echoed across the stage... and Dusty disappeared for the last time in a shimmer of shocking pink, they... said that was the very best they'd ever seen her." Mary O'Brien treated her parents to a display of every facet of her talent, from "The Look Of Love" to comedy routines like "What Did She Know About Railways?", a Peggy Lee medley that included "Love" and "Mr Wonderful", and her own material like "I Only Want To Be With You" and "What's It Gonna Be?".

But, it was her Shirley Temple routine which attracted most of the praise and newspaper column inches. "She originally wanted to do a number dressed as Carmen Miranda, until, ever practical, we reminded her she would have to sing and dance wearing a three-foot tower of fruit on her head while walking on six-inch platform soles, without glasses, on a stage with no rim to stop her falling off," recalled Fred Perry, her lighting manager. "What finally killed the idea [was] she would also have to wear a dress with a slit cut right up to there!" Wearing a small girl's red and white polka-dotted dress, a large bow in her ringlet hair, with white ankle socks completing the outfit, Dusty skipped and squeaked her way through "I Wanna Be A Movie Star" and "On The Good Ship Lollipop" against a backdrop of old movies flickering behind her. The audience loved every second. "It's the sort of me people don't often see," she explained afterwards. Dusty was relaxed, confident, totally in control, and when the 20-piece orchestra came in too slowly on one song, instead of losing the beat, she simply laughed it off saying "faster, gentlemen, faster". Any criticism was confined to her hesitant ad-libbing between songs which was difficult to understand, and the running order of her songs which, some believed, was unbalanced.

Of the many fans to meet Dusty backstage, Mike Gilbert was luckier than most as he recalled "Pat was there helping out but Dusty tried to say something to each fan and was signing autographs all the time. I was a young lad from Birmingham visiting the big city for the first time with my best mate. The time in Dusty's presence just seemed to fly by... and when I looked at my watch I realized that we had missed the last train back home. Pat must have sensed that there was a problem and asked if we would like to go back with her and catch the early morning train. We waited until everyone had gone, said goodbye to Dusty, and then Pat discovered that Dusty had not picked up her vanity case. We had to drop it off on the way to Pat's home, and swear that we wouldn't tell anyone where she lived." And they never did.

Mid-way through her season, the *If You Go Away* EP was issued. With a verse sung in French, her version of the Jacques Brel number was faultless. She was submissive and loving and was matched only by Scott Walker's version of the song. "Bringing out the emotion in a song is hard for me," Dusty said at the time. "They can't all be a cry from the heart... But there's one song I can always perform with emotion and that's 'If You Go Away'. It's about fear of rejection and abandonment, (and) that's what happened to me." "Sunny" and "Where Am I Going?" were the filler tracks, while "Magic Garden" was the second highlight. According to the song's composer, Jimmy Webb, it is difficult to sing, while Paul Howes believed that if Dusty had released it as a single she would have regretted it. Anyway, due to the lack of originality, it was her first extended play single that failed to chart.

From London's top nightclub, Dusty switched to the Cranberry Fold Inn in Darwen, and then back to Blackpool for a pair of concerts. She then returned to the studio to record three songs, including a Clive Westlake tune which he'd previously played to Vicki Wickham, who agreed it would be the perfect follow-up to "I Close My Eyes And Count To Ten". Clive's original version of "I Will Come To You" wasn't that commercial, and when Dusty took it over, she speeded up the melody and coated it in a dramatic musical blanket that wasn't the way he intended the song to pan out. He also believed the song, which was released in September 1968, was too soon after "I Close My Eyes And Count To Ten", which still had some chart life left in it. At the time of its release, Dusty was in Memphis laying down tracks for her first album with Atlantic Records, before performing in San Francisco. She interrupted her recording sessions to return to Britain to promote the single with interviews and on prime-time television shows. Few people actually realized that Dusty appeared on television sporting a black eye, gashed forehead and severe bruising. She claimed she had fallen out of a tree in Tennessee. Thick make-up and a hairstyle with a fringe disguised the damage.

Despite her support, and to everyone's surprise, "I Will Come To You" failed to chart. Clive Westlake said he couldn't help wondering whether it would have been a hit if Dusty had stuck to the original demo recording, while author Paul Howes remarked that, despite its poor chart performance, the song will remain one of her finest recordings. "Like many Westlake songs, it has about two or three different tunes running through it and is steeped in atmosphere, with Dusty's soft and wistful vocals in the verses becoming loud and dynamic for the chorus."

Two months later, *Dusty… Definitely* was released, where she deliberately mixed uptempo soul titles with tailor-made nightclub songs, aiming for both her young stalwart fans and a more mainstream market. The packaging was golden and black, with a smiling, relaxed singer dressed in one of her trademark sparkling long gowns, sitting on the floor. In the sleeve notes, she admitted she had chosen the songs simply because she liked them. Her brother,

Tom, reviewed the album for *NME,* saying that he believed it to be the best she'd recorded. "Side one was meant to be black, and the other, white. I prefer the white side because it's more melodic and has better songs on it." Starting with a version of The Temptations' "Ain't No Sun Since You've Been Gone", Tom felt his sister was sounding older, getting more depth to her voice. "This is certainly the best song on side one," he said of "Take Another Little Piece Of My Heart", first recorded by Erma Franklin, younger sister of Aretha. "I loved the sort of strangled sexy sound... it's a great song."

It was a song Dusty loved but, due to its high notes, was one she shirked the responsibility of actually singing. "However, with the help of several cups of Philips tea (a secret brew – too much of it and one retires ashen-faced to one's bed) I made it." Happily, it also survived the test of time – in 2005 Cadbury's Dairy Milk used it as the musical backdrop to one of their television advertisements. Tom also commented on Bacharach and David's "Another Night", first recorded by Timi Yuro and Dionne Warwick, saying he considered his sister's version to be similar to both. "Singing's good but what happened to the bass and drums though?" He admitted his attention wandered through "Mr Dream Merchant", the Jerry Butler original, while "I Only Wanna Laugh" was her "Dusty-Springfield-on-Broadway" track. "I liked the line 'no sad songs for me.' I've already used it in three songs." She sang "Who (Will Take My Place)" down the phone to him because she wanted to change one word in it but later didn't use it. Tom rounded off the review by saying it was a pity "Morning" was put next to the last track of "Second Time Around" because they were both "weird songs", adding, "Dusty has two or three different voices that she uses and they are all getting better and better, and I'm not just saying that because she's my sister."

During the recording of one of the songs, an unfortunate chap known as Fred interrupted the take by bringing a tea trolley into the studio. Dusty wasn't amused and the tray promptly went flying. She liked the sound so much that the effect of the crashing crockery was included at the end of the album, and Fred was found in the list of credits on the album sleeve. *Dusty... Definitely* peaked at number 30, ten rungs higher than *Where Am I Going?* Compared to the sales performance of some of her singles, this result was obviously disappointing.

For the remainder of 1968 Dusty spent most of her time on and off planes, flying to and from America, Europe and back to Britain again. She used this service as regularly as others boarded the number 18 bus. Her poor-selling album and singles were worrying her as, once again, her career appeared to be on the slide. However, all was not lost, because Dusty had been to Memphis.

Registration District *Hampstead*

1939.   Birth in the Sub-district of   *Hampstead*   in the *Metropolitan   Borough of Hampstead.*

No.	When and where born	Name, if any	Sex	Name and surname of father	Name, surname and maiden surname of mother	Occupation of father	Signature, description and residence of informant	When registered	Signature of registrar	Name entered after registration
245	Sixteenth April 1939 87 Fordwych Road	Mary Isabel Catherine	Girl	Gerard Anthony O'BRIEN	Catherine Anne O'BRIEN formerly RYLE	Accountant of 97 Lansdale Mansions Paddington	G. A. O'BRIEN Father 97 Lansdale Mansions W. 9.	Twenty third May 1939	Du Boreham Deputy Registrar *Registrar.*	

...sty's birth certificate showing her father as an accountant, although Dusty maintained that ... never sat formal accountancy exams.

...sty (far left) with her "Lana Sisters" partners Riss Chantelle and Lynne Abrams and ...anist Dave Lee in 1960.

A dark-haired Dusty with The Springfields, Tim Field to her right and her brother Tom to her left.

The Springfields' first hit, "Breakaway", reached No. 31 in the UK singles chart in August 1961.

usty had watched
V pop show *Ready*
eady Go and longed
be in front of the
mcra, little realising
at she would become
regular.

Dusty would progress
from *Ready Steady
Go* to hosting her own
television show on
BBC 1 in 1966.

Dusty was often reluctant to pose for photographers but, as this 1964 portrait shows, could play to the camera when she chose.

Over the years, Dusty had amassed a huge record collection and was distraught at having to leave much of it behind in America when she moved from Los Angeles to Amsterdam in 1988.

Always a pet lover, Dusty even became involved with a sanctuary for exotic animals when she moved to Los Angeles.

Dusty on BBC TV's *Top Of The Pops* in 1970 singing "Morning Please Don't Come".

In 1979, Dusty appeared on TV in the UK to promote the *Living Without Your Love* album but neither the album nor her UK tour managed to revitalise her career.

By 1985 Dusty's famous bouffant hairstyle of the Sixties was long gone and she had adopted a more dramatic, modern style.

Dusty with the Pet Shop Boys, Neil Tennant and Chris Lowe, dressed as reporters for the video to promote "Nothing Has Been Proved" in 1989.

Dusty died in her sleep at her home in Henley-on-Thames just weeks before her sixtieth birthday.

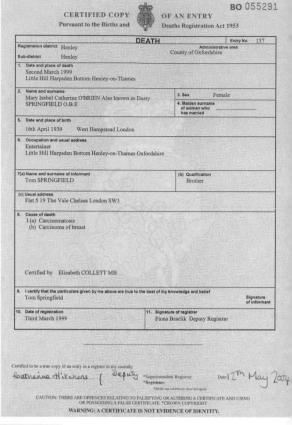

CERTIFIED COPY OF AN ENTRY
Pursuant to the Births and Deaths Registration Act 1953

BO 055291

DEATH
Entry No. 157

Registration district Henley

Administrative area
County of Oxfordshire

Sub-district Henley

1. Date and place of death
Second March 1999
Little Hill Harpsden Bottom Henley-on-Thames

2. Name and surname
Mary Isabel Catherine O'BRIEN Also known as Dusty
SPRINGFIELD O.B.E

3. Sex Female

4. Maiden surname
of woman who
has married

5. Date and place of birth
16th April 1939   West Hampstead London

6. Occupation and usual address
Entertainer
Little Hill Harpsden Bottom Henley-on-Thames Oxfordshire

7(a) Name and surname of informant
Tom SPRINGFIELD

(b) Qualification
Brother

(c) Usual address
Flat 5 19 The Vale Chelsea London SW3

8. Cause of death
I (a) Carcinomatosis
  (b) Carcinoma of breast

Certified by   Elizabeth COLLETT MB

9. I certify that the particulars given by me above are true to the best of my knowledge and belief
Tom Springfield

Signature
of informant

10. Date of registration
Third March 1999

11. Signature of registrar
Fiona Braclik Deputy Registrar

Certified to be a true copy of an entry in a register in my custody.
Catherine Hitchens   { Deputy   *Superintendent Registrar
                                  *Registrar
                                  *Strike out whichever does not apply

Date 12TH May 2004

CAUTION: THERE ARE OFFENCES RELATING TO FALSIFYING OR ALTERING A CERTIFICATE AND USING
OR POSSESSING A FALSE CERTIFICATE. ©CROWN COPYRIGHT
WARNING: A CERTIFICATE IS NOT EVIDENCE OF IDENTITY.

THE PARISH CHURCH OF
ST. MARY THE VIRGIN
HENLEY-ON-THAMES

Friday 12th March, 1999
12.30 p.m.

✝

**DUSTY SPRINGFIELD
OBE**

16th April 1939 — 2nd March 1999

The front cover of the order of service for Dusty's funeral in Henley on 12 March 1999.

Chapter Seven

DUSTY IN MEMPHIS

"It's become a rather overrated classic"

Dusty Springfield greeted the New Year of 1969 with a broken nose. She had finished Christmas lunch at her parents' house and had gone outside to collect more wine. Doug Reece and singer John Rowles decided to follow her and somehow knocked her down a three feet, six inch drop onto concrete. "I wouldn't have minded," she later moaned, "but I wasn't doing anything!" Nursing her nose, the singer subsequently spent five hours in hospital waiting to be stitched up. Forced to cancel a New Year's cabaret date for the Anglo-American Sporting Club at London's Hilton Hotel, she was fit enough to convalesce in the Bahamas, where it's thought she had her nose straightened.

On the upside, Dusty was once again a high-profile artist thanks to the runaway hit "Son-Of-A Preacher Man" – released in November 1968, the first from her September 1968 recording sessions in Memphis. Dusty explained how this happened: "When I lived in some rabbit warren block of flats in Ladbroke Grove, where it was all singers and performers. It was Goldie and the Gingerbreads and Leapy Lee. Anyway, one of Goldie and the Gingerbreads knew Atlantic Records' Ahmet Ertegun. He came over one day to their flat and I'd just done 'Some Of Your Lovin'" and they played it to him. He sat on the floor in a trance, then said to me 'if you ever get free, I'd like you in the States, please come to us'. I was very flattered that he liked it and that he'd realized I'd done a good record. And that he thought it might work out between us." Written into her recording contract was the condition that Atlantic Records' co-owner, Jerry Wexler, would be the project's producer. Along with Ahmet and Nesuhi Ertegun, Wexler (who had actually coined the phrase "rhythm & blues") had built Atlantic Records into a major recording force. In 1967 he was named Record Executive of the Year for his successful work with Aretha Franklin. So Dusty was taking no chances. She wanted to be part of the Atlantic Records' legacy, to be mentioned along- side the company's greatest acts like Sam and Dave, Wilson Pickett, Carla Thomas and, of course, The Queen of Soul, Aretha Fran- klin. Jerry Wexler would ensure her name became more closely linked with black soul music. This was, perhaps, a step further than her beloved Motown could take her as some of its music was by now categorized as "mainstream" which, of course, was not intense enough for the soul-smitten Springfield.

During 1968 Atlantic enjoyed its greatest year to date as record sales increased by 85 per cent over the previous 12 months, earn- ing 23 gold discs, more than any other label. Jerry Wexler said the company's secret weapon was his partner and recording associate, Tom Dowd. Both of them would work with Dusty because Wexler saw the chance to bring her greater recognition than she had ever previously known. With assistance from Mark Myerson and Jerry Greenberg, he amassed 80 titles to present to her when she flew to New York to meet him at his home in Great Neck. They spent the day and most of the night together, and he told singer/songwriter Warren Zanes, "We soon found ourselves ass-deep in acetates. As I played her song after song, I was hoping for a response. Would she like this one? If not, how about the next one?" And so it went on, until Jerry had gone through his entire inventory without any real decisions having been made. Dusty had simply been overwhelmed. When she visited him for a second time, he played her 20 from his original 80 and she loved them!

Originally earmarked for Aretha Franklin, who turned it down, "Son-Of-A Preacher Man" became a much-needed top ten hit for Dusty on both sides of the Atlantic. This prompted Aretha later to record it and, instead of following Dusty's vocal guidelines, she changed the emphasis on some of the lyrics. This change in styling was adopted by Dusty in her live performances. When her single entered the British Top 30, The Sweet Inspirations, who had recently released their own "What The World Needs Now Is Love" single in Britain, flew to London to sing with Dusty on *Top Of The Pops*. Sadly, their trip was cut short because the group fell ill with flu and couldn't perform. Prior to this, Dusty had never actually met the gospel group led by Cissy Houston, despite their obvious involvement with the album. She fobbed this off, saying, "Listen! I know a percussion player who played for Diana Ross on all her Motown records and never met her!"

Recorded at the American Studios in Memphis and completed in New York where The Sweet Inspirations' and Dusty's vocals were added, "Son-Of-A Preacher Man" presented a new, warm, sweet-sounding Dusty to the public. Relaxed, melodic and soulful. However, she was far from happy, saying she felt inhibited in the recording studios, preferring the British sessions because she knew the musicians, and she had wanted to re-record the vocal because she felt it was too 'white' sounding. Before this could happen, Tom Dowd agreed to release it. In 1994 the song was given a new lease of life when Quentin Tarantino included it in the *Pulp Fiction* movie, later earning her a gold disc. "I winced at the sound of my own voice… (the song) seemed to move people on a sexual level where it didn't move me at all…"

Working with young musicians like Bobby Wood, Reggie Young and Tommy Cogbill in the tiny Memphis studio that was tucked away behind a restaurant in a car park, Dusty noticed they rarely went home. "They work solely for Atlantic and will work 24 hours a day if you let them. They all come into the control room and listen to the tapes and if they're not pleased with something, they'll go back and do it all again." The more she got used to their ways, the easier she felt and this can clearly be heard in the other album tracks like "Just A Little Lovin'" written by Cynthia Weil and Barry Mann, who told Paul Howes, "She has a voice like silk that can make your heart melt. Her interpretation of the song is as good as it can get – and maybe even more."

When Dusty spoke of these recording sessions, she emphasized the absolute fear she felt when she first started. "I got destroyed when someone said 'stand there, that's where Aretha stood' or 'stand there, that's where Percy Sledge sang "When A Man Loves A Woman"'. I became paralysed by the ghosts of the studio. I knew that I could sing the songs well enough, but it brought pangs of insecurity, that I didn't deserve to be there. I just knew that Aretha's drummer was going to say 'ain't she a piece of shit.' It's the most deflating thing you can say to me that somebody I adore and worship actually stood there and probably delivered an effortless performance while I'm slogging away trying to get it right. They meant well, but they didn't realize what they were doing."

Years later, Dusty related these fears to George Michael who, in 1987, duetted with Aretha Franklin on "I Knew You Were Waiting For Me", an international chart-topper and winner of the 1987 Grammy Award for Best R&B Vocal Performance By A Duo. He agreed with her: "... and it was interesting we could talk about it because he and I understood those feelings. It was insecurity really, and that we didn't deserve to be there. They meant well with George but they didn't realize these little children were terrified." Dusty actually met Aretha Franklin once. Not in the studio, but in a lift – "She went 'girl'. And I thought 'hell, she touched me. The queen touched me!'"

Although she maintained she loathed the time she spent in the studios because of her personal fears and inadequacies, Dusty admitted the results showed the patience and dedication of the musicians and producers. "They worked with me until they got it out of me. Probably the irony of those whole sessions was that I was so crippled with laryngitis they could only record me two or three words at a time. Yet, there are notes on the album that I've never sung again; they're stratospheric, they're so high. I'd be revving up and I'd just go for it. When I didn't make it, I'd do it again until I did. It was rough." Rough or not, the result was her finest work; recognized as one of the greatest soul albums ever. "Dusty is the incarnation of white soul if there is such a thing," commented Jerry Wexler at the close of the recording sessions. "I don't know a singer with better intonation. She never hit a wrong note. She's certainly not an R&B singer, but she is as soulful as hell." And the musicians? They thought the album pretty good – for a white girl!

Two days before the release of her sixth album, Dusty celebrated her thirtieth birthday while fulfilling an engagement at The Chevron Hotel, Sydney, Australia. *Dusty In Memphis* was greeted with much media excitement, the critics adored it. But sadly not the public. The British album carried a different cover to the American version issued three months earlier but the track listing was unchanged. Blues & Soul reviewer Bill Buckley noted: "... Only rarely in recording does everything come together so magnificently – artist performance, choice of songs, creative production, the right studio, sympathetic session players – it's all here. It would be churlish to pick out highlights... the measure of this album's excellence is the fact that even a fairly banal song like 'The Windmills Of Your Mind' becomes a tour de force... if you've ever doubted Dusty's status as a real soul singer prepare to be converted." One of the highlights was Hinton & Fritts' "Breakfast In Bed" with its many connotations, her sensual teasing and breathy vocal across the song which, however, rendered it too strong for a British single from her. Young boy with mature woman: but not as refined as Mrs Robinson and her graduate. This was new territory for Dusty, yet the result indicated she'd been a teaser all her life! When Chrissie Hynde and UB40 enjoyed a hit with the song during 1988, she regularly referred to Dusty's version as inspiring in her interviews.

Other highlights were two (of the four included) Goffin & King classics at the close of the album – "No Easy Way Down" and "I Can't Make It Alone". The first contained lyrics predicting Dusty's pending drop in popularity (which was obviously not the intention) against a systematic musical backdrop supporting her resigned vocal of failure. It crossed sadness with despair which the composers cleverly intertwined. As for "I Can't Make It Alone" – from the compelling, subdued, haunting entrance, introducing a seductive Dusty pleading her way through a song that builds to a peak; where The Sweet Inspirations cuddle her cries in song, to bolster the sound to its climax until a deflated singer moans "oh help me", was pure perfection. *Dusty In Memphis* was faultless. It should have elevated her into iconic stardom, but, explained Paul Howes, "It was treated as a flop because it never entered the *Record Retailer* chart which was for a period limited to the top 15 albums. It did, however, get to number 14 in the *NME* chart which suggests that had there been a *Record Retailer* top 30, it would probably have charted around number 20. I think, also, its sales didn't live up to the expectations of what was considered to be a milestone album."

The album then scratched its way into the American top 100, signifying her slow decline. "It's become rather an overrated classic," the singer later admitted. "It's not as if it's some magnificent work of art. It's a good record." Despite her bravado, she was worried at the effect this would have on her career. The dark thoughts of failure that plagued her could suddenly become real, to the point that she seriously thought her time as a charting singer was over: "… I wouldn't know how to do an ordinary job. All I know… is what I've done for 30 years."

While his sister was mulling over her future, Tom Springfield was still making money with The Seekers when their *Best Of...* album replaced The Beatles at the top of the chart. The Australian group had disbanded by now. Tom believed that, like The Springfields before them, they had tired of singing the same material over and over. Confirming he never liked performing anyway, Tom confessed this was one of the reasons The Springfields had so often fooled around on television performances. "Those were the days when you could still mime to records and we would mime totally different words to the song." Dusty rarely remembered lyrics anyway, he pointed out, "Even now, when you see her dancing away, bringing her hands up to her face, it's probably because she's got the words written on her arms." As for himself, he'd recently recorded an album of Latin-American material titled *Sun Songs* which he'd recorded for the fun of it. *Love Philosophy* followed in October 1969 featuring "Morning Please Don't Come", a duet with Dusty. The guitar-backed song, mostly highlighting her gentle, kid-gloved, easy manner, was later released as a single in February 1970 but, despite considerable promotion by them both, it was a poor seller, prompting him to concentrate on his songwriting in future.

Dusty threw herself into her busiest year to date, with the emphasis on international tours and performances. During April and May 1969 she toured Canada and America, but things didn't go entirely according to plan. Even with the release of "Windmills Of Your Mind" giving her a Top 40 charting single, the tour was poorly attended, leaving her out of pocket to the tune of £12,000. She blamed the lack of promotion. "It was the interim dates which went wrong. Nobody knew I was even appearing. I was very upset at the complete lack of co-operation. The first and last dates, which were well advertised, were packed out." Although it was a major disappointment for all concerned, a further college tour and a performance at the Hollywood Palace were earmarked for October. While in America she returned to the studios in New York for a ten-day recording session for Atlantic Records. The result was three tracks – "To Love Somebody", "That Old Sweet Roll (Hi-De-Ho)" and "Willie And Laura Mae Jones", later an American single. A strange song by her standards; written by Tony Joe White, it was mildly reminiscent of "Son-Of-A Preacher Man" without the edge that benefited the hit. Despite Dusty being committed to recording a second album with Jerry Wexler, this trio was all she delivered.

Postponing a cabaret season at New York's Americana Club, Dusty made an early start on her third BBC1 television series *De-*

cidedly Dusty, due for screening for eight weeks from 9 September. Dusty romped her way through a huge selection of material, ranging from her own hits to Motown and show tunes, supported by backing singers Madeline Bell, Lesley Duncan and Kay Garner as well as dancers Cassandra Mahon and Peter Newton. Valentine Dyall also appeared regularly, and he featured an anagram of 'Dusty Springfield' in each show.

On the first programme she paid tribute to her Motown peers and gooned around with Spike Milligan, while others included her singing "Private Number" with Jimmy Ruffin, and larking around with her friend Danny La Rue who was dressed as her singing "I Just Don't Know What To Do With Myself". On other shows she sang with The Bee Gees and listened to Dr Murray Banks, one of the most sought-after speakers in America. His unusual mixture of folk psychology and Jewish stories had elevated him into a major recording artist, with oddly titled albums like *What To Do Until The Psychiatrist Comes*. The sixth show was a family reunion because her parents were in the audience and she sang "Morning Please Don't Come" with Tom. To round off the family evening, photos of Dusty as a teenager later provided a visual backdrop. Opening the show with the funky dance number "Ain't Nothing Like A Houseparty" with Madeline, Kay and Lesley, she included a medley of The Seekers' hits to underline her brother's contribution to the group's remarkable success. Ornithologist and animal impersonator Percy Edwards contributed to the penultimate programme along with 1969's Eurovision co-winner Frida Boccara, while the ventriloquist Shari Lewis and her puppet Lamb Chop replaced soul duo Bob & Earl in the line-up for the final show – hardly adequate for the avid soul fan hoping to hear their classic "Harlem Shuffle"! Dusty and Valentine Dyall then closed the series by sending up *The Sound Of Music* as they left the television studio.

As much as she had enjoyed filming them, Dusty was tired of the format and this time her audiences had expected new material from her which hadn't been possible. "In a way it's a bit boring, but I suppose you're very limited in 25 minutes, so apart from singing hanging from the ceiling, it's hard to think of new things to do."

Clothes were also a huge problem, she said, due to two costume changes per show. She felt more of a lady in long dresses and they allowed her the freedom to leap around without having to worry about her legs being on show. Usually designed by Darnells of London they were costly at £120 each. On the other hand, she shopped for her shorter stage clothes explaining, "however nice a short dress is, it never looks quite so good in front of the camera." Always conscious of her appearance in public, Dusty was constantly on edge that someone would find a reason to look down at her, and used the following as an example – "[People] will stare in horror if I've a ladder in one of my nylons. They simply won't bother to consider that I might not have had time to change them, or buy a new pair." She usually wore Aristoc's Bitter Chocolate mesh stockings at 6s 11d a pair, often with a very thin, diamond-shaped pattern on them, and often wore flesh-coloured ones underneath to hide her non-existent varicose veins.

Having her photo taken was another trial for her, not just at this time but throughout her whole career. She disliked being photographed from the left side claiming that to be a bad profile, worrying that two lines running from her nose to the corners of her mouth were too prominent. Her attempts to conceal them under layers of make-up failed, yet it was those same lines that opened up her face when she laughed. Inevitably, she clashed with photographers more than once – David Redfern was one. He first crossed swords with her as a member of The Springfields as he wrote on his website. He'd been hired by their record company, Philips Records, to photograph the trio at a television show being filmed in Bristol. Arriving at the studio, Redfern was told the shoot wouldn't happen after all. Following numerous phone calls to and from London, there was a stalemate situation until Dusty suddenly instructed – "Oh, take your fucking picture!" He did before she changed her mind. Redfern went on to snap her and a host of other artists at the *Ready, Steady, Go!* studios when she warned people about him saying, "Watch him, he's an evil one, he always gets his picture!" Harry Goodwin also recalled a situation involving Dusty and Vic Billings, and their combined unwillingness to let him photograph her. They argued in Goodwin's hotel room for a while until he left them alone to ask the hotel's doorman to interrupt them, by saying there was a transatlantic phone call for Billings. "He kept arguing until Dusty said you'd better go and take that call. He went out and they kept him hanging on the phone for three minutes during which time I shot three reels of film with Dusty." On the other hand, the singer always happily posed for her fans in the street, backstage in her dressing room, and so on, because she knew they wouldn't be published.

While the series ran, "Am I The Same Girl?" was issued as a single. Doug Reece recommended she record it after hearing Barbara Acklin's beautiful interpretation (a vocal version of the original Young-Holt Unlimited's "Soulful Strut"). Equally infatuated, it took Dusty less than a week to record it with producer Bill Landis replacing Johnny Franz, who was on holiday. A film of her singing the song was slotted into the show being screened nearest its release date on 12 September 1969, while a spot on *Top Of The Pops* was remembered, not for her performance but her hair which was in the page boy style – and red! Dusty later conceded it had been an unwise choice! One critic went further by saying he believed she wasn't (the same girl) and suggested she looked ridiculous in her old rags and wig, although both complemented the worst performance he had seen of the worst record he had heard!

Struggling to chart, "Am I The Same Girl?" entered the British top 50 twice before peaking at 43 in the listing. To be fair, the public was confused because Dusty's voice had changed. It wasn't its customary full-volumed range, but soft, subdued and whispery, similar to that used on "The Look Of Love". Perhaps if she had insisted that a second track from *Dusty In Memphis* be issued instead, she wouldn't have been in the quandary of where to go next.

Certainly, "Just A Little Lovin'" was a prime contender for single release. Meanwhile, she had spent a lot of time on the continent, kicking off in Holland. She was there to perform at a song festival staged at The Kurhaus in Scheveningen, where her 45-minute set was transmitted live under the title *Dit Is Dusty*. A week in Cannes, and concerts at The Tivoli in Stockholm followed.

Away from the public glare, Dusty's social life was full to bursting with family and friends. As Martha and the Vandellas' career escalated in Britain, the girls would visit for promotional trips and tours, so Dusty and Martha invariably spent time together, often with mutual friends. Dusty had already introduced her to her circle of friends that included Elton John. The two shared a mutual admiration which had grown through the years following Elton's crush on her. As a youngster, he had pictures of Dusty from *Reveille* magazine plastered over his bedroom wall alongside football heroes. He was hypnotized by her "Barbie doll glamour, spun-up bouffant hair, bow-tied balloon-skirt dresses and enormous black-smeared eyes" Philip Norman wrote in his definitive biography *Sir Elton*. And when Elton and Bernie Taupin started writing together in earnest, they aimed their material at singers like Dusty.

After securing a publishing deal with Dick James Music in 1967, their demo work was given to Johnny Franz in the hope he would pass it on to her. Franz decided it was unsuitable and she never heard it, which devastated Elton but led to him recording his own work in future. The two had a lot in common. They were both gay but their closet doors were tightly shut. And, like Dusty, Elton John reinvented himself from Reggie Dwight, a name he believed befitted an accounts clerk. He had his wacky, colourful glasses and clothes; she had her beehives and heavily mascared eyes. Both were extrovert on stage, painfully shy off, and both later suffered drug and alcohol abuse. By March 1970, Elton was enjoying his first charting single "Border Song" and was performing it on *Top Of The Pops* when he met Dusty. Her enthusiasm for the song led the star-struck Elton to say "she made my year!" With his star on the rise, Elton launched his own record company with offices at 101 Wardour Street, London. One of his first recruits was Penny Valentine, then an established and respected music journalist and, of course, personal friend of many a celebrity, including Dusty. Penny noted that they shared a particular quality, that of a complete lack of sexuality, while being obsessed with the "trivia and minutiae of show business".

Elton was unable to sign Dusty for his label but clinched a deal with one of her session singers, Kiki Dee, being attracted by the same mixture of smokey soul that had originally drawn him to Dusty. As Kiki's personal A&R man, Elton rejected Motown-style songs in favour of "Amoureuse", a beautifully haunting French song. It was Rocket Records' first hit in the top 20, and finally Kiki Dee had the recognition she deserved. Her second hit was "I've Got The Music In Me", but it was her love duet with Elton that most people remembered. "Don't Go Breaking My Heart" was their first number one single (Kiki's only one) in July 1976. She went on to enjoy intermittent chart success until 1993 when, once again, she sang with Elton on "True Love", a top two single.

Returning to September 1969, Dusty began a two-month stay in America. She first recorded in Philadelphia with Kenny Gamble & Leon Huff, then taped appearances on *Hollywood Palace* (with Burt Barcharach and Angie Dickinson), *The Andy Williams Show* and other peak-time television programmes. She returned to London on 11 November then left for Cologne on the following day to record her own German television spectacular, to be screened in December. With Dusty now recording in America she had little use for her regular support singers who had added the familiar rich gospel/soul fullness to her songs, which was just as well for Madeline Bell who was enjoying herself as a member of Blue Mink. Formed to record "Melting Pot", a song composed by Roger Cook and Roger Greenaway, the group's success escalated almost overnight. With Madeline and Roger Cook on vocals, and musicians, who included Herbie Flowers and Alan Parker,

"Melting Pot" hit the top three in late 1969. Further hits "Good Morning Freedom" and "Our World" quickly followed. Blue Mink enjoyed a chart career until "Randy" became their seventh and last hit in 1973. They disbanded while at the top, leaving Madeline to pursue a solo career.

Two months after "Am I The Same Girl?", "A Brand New Me" was rush-released to coincide with its success in America. Soul music aficionados believed Jerry Butler's 1969 version to be the ultimate interpretation, while Dusty fans thought she held that honour. To be fair, each held a unique charm; Butler, who had been instrumental in propelling the Sound of Philadelphia with Kenny Gamble and Leon Huff, delivered a mature, deep, earthy sound, while Dusty chose a looser, lighter interpretation. Critics raved but, once again, the public didn't. "A Brand New Me" was to have been the title of Dusty's second Atlantic album but, due to the poor British sales, it was re-named *From Dusty...With Love*. Eventually, she dropped the song from her live performances.

This was a confusing but interesting year for music because anything and everything was a potential hit. For instance, Jane Birkin and Serge Gainsbourg's panting, sexual "Je T'Aime, Moi Non Plus" clashed with the protesting "Give Peace A Chance" from John Lennon, Yoko Ono and The Plastic Ono Band. Eden Kane's brother, Peter Sarstedt, enjoyed passing success with the sugary "Where Do You Go To My Lovely?", while Motown showed its musical strength with Marvin Gaye. Apart from his duet success with Tammi Terrell, he enjoyed his first British chart-topper with "I Heard It Through The Grapevine". Other hits were released by Joe Cocker, Bob Dylan, Donovan, The Rolling Stones and The Beatles who bid farewell with "Get Back". The group who had changed the face of music for ever, was no more.

Before returning to the States in the New Year of 1970, Dusty topped the bill at the *Save Rave '69* gala held at The London Palladium. Attended by Princess Margaret, the concert was in aid of one of her charities, the Invalid Children's Aid Association. Wearing a sequined, powder blue, full-length gown, her performance was devoted to material she liked, with only one of her hits included – "I Close My Eyes And Count To Ten". She gave a marvellous show but it wasn't what the audience had been expecting. The princess, on the other hand, was delighted at the support Dusty had given to the charity; unfortunately, that wasn't the case when next they met.

After recording another guest spot for *This Is Tom Jones*, Dusty joined Cilla Black for a live television transmission of *Cilla*. The singers' paths often crossed but never did they view each other as competition. Dusty was too consumed with achieving the high standards set by her American peers, while Cilla battled with home-grown songstresses like Helen Shapiro whom she considered "had a great voice". Cilla first met Dusty on a television show, and wrote in her autobiography *What's It All About* that "I think she learned a few things from me, not vocally so much, more in terms of dress sense." She was also amused to learn that one of Dusty's wigs was named after her (Lulu and Sandie too) but was shocked about her friend's treatment of crockery which, Cilla said, wasn't an act of anger but rather boredom. "For me, brought up in a total thrift in the North… I could never have broken good china in the way Dusty did. I'd have thought 'my God, what a waste – how much did that cost?'!"

Like her work pal, Cilla also hosted her own BBC1 television series which had run for nine weeks from January 1968, attracting an audience of 13 million. The series bridged the sixties and seventies, with the third one running through the 1969 Christmas into the New Year. Her self-propulsion kept her in the public spotlight, and when she switched from the charts, cabaret and pantomime to television shows like *Surprise Surprise* and *Blind Date*, Cilla became a fully paid-up member of the British institution. This, however, was not for Dusty, and she rebelled against it. She never wanted to endure the cabaret treadmill for longer than she had to, and certainly had no intention of slapping her thighs as a leading character in a Christmas pantomime. Some believed her foolhardy; others admired her stand against convention.

Often told was the story of how Cilla's first manager, Brian Epstein, tried to offload her onto Tito Burns in exchange for Dusty. Apparently, Burns bumped into Epstein as he left Cilla's dressing room at an awards concert staged at Wembley Stadium. Looking as white as a ghost, Epstein said he was having a hard time with his artist. "I'll do a swap with you" he said to Burns, who immediately responded – "Thank you Brian, but I like the way Dusty sings."

Chapter Eight

LEARN TO SAY GOODBYE

"...I know I'm perfectly capable of being swayed by a girl as by a boy"

When 1970 dawned, the British music scene was struggling with a hangover from the runaway excesses of the swinging sixties. The break up of The Beatles put pressure on the individual members to prove themselves musically, while the first stirrings of glam rock introduced the flamboyant elf-like Marc Bolan and T Rex, who in turn paved the way for Rod Stewart (himself a Dusty fan), Sweet, Queen and Wizzard among others. Tom Jones, The Rolling Stones and The Hollies were among the regular British charting artists, while Detroit's Motown music continued to make its presence felt. A musical pot pourri for sure.

By now, Dusty lived with Norma Tanega in a house at 38 Aubrey Walk, situated between Holland Park and Notting Hill Gate which she'd purchased for £20,000 in 1968 between trips to America. The house had been empty for a while and needed at least £6,000 worth of work done to it. The third floor was "a work and madness section", with two bedrooms, a bathroom and a kitchen which Dusty intended to have knocked into one room to house her piano. Two further bedrooms were also to become one with an ensuite dressing room. Downstairs, the double reception room ran the length of the house to open up onto a courtyard, and the small kitchen needed enlarging to include an eating recess which would feature labour-saving devices. "I'm not a great cook," Dusty laughed at the time "but I can rustle up steaks and salads. Besides I like nice kitchens!"

Dusty had met Norma Tanega in 1966 amid the cables and

cameras at the BBC's television studios in Manchester. Dusty was due to rehearse "You Don't Have To Say You Love Me" for an evening's slot on *Top Of The Pops* but, as she left her dressing room, the studio technicians decided to take a tea break and turned down the lights. It was then she spotted Norma who was also on the show, standing in the shadows. A painter-cum-singer, with an open attitude to life, who had campaigned to end the Vietnam war, Norma had written a strange song with whimsical lyrics titled "Walking My Cat Named Dog". With her long dark hair, she was the opposite to Dusty's blondeness, and was totally at a loss why she should be standing in darkness. Dusty explained about tea breaks being part of the British way of life to the bemused American. "Walking My Cat Named Dog" was a top 30 British hit – the first and only for Norma – whereupon she returned to her painting, while keeping her finger firmly on the musical pulse.

When Norma returned home Dusty kept in touch, and then flew to New York to persuade her to live with her. By now Dusty had left her rabbit warren block of flats for an apartment in Earl's Court, and later a £55-a-week ground floor flat in Ennismore Gardens, off Kensington Road, Knightsbridge. It was here that she first lived with Norma, with Dusty admitting that this was the first time she had enjoyed such a close relationship with a woman.

Seventies pop music may have visually flaunted homosexuality through its dress style and campness but it was never publicly discussed, although many suspected and the industry protected. And Dusty fell into that category. She was the first woman in modern pop music assumed to be gay, and the media hounded her hoping for an exclusive submission. It's true she had considered going public knowing it would kill her career dead. But there was more she wanted to achieve, so she held her tongue and suffered the hurt from the tabloid misquotes and personal rumours. "Whatever I did made the front page. Actually, the more I read it, the more I lived up to it." She recalled a trip she made to Holland. Her record company there had confirmed there would be no photographers when she arrived. "But there were and I lost it. I hit one of the poor bastards with a bunch of flowers. They nearly threw me out of the country!" But it was the persistent probing about her non-marital state that prompted Dusty to tell the *Observer*'s journalist Marcelle Bernstein "I have a certain pride in myself as a woman, and it upsets my femininity. ... I've done nothing wrong and I refuse to invent a relationship to appease them." Being in a business that enjoyed excesses of everything, Dusty was a rare creature. She was neither promiscuous nor a headline seeker, and it was this aspect of her that annoyed journalists to the extent that they invented stories. However, even she realized the acting had to stop, and when she attempted to "come out" in a 1970s interview with Ray Connelly for the *Evening Standard* it was an incredibly courageous step to take – "A lot of people say I'm bent, and I've heard it so many times that I've almost learned to accept it ... I know I'm perfectly capable of being swayed by a girl as by a boy." She had nothing to lose because her sights were set on America where she could freely live her life the way she wanted without being the subject of newspaper headlines. "I can't stand to see anybody caught up in a world that inhibits them so much" Norma Tanega said at the time. And in 1999 she told Peter Sheridan of the *Mail On Sunday*, "She was a very gifted person but she had a difficult life. It's unpleasant for anybody to have to deny their sexuality." After Dusty's death, Ray Connelly said, "It was an honest and brave thing to do. I don't know whether she had any regrets."

There was another side to Dusty which also wasn't often discussed – her desire to be a mother. On one occasion she asked The Searchers' Frank Allen to make her one. Norma wasn't fond of hitting the London nightclubs, so Dusty usually partied with Peppi Borza and, on this particular evening, Frank Allen. They headed for The Sombrero in Kensington High Street. The atmosphere was soon buzzing because Dusty was there. She got drunk on vodka and coke while Frank, who was driving them, remained sober. They spent most of the evening engrossed in each other's company, whereupon Peppi, feeling ignored, left on his own. It was on the journey home that Dusty told Frank of her desperation to have a child as her body clock was ticking away, and asked him if he would oblige. "By this time her hand had moved over onto the part of my anatomy where a hand should really not be placed without prior permission from the owner", he wrote in his autobiography *Travelling Man*. "The appendage that was only separated from the superstar's skin by the thickness of a piece of cavalry twill, was certainly not rising to the occasion as one might expect would be the case." Noting his discomfort, Dusty explained she would take full responsibility for the offspring, but for Frank the moment had passed and her hand withdrew. Accepting it was the alcohol talking, he drove Dusty home to Norma who was, he said, highly amused at the sight of her. When Frank attempted to tell Dusty about the incident years later, she remembered not a thing. He was devastated: "…my idol had absolutely no recollection whatsoever of fiddling with my willy. Sometimes life is very cruel." Pat Rhodes added "Dusty would have made a wonderful mother and was aware that her body clock was ticking away. Despite the constant rumours of so called pregnancies and abortions, she never was one."

Norma, however, co-hosted Dusty's infamous parties in their Aubrey Walk home, as Cilla Black remembered after attending one with her future husband Bobby. When Dusty opened the front door, the couple was greeted with a heavy waft of joss sticks, and the house, which reverberated with music from two stadium-sized speakers, was painted in purple and pink. Cilla believed they had been invited to prove to Dusty's parents – who were also guests – that she had some non-gay friends. Indeed, she spent the evening in their company, while other guests like Martha and the Vandellas, Billy Jean King and Rosie Casals acted crazy. At one point Dusty had introduced Elton John to the tennis players: he became addicted to the game but she larked around on the court. The last time Dusty had played tennis was in the fourth year at school, but when she couldn't maintain the high standards of her team, she gave it up. She did, however, support Wimbledon fortnight by ensuring that her work schedules were free. She followed Illie Nastase and Rosie Casals in particular, saying "I admire them for their courage ... and there is something so attractive about the way they both play." They were all friends for life. Elton went on to support the Philadelphia Freedoms, Billie Jean King's World Tennis League team, by writing the song "Philadelphia Freedom" for them which in 1975 became an American number one single.

Partying was Dusty's speciality; she was one of the original IT girls. They were renowned as much for their American soul music as their food-slinging episodes; shambolic, entertaining and great fun. Whatever new dances she had learned, she'd take great pains to teach her guests, insisting they danced until they dropped. But it was the flying food that attracted most comment. "I always remember Kim (Weston) coming to one of my parties. She came in this fur coat, arrived at the door ... the party had really disintegrated by then and she trod on a sardine or something and went flying. She was a good sport." Dusty remembered, with a grin on her face, in 1990. "So were Martha and the Vandellas. First they hid because they thought they'd get coleslaw in their wigs, but they came out swinging! (Dusty demonstrated how they used French sticks as baseball bats.) They were hiding behind chairs... Martha was the first one out with a French loaf and she started batting at things. She was a good sport too. I don't think she'd do that now. I saw Martha in San Francisco a few years ago ... she has that way of kinda looking at you and frowning, and you don't know whether she's being friendly or frowning at you. She has an assessing look and that's just her. I got used to that. It had been some time since we'd met and it was one of those things – 'oh, we must get together sometime' but sadly it never happened."

Dusty may have felt her career was slipping away from her, but she still held on to the top world's female category in the *NME's* readers' poll, losing the British title to Lulu. When the results were published Dusty was in the States appearing on prime time television specials like *The Johnny Carson Show*. She also recorded further tracks with Gamble & Huff in Philadelphia before holidaying in the West Indies, where she planned to relax in anonymity before embarking upon the British promotional trail for her new album. She laughed as she recalled that "...while lying on the beach with a towel wrapped around my head, burnt to a crisp with a nicely toasted nose and dark glasses, up comes a complete stranger and says 'hello Dusty!'. They were engineers from Birmingham... and [I] never know whether to be pleased or insulted when [I'm] recognized looking like that!"

Following the American release of the album track "Silly, Silly Fool" on 25 January, the British version of *A Brand New Me* was issued. Re-named *For You... Love Dusty* it was released under the further amended title *From Dusty... With Love*. It also carried different packaging of soft pinks and mauves, rather flowery and girlie for a white soul singer, against its American cover with the same picture of her mirrored across the front encased in green.

Recorded at the Sigma Sound Studio, Philadelphia for Atlantic Records, it was the only one of her albums at that time to feature songs predominantly by the same composers, namely Kenny Gamble and Leon Huff, who also produced the project, with arrangers Thom Bell and Roland Chambers. Musicians included the finest Philly talent like Norman Harris, Earl Young, Vince Montana and Ugene Dozier. From the opening track, another Jerry Butler original called "Lost" through to the riveting "Let's Talk It Over", with her bluesy voice over wonderful gospel vocals from the Sweethearts Of Sigma, this was a ground-breaking Philly-Soul album. There were tracks of genius like the velvety "Bad Case Of The Blues", and the soulfully hypnotic "Never Love Again" that so easily merged with her soulful yearning in "Let's Get Together Soon". Dusty smouldered her way through "Joe" from its subdued beginnings to the crescendo; whether she found him remains to be seen! Changing mood with "Silly Silly Fool" she adopted a simmering rhythm on this lightweight track, whose very title could have led to its dramatic demise as an American single. It was a submissive album where the songs reflected a certain sadness yet, despite delivering a stunning performance, Dusty – true to form – wasn't happy with the results. But her fans were. It was a top 40 British hit, her first charting album since *Dusty… Definitely* in December 1968.

Kenneth Gamble and Leon Huff went on to open Philadelphia International Records, establishing their own brand of music via artists like The Three Degrees, becoming to the seventies what Motown was to the sixties. Author Paul Howes believes that if Dusty had waited until the record company was established, she'd have enjoyed a major international seller rather than a lukewarm one. Most of the tracks from her entire Philadelphia sessions were released at this time, with two released shortly after her death, and the remaining three a couple of years later.

Spending much of the year outside Britain, Dusty did return to attend her secretary Pat Rhodes' wedding at Harringay Civic Centre on 13 June 1970. She went with Madeline Bell and Norma Tanega and, to ensure she didn't steal the bride's limelight, dressed down in a long off-the-peg cotton dress. "I could have killed her because I wanted her to be noticed!" Pat remembered. "The funny thing is Dusty could wear a headscarf and dark glasses and there's still a presence about her. You can feel it." From her secretary's wedding she went to the recording studio where she was experimenting with new material for her next album. During August "Lost" was American released, and a month later Dusty promoted her new single, a revival of The Young Rascals' "How Can I Be Sure?" in Britain. Her version began softly before hitting the chorus in a melee of strings and emotion against a sweeping, lilting melody. Recorded specifically for her home market, it was a song she had loved for some time and believed the public would share her enthusiasm. She wrong-footed them; the single peaked at number 36, was her last British single for nearly a year and her last British hit for nine years. When teen heart-throb David Cassidy took his version to the top of the charts in 1972, Dusty's already fragile ego must have taken a huge knocking.

By now, it was reported that Dusty's relationship with Norma was rocky, and that she had returned to Los Angeles, leaving Dusty to fend for herself. Not an easy option for her, regardless of who was to blame for the break up. However, the two would spend time together when Dusty was in America. Meanwhile, Dusty's home was raided by the police looking for drugs but they had found nothing. Apparently, they had been tipped off by a woman whose advances Dusty had rejected yet, unlike police raids on properties owned by The Beatles and The Rolling Stones, her raid passed by unreported in the press.

Early in 1971 Diana Ross replaced Dusty as the top world singer in the *NME* readers' poll, with Cilla Black pushing Lulu from the top of the British female singer category. Dusty was third in both sections. Spending the bulk of the year in America, Dusty's recording output was regular thanks to the 13 or so tracks she had already recorded with writer/producer Jeff Barry for Atlantic Records, like "Haunted " in August and "I Believe In You" three months later. "Haunted" was earmarked for her next studio album "See All Her Faces", but Dusty's product manager at Philips Records changed his mind and the track remained unreleased until 1980. On the other hand, "I Believe In You", a mid-tempo rock track, was the second of two singles to be US-released from the Jeff Barry sessions. The album was never released because Dusty reputedly fell out with Atlantic Records executives or, as more likely, it was canned because the lifted singles were poor sellers. The master tapes were later destroyed by fire but, luckily, Jeff Barry had kept safe copies of the intended final mixes.

With the Jeff Barry project finished, Dusty returned to London in June. During her stay she recorded appearances on *The Marty Feldman Comedy Machine* and *It's Lulu*. Dusty's American recordings weren't released in Britain, so fans contented themselves with the maxi single containing "Some Of Your Loving", "Son-Of-A

Preacher Man " and "You Don't Have To Say You Love Me". And, as if to add insult to injury, their star announced she had moved to Los Angeles and hired a new manager, Alan Bernard! While working on a couple of Andy Williams' shows, Dusty had met Bernard, Andy's manager of 13 years. "When he expressed an interest in me, I didn't take it too seriously" she said. "But the way he talked intrigued me and I signed with him. He has my absolute trust and respect."

With no British single to promote, Dusty declined invitations to appear on television music shows and headed towards Germany for a solitary performance. She then headed back to the States to begin a series of hotel concerts during 1972. Fred Perry was in charge of her stage lighting for all the dates. The first was at The Persian Room, in the New York Plaza Hotel, followed by an April – May season at the Fairmont Roosevelt's Blue Room in New Orleans. She opened her act with the words, "The astronauts finally landed on the moon, but I can't seem to make it down here from the eighth floor on time!" Wearing a clinging, hot pink Ray Aghayan gown, she opened her 45-minute act with "But Alive" and admitted she was a little nervous as she cautiously continued with her act. With her repertoire including "You Don't Have To Say You Love Me", "Son-Of-A Preacher Man" and "Since I Fell For You", she electrified her audience with a medley of "Joy To The World", "Take A Look Around You" and "Higher And Higher". On the faster songs she came across like a full-volumed jukebox in a classy dive, with her little dance steps and precision support from a trio of back-up singers. The orchestra often overpowered her, but most critics agreed she was the world's top female singer.

Rosie Casals caught her act, and when the tour closed at the Century Plaza Hotel, Century City, Diana Ross and Dionne Warwick were in the audience. Performing in these top-class hotels, Dusty was given a large, luxurious suite to live in with 24-hour room service. Thankfully her love of hotel life saw her through these long seasons where, more often than not, she stood in the hotel's noisy, working kitchen waiting to go on stage, perform for an audience who weren't necessarily her fans, then return to her hotel suite too tired to eat anything but a sandwich. Despite her bravado in interviews, the lady was lonely.

Recorded in 1970, Dusty turned to Charles Aznavour's compelling composition "Yesterday When I Was Young" as her next single. Befitting a cabaret performance, it was strange choice for a mainstream market release in May 1972. Viewed with scepticism, her public had waited so long to hear that treasured voice again they felt Dusty had failed to deliver the goods with a song that started with her speaking, building slowly until she ended up battling with the orchestra. It was a poor choice which was reflected in its sales. As the single floundered, Dusty lent her voice to ex-Move Carl Wayne's debut solo album recorded in London's Piccadilly. Produced by Don Paul, the project was a departure from his recordings with the group and Roy Wood, and demonstrated the full range of his incredible voice. The album also had a secret, Dusty's uncredited backing vocals, and it was through Don Paul that she became involved. Carl Wayne explained that "She sang on four tracks … one o'clock in the morning, Dusty and I would be pissed out of our brains, sitting in the studio. You can hear her clearly on 'Spirit In The Sky' … it was great!" Re-mastered for CD release, *Carl Wayne* was re-issued in 2001.

From Carl Wayne, she turned her attention to her own new project for ABC Dunhill, now that her contract with Atlantic Records was finished. This time Steve Barri, Dennis Lambert and Brian Potter were given the task of working with her. Soul fans went on to love their work with ex-Motowners, the Four Tops, particularly the *Keeper Of The Castle* album during 1972 and *Main Street People* a year later. Both projects had spawned hits and their sympathetic attitude to music was considered ideal for Dusty who, like the Four Tops, needed hit material. With the working title *Cameo* they locked themselves in the ABC Recording Studio, Los Angeles, with backing singers Clydie King, Sherlie Mathews,

Myrna Mathews and Venetta Fields, and some of the finest musicians of the day, to produce an album that would elevate Dusty into
the international charts. The sessions weren't without incident; in
frustration she threw her multi-thousand dollar jade and diamond
wristwatch to the studio floor – "It was so beautifully made that
it even fell apart neatly!" Some of that frustration arose from her
sense of not belonging "... and for the first time in my career I lost
creative control" she explained to *Billboard* magazine's Peter Hartz.
"*Cameo* was a good record but also quite plastic. They wanted
me to record material they had selected. It didn't sit right. I was
terribly galled that they had done some tracks without even asking
me what key. I became terribly unco-operative and just dug in my
heels... It was all wrong. I wanted out."

Meanwhile, in her absence *See All Her Faces* was released in November 1972 and, as if to push the point home even further, the album featured eight different producers including herself, and was a
collection of varying musical styles, none of them reaching the high
Springfield standards set down in previous albums. With tracks from
her American buddies like Tom Dowd, Arif Mardin, Jerry Wexler,
Jeff Barry and Ellie Greenwich, fans expected better, particularly
after a two-and-a-half year wait. Buyers should have realized from
the wishy-washy cover, which showed three drawn faces of the
singer as sad, fine and happy, that all was not as it seemed. Kicking off with "Mixed Up Girl" (beautifully delivered by soul star
Thelma Houston on her evergreen *Sunshower* album which Dusty
had in her collection) the lyrics seemed to sum up Dusty's state of
mind at the time. She then launched into "Crumbs Off The Table", originally recorded by the Invictus group Glasshouse which
included Scherrie Payne (who co-wrote the song), a later member
of The Supremes. Scherrie is also sister to Freda, known for her
blockbusting "Band Of Gold". "Crumbs Off The Table" was her
favourite track on the album; she produced it with Johnny Franz
and believed it to be a very powerful song. Indeed it was, with the
help of Lesley Duncan and Kay Garner. Originally recorded by

Tom Springfield for his *Sun Songs* album, "Come For A Dream" was another of Dusty's favourites. Norma Tanega penned new lyrics for her version but only one of the original writers Jobim (not "and Duran") was credited on the album. Four tracks share the same underlying smoothness of emotion – "What Good Is I Love You", "Willie & Laura Mae Jones", "Someone Who Cares" and "Nothing Is Forever". With their sweeping melodies, they showed the fire in Dusty's soul. Originally recorded by Rick Jones, the album's title was the penultimate track. Rather nondescript, it battled against the wonderful American productions. All in all, *See All Her Faces* was a collection of songs, presented indifferently by an artist who should have known better!

As *See All Her Faces* struggled, Dusty began rehearsing for her next season at London's Talk Of The Town where, following an absence of four years, she was due to open on 4 December. Her previous seasons were hugely successful, with capacity audiences and there was no reason to think this would change. Negotiating a four-week contract worth £6,000, topped up by another £4,000 as her percentage of the theatre's takings, it was a lucrative deal. Before she stepped foot on the stage, she had spent £10,000 on musicians, singers, sheet music and, of course, her gowns. However, all didn't go according to plan because Dusty had flu and laryngitis. The opening performance of her British "comeback" was due to start at 11.30 pm but, unknown to the audience, Dusty was receiving emergency treatment from a Harley Street specialist which included a cortisone spray. It was after midnight before she crawled on stage, opening with the aptly titled "But Alive". During the second song she waved the orchestra silent to cough and wipe her perspiring face. "There are many songs I'd like to sing but I can't because they would be an embarrassment to you and me. I thought I'd just say 'hello'". As she chatted, her humour covered her desperation to save the show, and even the risqué send-up of Ivor Novello's "His Mother Came Too" was well accepted. Clearly, her jangling nerves were in the same state as her painful throat, but her Irish bravado won through as she battled on with "I Just Don't Know What To Do With Myself", "Son-Of-A Preacher Man", "You Don't Have To Say You Love Me" and "The Look Of Love", achieved after several false starts. During this section, she told her star-studded audience that included Elton John and Rod Stewart – "I might as well have a bash. No harm done; it's the spirit that won the war!" Indeed, it was the sympathetic audience that helped her through, until she left the stage to a standing ovation. In retrospect, Dusty should never have attempted the performance but she refused to let her public down. However, one reviewer didn't agree with her decision. "If I'd have been the manager of the Talk Of The Town, I'd have fired you after the first night when you were nearly three-quarters of an hour late, dried up once and twice flew in self-pity from the microphone."

When the theatre's manager received a phone call advising Dusty had been ordered to rest, he sacked her. "I was up to my ears in drugs" the angry singer pointed out at the time. "I was ill but was willing to go back to work when I recovered. But they gave me the boot." Bruce Forsyth replaced her for the month's booking. Her lawyers sued the theatre (the case was settled out of court) and her American management team told the media she would never appear there again. And she didn't… until the theatre became The Hippodrome that is.

By the close of 1972 Dusty had decided to relocate to America for a short stay and to this end sold her beloved 38 Aubrey Walk, said farewell to Pat Rhodes, her backing group The Echoes, particularly Dougie Reece, and of course her friends and family. Her gowns, wigs and personal effects were already en route to their new home. Although she sympathized with Dusty's reasons to move on, Pat believed she could have enjoyed a different kind of career if she remained in Britain. That of comedy acting. "Her heart is in that medium; she is so funny and has a fantastic sense of humour". She also understood the need to break away from the "pop singer" image, saying "She can do other types of music, country and western, and she's got the perfect Blues voice, but people here wanted her to do pop songs, and that was it. With all this going on in her mind, I think she thought if she went to America, perhaps she would be able to open up." The singer's public were confused by her actions. These were two typical reactions "Really true fans will realize this decision was a foregone conclusion" wrote Gillian Holt. "For although we put her records in the chart, Dusty has never been appreciated in this country for the true artist she is." Fiona Shoat, on the other hand, asked "Is this her way of saying thank you to the thousands of fans who have stood by her for all these years?"

"For as long as I can remember, I've been in love with the idea of living in California. It came first from the Hollywood musicals I saw as a child, and later through friends in the music business. I was determined to go, and once there, determined to be as Californian as possible." On a more serious note though, and probably nearer the truth, Dusty had been hounded by the British press and felt she had totally lost control of her personality and her life. Admitting they were "nice to me for a long time and then they got bored and got a kick out of trying to cut me. That was one reason why I didn't want to stay here. I had everything coming at me." Further probing into the singer's life had led to revelations about her self-harming. In fact, she had been seen running with a friend into St Mary's Hospital, London, late one evening. Dusty had slashed her wrists and was screaming obscenities, but reputedly the nursing staff protected her identity. However, she wasn't so lucky when she spoke to Kenny Everett during one of his Capital Radio shows. Dusty was in Los Angeles at the time with his (then) wife Lee, and they phoned him during his programme. During the exchanged banter Kenny said Dusty's arms should have zips. This time, the comment was reported in the music press. The two enjoyed an easy relationship, both sharing a zany, often black, sense of humour. Indeed, when the singer guested on one of his extremely successful television programmes, viewers were shocked/delighted to see her suspended in chains while Kenny whipped her, extracting the confession "I love it, I love it... and I love the show too!"

Early in 1973, there were British dates to honour, starting with a string of nightclub dates where she performed her Talk of the Town act to audiences in Manchester and Batley. She then pre-recorded the first of a series of half-hour specials titled *Music My Way* for the BBC to be screened in July, marking the last time she was seen on the small screen for nearly five years. And on 28 January, the singer took her act to the London Palladium for two concerts. With a softer, shoulder-length hairstyle, Dusty was subconsciously adopting the American cabaret artist image befitting a 33-year-old. A 45-strong orchestra marked her arrival on stage before a packed theatre when she opened with "But Alive" from the musical *Applause*, with its lyrics of feeling "twitchy, bitchy and manic". Sung with a humorous edge to her voice of course! This was followed by "Just A Little Lovin'", "Magnificent Sanctuary Band" and "Yesterday When I Was Young". "Dorothy Squires loaned me her gown for the evening" she laughed. "But she must have it back by 12 as she's hired the Vatican for the night." After a string of hits which brought a memorable evening to an end, critics glowed that Dusty still reigned supreme in the Kingdom of Pop!

The first single to be extracted from her new album *Cameo* was "Who Gets Your Love" in March 1973, a month after its American outing. The album was also released in March, and two months later in Britain. Originally intended to be released in a felt cover to highlight the front cover showing Dusty's face within a cameo brooch, the idea proved impractical and was abandoned in favour of laminated card. The American gatefold sleeve was available in two different label designs, while the British version was a poor relation, a one-sleeve package! With strings a smidge over-loud, shimmering piano and guitar playing, Dusty's performance was immaculate on "Who Gets Your Love" but, without her personal promotional touch, it bombed without trace. Opening the album, this track was one of five written by Dennis Lambert and Brian Potter; the others – "Breakin' Up A Happy Home", "Mama's Little Girl", "Comin' And Goin'" and "Of All The Things" – were emotionally charged and high octane in melody and vocals, yet Dusty said she "wasn't proud of the sounds coming from her throat and didn't think she could tell what was a good song anymore." Her Motown heroes, Valerie Simpson and Nickolas Ashford, penned "I Just Wanna Be There", an easy musical journey for her to travel, while perhaps the unusual inclusion of Van Morrison's "Tupelo Honey" and David Gates' "The Other Side Of Life" might have given her cause for concern. Despite Dusty's moanings, the album's heart was "Learn To Say Goodbye" from the 1972 ABC movie *Say Goodbye, Maggie Cole*, starring Susan Hayward. The song was throat catching from the opening note, a tear jerker in the finest overwrought Springfield style. Loaded with a remorse almost too painful to bear, it reached such an emotional level that listeners were hard-pushed not to grab a Kleenex. Certainly the saddest song of all, but to her it represented the worst of Hollywood because when she recorded the song for the television movie "They made me stand in the middle of an enormous sound stage, with one microphone and no earphones, and expected me to come up with a good sound." She did; it was perfect! Although the film had a British screening, Dusty didn't promote the single, so it followed the same fate as its American release. With no hit singles to promote it, *Cameo* bombed on both sides of the Atlantic.

While this project lived in Britain, Dusty was guesting on several peak-viewing US television shows like the NBC daytime programme *Dinah's Place*. Believe it or not, the host, Dinah Shore, prepared an Enchiladas Verdes dish for Dusty, and viewers saw the two chatting and cooking in a studio kitchen. With her hair in a bob cut, and a twinkle in her eyes, Dusty showed an unhealthy interest in the chicken filled tortillas and green tomato sauce!

In the succeeding months, contractual complications, a growing disillusionment on her part, and an escalating drug and alcohol habit, brought her career to a halt. She parted company with her management team – telling them they didn't know what they were doing – and was in no hurry to sign to another record company.

"It was very good for me to stop because it gave me time to soak up Los Angeles ... After a period of time I discovered I did know what was best for me and that my instincts were right."

In July, Elton John launched the American opening of his label, Rocket Records, at a party held on the back lots of Universal Studios, Los Angeles. By now, he was an international star and was riding high on the rock single "Saturday Night's Alright For Fighting", with his *Goodbye Yellow Brick Road* project due for release. Dusty was invited and, according to Fred Perry who escorted her, was determined to keep a low profile "... when suddenly she was dragged up onto the stage and, with Elton and Kiki Dee, did about 20 minutes of harmony... the audience reaction was incredible and these were hard-boiled music industry types." Having worked with Elton on his 1970 *Tumbleweed Connection* album ("Ballad Of A Well Known Gun" and "My Father's Gun"), Dusty held on to the hope that he'd produce her one day. In fact, when he publicly announced this was his intention, he quickly withdrew the offer via a letter on Rocket Records notepaper, without Dusty really knowing why. "Elton was very enthusiastic but I think my management at the time made absolutely outlandish demands on him, creatively and financially." However, she went on to sing with him on "The Bitch Is Back" and an unreleased alternative version of "Don't Let The Sun Go Down On Me", tracks for his 1974 album entitled *Caribou*.

During what she called "her quiet period" between 1974 and 1976, Dusty lent her voice to third-party projects, none of which followed any particular pattern. She was a session singer on fellow ABC Dunhill act, Thomas Jefferson Kaye's album *First Grade*, where she was clearly heard on a trio of tracks – "American Lovers", "Sho-Bout" and "LA". She can also be heard on Bob Neuwirth's eponymous album released by Asylum Records. A happy reunion with country star Anne Murray (who, with her husband Bill, was in the audience for one of her London Palladium concerts in January) led to Dusty being a session singer on her 1975 *Together* album, notably on the Michael Omartian produced tracks "Sunday Sunrise", "If It's Alright With You", "Player In The Band" and "Blue Finger Lou". (Omartian had been a featured keyboardist and strings, horn and flutes arranger on *Cameo*.) Dusty said they had marvellous times together, recording in Toronto: "...This was really an honour for me because I am a big fan. So they flew me up and I sang a couple of notes, here, there and everywhere, and it was a wonderful experience... I was with Dianne Brookes, who was also a singer from Toronto." Anne Murray added, "She was clean at the time and we had just the best week together." From country music, Dusty joined others like Lesley Gore and Brenda Russell to work with songwriter-cum-cabaret star, Peter Allen, on "Back Doors Crying", a track on *Taught By Experts*, an album produced by Brooks Arthur. Dusty was so impressed with Allen that she adopted his composition, which he co-wrote with Carole Bayer Sager, titled "Quiet Please There's A Lady On Stage" as her very own.

From cabaret Dusty switched to Evie Sands (who recorded the original of "Take Me For A Little While" which Dusty covered on her 1967 album *Where Am I Going?*) to sing on "Lady Of The Night", a track on her 1979-released album *Suspended Animation*. Unfortunately, fans were hard-pressed to hear Dusty and, if her name hadn't been included in the recording credits, few people would have known she was there. And, probably, the last publicized session work during this period was her work with Rough Trade (Carole Pope and Kevan Staples) on their *For Those Who Think Young* album. Crediting her on the packaging with "vocal assistance by Dusty Springfield", it was considerably clearer than that given by Dusty on her 1982 album *White Heat* which read "this vinyl thingie was made in part because of (and in spite of) J. Tone". Pope and Staples had contributed "I Am Curious" and "Soft Core" which, many claimed, were the album's highlights.

Back in 1974, from July to September, Dusty worked with Brooks Arthur in New York on what would have been her second album for ABC Dunhill. So keen was the company to advertise the fact, that, before the year had ended, a slightly cropped illustration of the cover was included in full-page advertisements alongside other ABC Dunhill albums due for release. The advert was misleading because Dusty's project had been shelved, with a company spokesperson saying, "If the album sees the light of day, it'll be the kiss of death for Dusty's career." During 1994 Springfield historians unearthed the tracks which showed a varying musical road, quite alien to the lady's style. Barry Manilow's "I Am Your Child" was one, which was the first song he'd written with his partner Marty Panzer. "When, as a young singer-songwriter, I was told that she was about to cut the first song I had ever written, I was thrilled beyond belief" Manilow wrote in the CD notes. "When Dusty and Brooks Arthur requested I play for them, I was honoured." Stephen Swartz's "Corner Of The Sky", which likewise featured the composer on keyboards, was released 33 years later when fellow British singer, Petula Clark, added her own vocals to release it as a joint effort on her 2007 CD *Duets*. Melissa Manchester who was featured on "Home To Myself", a song she wrote with Carole Bayer Sager, said she was "over the moon" when she heard Dusty's interpretation. Petula Clark's accompanist, Frank Owens, played Fender Rhodes electric piano on "Exclusively For Me", and piano on "Angels" and "In The Winter". The songs were either incomplete, or abandoned because Dusty was unhappy with them, or had just lost interest. She was going through personal traumas, and battling with drug and alcohol abuse; in fact, her well-being was causing concern. Not so long ago, she'd have found security and comfort within the confines of the recording studios, but now she found it impossible to face the day, let alone hold a song together with people she didn't know. Brooks Arthur told Paul Howes that "She was in a tricky spot in her life and she wasn't confident about ... revealing ... her full emotions, and also she would hide that behind whatever other kind of nonsense she was doing to herself." Jay Lasker, head of ABC/Dunhill Records, was reluctant to keep investing in Dusty;

he told Arthur "I don't want to keep on throwing good money after bad ... I know she's not showing up for various sessions and, if she shows up, she's eight hours late and then in the eighth hour Bruce Springsteen's in there." Dusty actually believed Brooks Arthur had dreamed up this Springsteen feller because she never saw him. They eventually did meet and she was struck by his talent – and looks.

However, a handful of gems not only survived the sessions but were completed, like "Beautiful Soul" and incomplete versions of "Make The Man Love Me", "Turn Me Around" and "A Love Like Yours", the last two titles being re-recorded for the 1978 album *It Begins Again*. Even though the project was incomplete, it's thought that some of the songs were hawked around American record companies. Tapes also reached the manager of the MOR division at EMI Records in London. He reluctantly turned it down because his immediate boss feared she was too much of a gamble. Thankfully, this attitude changed in 1987 when the Pet Shop Boys presented her to the company.

By now Dusty had moved four times; she blamed her restless spirit and her hatred of becoming involved in serious homemaking. Each apartment was rented and impersonal with the same qualities of a comfortable hotel suite. The only difference was the facilities for her cats. She described her then current house, on the valley side of Laurel Canyon, as having "a fantastic view with a big pool... sort of nouveau riche. The trouble was, I wasn't very nouveau and not at all riche!" Dusty couldn't swim but sat instead by the pool eating quaalade sandwiches – "I tell you, if you eat enough of (them) it's gonna be a lifetime before you learn how to swim!" She later sold the house to move into a smaller property in Beverley Hills.

When Dusty was ready to concentrate on her own career again, Vicki Wickham recommended Cat Steven's manager Barry Krost. He negotiated a recording deal with United Artists where one of the conditions in her contract was her creative control in material selection and production. But even that brought problems!

Chapter Nine

I'M COMING HOME AGAIN

"I'm a lady who has learned not to expect too much from life."

With Barry Krost taking over as her manager, Dusty's fans hoped she would once more be back on track. Things certainly looked more hopeful when she signed a recording deal with United Artists in America and almost immediately started working at the Cherokee Studios in Los Angeles with producer Roy Thomas Baker, known for his work with Queen. They had met at a Los Angeles party and not for one moment did Dusty consider him as a producer with whom she could work. In fact, when the suggestion was put to her, she considered it to be too bizarre for words. Eventually, he was to become one of the few producers she trusted. Dusty chose the songs and musicians for the album because Roy was involved in other, more pressing projects.

"We went through all the material together and I decided which songs to do by watching the reaction on his face," she later told *Music Week*, the British trade paper. "He is the most understated person. If he says something is good or quite nice then it usually means it's terrific. It took me quite a while to read him." Elton John's producer, Gus Dudgeon, was also approached, but he insisted Dusty record in Britain and that wasn't on her agenda.

Dusty recorded her debut single for United Artists independently from the proposed album with Roy Thomas Baker. Titled "Let Me Love You Once Before You Go" from the pen of Steve Dorff, who also produced it with Dusty, it was released during June 1977. The American trade paper *Cashbox*'s reviewer wrote, "One of the world's most soulful ladies puts in a command performance with this ballad." Dusty, however, wasn't happy because it was heavily "un-promoted" and urgently needed a remix, although she conceded "as a song it's quite poignant and quite strong." The title was officially released in Britain 17 years later as a bonus track on the *Goin' Back* CD compilation.

The fate of the "un-promoted" single which struggled for American sales had a lot to do with Dusty herself. Barry Krost told United Artists' executives that she was too ill to attend the launch party. In actual fact, that wasn't the case. As he later explained, "She didn't have time to get her hair done so we told the president of the company she didn't feel well to get out of having photographs taken." He also stipulated that when she did grant interviews, questions about her personal and previous life were banned. This attitude certainly contributed to Dusty missing out on her first taste of success with her new record company.

By January 1978, Dusty was back in business. Following Christmas with her father in her Los Angeles home, she flew to Britain to promote her first single of the year, a brave version of "A Love Like Yours (Don't Come Knocking Every Day)". Written by Holland, Dozier and Holland, it was first recorded by Martha Reeves and the Vandellas during 1963, and was a British hit three years later for Ike and Tina Turner. Dusty adored Martha's version from the first hearing "because it's jolly and superficial, and I wanted to get away from the weepies because everyone still thinks that I'm such a drama queen." The song was one of the unfinished tracks from the Brooks Arthur sessions for the *Longing* album in 1974.

Some considered Roy Thomas Baker's production on "A Love Like Yours" to be a little fussy while others believed he was "bringing Dusty up to date", as was the bulk of the song's mother album *It Begins Again*. To kick start the single's January release in Britain, a slimmer, conservatively dressed Dusty with a soft-waved hairstyle and downsized eye make-up, flew to London for 10 days. Scuffles broke out and swear words were exchanged at Heathrow when her record company executives tried to smuggle her out of the airport without being photographed. As she emerged from Customs, they ushered her away from the angry photographers and into the back of a waiting black Rolls Royce. As she was whisked away, she shouted "it's good to be home" to the photographers. Dusty later said "For some reason they had it organized that I would be kept under wraps like some statue until the press conference. I didn't know. I was smiling my head off, even at 5.15 in the morning. I was wonderful… and I said wonderful things to nobody in particular and it got printed as 'Dusty In Airport Scuffle!'"

Phonogram Records held a press conference for their star at the Savoy Hotel on 2 February, where journalists were keen to probe into Dusty's private life. She fielded their questions with remarkable articulacy and poise and, although she was quite frank about her life in America, she omitted to say that she shared that life with women. Perhaps her courage failed her and she just didn't feel able to open up, but in the free-living seventies, would it have mattered that much? Naturally, she also managed to mention her new single and album due for release in six days' time. Ray Coleman wrote in *Melody Maker*, "This was no ordinary press call. Few warm the cockles of a pop fan's heart as much as the return of Dusty because she was, and is, a great singer who always had taste, style, and that elusive star quality."

In countless later media interviews Dusty claimed to loathe the word "comeback" because it was associated with drama and tragedy, and people like Judy Garland. She also defended her relocation to California, admitting she had run away from her life in London and a career that had rapidly gone stale. She had been unhappy and restless, so followed the American dream, intending it to be a temporary break. "I had only just bought a house in Britain, so I wasn't likely to leave for good, and if I stayed in America for more than six months I had to pay their taxes." But stay she did, after signing with a management team. "When I arrived they took me out for breakfast and I thought 'this is going to be good'. But after that I could never get them on the phone."

And in another interview she said, "They tried to make me into this slick, Las Vegas-style act, but I was quite hopeless at it. In the end, I got so depressed that I more or less gave up singing altogether." It was demoralizing, she said, performing for jaded businessmen, or for people who were resident in the hotel and wandered through to see the evening's act. "I knew they weren't coming to see me. My ego was severely crushed... [and] playing to those audiences wasn't helping my recording career." It took her two years to wriggle free from this depressing way of life.

Among the television spots, Dusty promoted "A Love Like Yours" on *Top Of The Pops*. Beforehand, she contacted Madeline Bell for advice on backing singers to join her on the programme. Staying with Madeline was singer Simon Bell who had been a Dusty fan since The Springfields. He tells the amusing tale of his first meeting with her in 1964 after a show at The Odeon in Glasgow. When Dusty emerged from the stage door, she quickly jumped into a taxi and, not to be beaten, Simon gave chase in another cab through the town to the North British Hotel. He followed her into the hotel where his reward was Dusty autographing his wrist. "I didn't wash for weeks," he laughed. Cutting his musical teeth singing with Glasgow soul groups from the age of 15, he relocated to London during 1970 where he later met Doris Troy, and became a session singer with her and Madeline. "I had the good fortune to be in the right place at the right time and sang with her on *Top Of The Pops*."

Wearing an outfit that was lacy, light and flowing, trousers and boots, Dusty looked remarkably like actress Sharon Gless as she funked and sidestepped her way across the studio's stage. "Thank goodness, she's back," announced the show's DJ host. Despite Dusty's high profile, "A Love Like Yours (Don't Come Knocking Every Day)" failed to chart, and wasn't the perfect advertisement for *It Begins Again*, her first studio album for five years. Nonetheless, no expense was spared by Phonogram Records to ensure their star wouldn't fail. They embarked upon one of their most expensive promotional campaigns, one that included 500 in-store displays where a grainy, autumn-coloured Dusty gazed defiantly from shop windows.

"*It Begins Again* is the first album I have liked on first hearing; I hope that's not the kiss of death," Dusty told journalists at the time of its release in February 1978. She explained she hadn't winced, yelled or gone beyond her vocal limitations, resulting in a much softer, warmer voice. Through the songs she explored and ana-lysed Californian life, dissecting and rejecting storylines to present a gloriously inviting and wholly satisfying musical journey. "Turn Me Around", which she had previously recorded with Brooks Arthur, was re-cut for inclusion here, providing a rather subdued start to an album with much promise. Nona Hendryx's composi-tion "Checkmate" followed, given to her by the composer two years earlier. Weaving around a strong melody with a storyline that was strangely old-fashioned, "I'd Rather Leave While I'm In Love", from the pens of Carole Bayer Sager and Peter Allen, was a rare gem in true Springfield fashion. Dusty insisted it wasn't a personal message: "I'm hopeless at leaving before things get stale... But it's funny, that song sums up the professional side of me." Many critics believed "Hollywood Movie Girls" to be the album's highlight where Dusty immersed herself in the frustrations of chas-ing the dream, living the lyrics, mesmerizing listeners as she did so. A stunning track which, surprisingly, never achieved A-side single status, it was confined as the flip to "A Love Like Yours (Don't Come Knocking Every Day)". While Dusty had considered and rejected taking up the option of an acting career, she does act on vinyl on two shattering tracks – Barry Manilow's "Sandra", the tale of an extremely unhappy and suicidal housewife, and Lesley Gore's "Love Me By Name", telling of the desperation of one-night stands. Of "Sandra" she said, "Although I've never been a housewife, I can identify with it as a woman. It's about people who get trapped (and) I have great sympathy for her." Of "Love Me By Name" she admitted she had fumbled her way through furtive one-night gropes. "When not done too often, they're great fun. They can be very good for the ego but they can be soul shattering as well." She added, "I never got involved with anyone until I was 25. I never felt I was worth being loved. Once I felt that I was worth it, it was all I wanted."

From fumbling on one night stands, Dusty switched to the dance floor with "That's The Kind Of Love I've Got For You", the album's oddball. An excited Roy Thomas Baker gave Dusty a demo of the song but she disliked it, believing it to be too repetitive. She changed her mind when he introduced her much-loved Brazilian music among his "crazy noises", and the song took shape to her satisfaction. Released in June, it was Dusty's second single from *It Begins Again* and was her stab at the disco market – the pounding beat and phased vocals – with 12 inch copies of the single already shipped to nightclubs to promote the mother album. Perhaps it was too different because, once again, she faced sales failure in the British marketplace where Boney M, the Bee Gees, Tavares and Rose Royce numbered among the high-flying dance acts.

In retrospect, maybe *It Begins Again* lacked the familiar Springfield hooklines that were so much a part of her musical personality, and maybe she was unwise in her choice of material. The album sold poorly and struggled into the top 50. By the time it peaked, Dusty had returned to America where its sales were likewise disappointing. The "comeback" hadn't gone according to plan, and the pressure, she said, "nearly killed me!" Unfortunately, this wasn't the only setback she had to face in the immediate future.

From the end of June through to September 1978 Dusty returned to the recording studio with David Wolfert to work on her next album for United Artists. Her version of Smokey Robinson and the Miracles' 1963 hit "You've Really Got A Hold On Me" was one of the first completed tracks and would later kick off the new album. In October she appeared on Rod McKuen's *Christmas*

In New England special, and recorded "Bits And Pieces" during December/January for *The Stunt Man* movie soundtrack, which was released as an album two years after the film was shot. And 24 years after that, the song was on Dusty's *Classics & Collectibles* compilation. In between times, it appeared on the American release *The Dusty Springfield Anthology*.

Within record time by Dusty's standards, the second album *Living Without Your Love* was American-released in January 1979, with its title track issued as a single. The album was originally called *Never Trust A Man In A Rented Tuxedo* and, according to Paul Howes, the cover design showed a (seemingly) naked Dusty standing in a room, clutching a coat to cover her modesty. A man wearing a tuxedo was pictured fleeing stage right. The *Living Without Your Love* design was tame by comparison, with a laughing Dusty throwing a coat away from her person against a black and mauve background.

When *It Begins Again* had failed to revitalize her career, the public greeted this new album with some trepidation. Anne Nightingale wrote in the *Daily Express*, "She has released an album to be proud of [and it] demonstrates that Dusty still possesses a unique tonal quality." Yet Penny Valentine in *Time Out* felt her stylistic desperation was subdued: "She seems no longer to enjoy the challenges of vocal risks that were once her forte." With her tribute to Motown over with the opening track, Dusty turned to the jazz influenced "You Can Do It", co-written by Evie Sands, easing listeners into a version of Melissa Manchester's original song "Be Somebody" which Dusty took at a faster pace. Interesting but not compelling. "Closet Man", by its very title, attracted all the attention. Its suggestive lyrics told a confidential tale of a woman who told her man that his secret was safe with her, that it was fine for him to continue with his lifestyle. The story ended when the ring she'd given him, he now wore in his ear. And Dusty told the tale in the only way she knew – with sensitivity. David Wolfert, who co-penned "Living Without Your Love" with Steve Nelson, had little experience as a producer before this project, yet he and Dusty were responsible for the whole project, following a production deal signed with The Entertainment Company. "She gave me a trial period which luckily I passed," he smiled. The uptempo track didn't do Dusty justice, as it chugged along to nowhere. Side two kicked in with the Barry Gibb song "Save Me, Save Me", already adequately recorded by Motown's Rare Earth group and Frankie Valli (of The Four Seasons). Support vocals from Patti Brooks, Brenda Russell and Diane Brooks – who appeared on the entire album – certainly helped. Introducing a touch of gospel, Dusty made hard work of "Get Yourself To Love", but thankfully "I Just Fall In Love Again" pulled her back on track. Not a new song by any means – Anne Murray and The Carpenters recorded excellent versions – but when Dusty injected her personality and unique styling into the romantic ballad, she beat them both. A pair of Carole Bayer Sager tracks closed the album – the flimsy, yet catchy "Dream On", and the gloriously flowing "I'm Coming Home Again". Crammed with tear-jerking emotion, it was the perfect vehicle for Dusty's own brand of pop/soul. "No other vocalist can sustain the balance between intense vulnerability and passionate generosity" a *Rolling Stone* reviewer noted. But it was *Melody Maker's* Susan Hill who summed up everyone's feelings – "Dusty's become so tasteful. The singing is breathy, smooth and true, but with a further depth of maturity … Ten 'safe' songs cut of an enduring sixties' cloth is a funny 1979 comeback."

Two months later, a curly haired Dusty returned to London to support its British release. Despite the failure of her previous visit, she shrugged off her disappointment, looked fate in the eye once more and gave it her best shot, starting with guest spots on BBC1's *Shirley Bassey Show* and *Saturday Night At The Mill*. Yet fate played tricks on her again, when her planned British tour to coincide with the new album, promoted by Rod Stewart's manager Billy Gaff, was pulled except for three dates at the Drury Lane Theatre, London in April 1979. The cancelled dates in Manchester,

Birmingham, Edinburgh and Brighton were a tremendous blow to her professionally and a great heartache on a personal level. Her triumphant return had virtually collapsed due to poor ticket sales. Fred Perry believed the posters were wrong because they made her look like Petula Clark: "I have always felt that a picture of the 'old' panda-eyed Dusty, and the words 'she's back' would have made such a difference." Dusty cried, "I've got a badly dented ego... I've learned a few lessons... it's a real disappointment." She lost out financially but insisted her real investment in the tour was in emotion and music.

The regions missed the show of a lifetime. It was emotional beyond words when the capacity audiences celebrated the return of their prodigal daughter. Their loyalty was unequalled when Dusty, clearly tearful, took to the stage to show that time had stood still for her as she performed with a dynamism that had elevated her to solo stardom a decade earlier. Nostalgia played its part, of course, with hits like "You Don't Have To Say You Love Me" and "I Just Don't Know What To Do With Myself". When she forgot the words during her second song, she dissolved into a fit of the giggles, and when she commanded, "I want to hear a nice butch roar and a nice girlish shriek. I want to know who's out there!" she was overpowered by the response. She later explained, "I make it up as I go along. I can cover mistakes like the band starting in the wrong place, or not finishing in the right place, the wrong key, that sort of thing, but not when it comes to lyrics. I have to make them up because I'm incapable of doing two things at once, like singing and remembering the words. Some of the songs I've sung a million times, but I still forget the words. It's alright, the fans forgive me, they sing in my place..."

Taking the Kate Bush song "The Man With A Child In His Eyes" to perfection, Dusty broke down during "I'm Coming Home Again" which was greeted with cries of "welcome home". Perhaps the most bizarre idea was the roller skating sequence built around the song "Rollerina". As her three backing singers – Simon

Bell, Doreen Chanter and Barry St John – and the dinner-jacketed orchestra struck up the music, Dusty skated onto the stage and fell over. It appeared to be intentional but was still an embarrassing moment. Solitary roses where thrown on stage during "Quiet Please There's A Lady On Stage" – "To me", she said, "it's... about all women who have been legends. There are very few, but enough to make the song have a different kind of poignancy when a woman sings it." Slices of high drama like "Sandra" complemented perfectly the disco medley featuring Elton John's "The Bitch Is Back" and Chaka Khan's "I'm Every Woman". Fred Perry insisted "Drury Lane was a smash, but the whole tour could have been like that."

The critics agreed. Ian Birch wrote in the *NME* that Dusty's strongest points have always been pop melodrama and the voice. "When on form, she embodies all the best qualities of a white soul singer. There's an innate understanding which brings out a song's emotional complexities: husky laughter sits alongside heart-broken regret; self-parody mingles with complete commitment. It was a significant week for Mary O'Brien. Not only did she turn 40, but she finally mounted a UK stage for the first time in six years."

Simon Bell, who had bought his ticket for the show before Dusty booked him for the dates, remembered they rehearsed for two weeks before the performances. The atmosphere was relaxed and funny – "She was very friendly throughout. And when she didn't show up, I'd do the rehearsal... At one point Dusty sings 'it had nothing to do with the wine – wanna bet!' on 'I Close My Eyes And Count To Ten'. We'd stop to talk about things, the gay pubs, and things and I still have the tapes of these wonderful times. The concert was among the most thrilling memories of my life."

Dusty also told him that, given half a chance, she'd throw all the songs out "and pinch a lot of Tina Turner's act." But that wasn't what people expected "... I can't throw away all of the past."

She also believed stage presence was something artists were born with because "You can be the best singer in the world but if you can't connect with your audiences there's something lacking.

I connect because it's all very hit and miss with me. I feel half the audience are thinking 'is she gonna get through this?' which adds a certain tension to it, and some people come to see me because they get off on that. I'm afraid I attract the same kind of people who used to go to see Judy Garland. They went because they get a kind of excitement of wondering 'is this gonna be her last breath' which builds a kind of tension and they actually enjoy it. I'm trying not to get locked into that, and that's partly why I don't like live performances. To me, it's very hard work, and it's very uneven, I go in and out of emotions on stage and I can't sustain it. I actually stop still sometimes. I can't move my feet. Then suddenly I'll go raving off because I suddenly lose my inhibitions. It's a very draining experience because I constantly feel I've got to keep going."

Fans were allowed 10 at a time backstage at the Drury Lane theatre following the show, when Dusty signed everything put in front of her. While other artists relied on aides to sign their autographs, Dusty signed each one, a throwback to the time when she was collecting autographs and was fobbed off with rubber-stamped versions.

"I'm Coming Home Again" was released as a single but, despite it being a show highlight for her audiences, the record buying public ignored it.

In May 1979 Dusty returned to Los Angeles where she later announced her future career would be handled by Kevin Hunter following her split with Barry Krost. And, two months later, she was in a Surrey studio recording "Baby Blue", her first single to be recorded in Britain since 1971. With Simon Bell joining her on support vocals, Paul Howes reported that "because of Phonogram's investment in her and her previous lack of success with material she had chosen, the company had put its corporate foot down and got her to record a disco song chosen for her." It was another passable stab at the dance market which, when released in September, sold reasonably well to reach the top 70, her first charting hit since "How Can I Be Sure?" in 1970. If Dusty had promoted it, chances are she'd have enjoyed a bigger hit but that wasn't to be. All she would say on the subject was: "The single was too fluffy for me (but) it should have done better than it did!"

Sadness hit her in November when her father died alone in Rottingdean, East Sussex. His body was discovered when a neighbour noticed that the milk bottles were piling up outside his door. "And that has haunted me," Dusty told Louette Harding in *You* magazine, in 1995. "I feel badly not because I wasn't there, but because no-one was there. I wonder if he was in pain. Was he incapable of reaching the phone? Did it happen fast? I'll never know." Dusty's mother had died from lung cancer some time previously in a Hove nursing home, and she remembered how appalled she had been when she saw her. "She looked like one of those horror masks, all sunken. Her eyes were glassy from the drugs, but suddenly they focused and she reached up this claw and tweaked my nose. I don't remember her ever doing this to me before." Following this visit, Dusty had to return to America, but she phoned immediately she reached home only to be told her mother had died. "So the tweak was important... I handled it very badly. Partly guilt because I wasn't there. I hadn't been there for some time."

A month later she faced another type of sadness when she felt she was snubbed by Princess Margaret following a performance at London's Royal Albert Hall for one of her charities, the Invalid Childrens Aid Association. Prior to the performance, Dusty told Fred Perry she wanted to say something lighthearted, like John Lennon had done at a previous Royal Command Performance when he quipped to an amused audience, "Will all the people in the cheaper seats clap your hands. All the rest of you, if you'll just rattle your jewellery!" Fred suggested that as her audience would be predominantly gay, she could say, "It's nice to see that all the royalty is not confined to the royal box." It was not a wise move.

With television cameras present, royalty in attendance and TV personality Russell Harty's pompous introductions, Dusty's performance turned into a wild celebration of her rejuvenation.

Her fans weren't content to deliver a standing ovation at the end of a song, but applauded during the songs. The heavily charged emotional excitement of her Drury Lane concert continued here with a considerably tightened act – "Rollerina" was dropped, for example. Shortly into her performance, Dusty dropped her clanger as she pointed to the "queens" in the audience. The Princess was thought to have taken offence and was seen to leave, only to return in time to catch her last two songs. However, according to Fred Perry, when Dusty was raising the smiles, the Princess was distracted and missed the quote: "One of her ladies-in-waiting said that Dusty had said something rude about the Queen. That's what really happened. I was there."

Dusty balanced her act between contemporary, nostalgia and disco funk with remarkable ease. Her charismatic confidence incorporated the glamour and voice with the Californian cool acquired in recent years. Flowers rained down on her, and fans chanting her name rushed the stage. A less seasoned artist might have been taken aback by this, but Dusty basked as she strode the stage, clearly enjoying herself. At one point she laughed, "It's a big hall to cover, dear, but mother will do her best!" Simon Bell, who was one of her backing singers, added "She was on great form. Getting her on the stage was a little more fraught. She had me do the singing for her while she checked the sound out front... I made her howl as I couldn't get through the songs without doing her hand movements."

Dusty was a huge success with her audience, but friends said she ended the evening in tears. After the show there was a reception attended by Princess Margaret, who received an £8,000 cheque for her charity. Since Dusty's hour-long performance was so well received, it was expected that the Princess would chat to her about it. Instead, she shook hands with all those present at the reception and left. "Dusty was terribly disappointed," said one guest. "I thought she might burst into tears there and then." To add insult to injury, Dusty later received a type-written letter from Princess Margaret requesting an apology for bad mouthing the Queen, which Dusty had to sign and return! Simon Bell said "She didn't deserve that."

The audience, too, had been unhappy with the Princess because they thought her thirst was responsible for the half-hour interval following John Miles' opening act, before Dusty's appearance. So when the unfortunate Russell Harty came on stage to introduce the star of the evening and talk about the Princess's charity, he was loudly booed. Known by the nickname Yvonne in the gay fraternity, a news item in the *Daily Mail* in 2007 suggested that Princess Margaret "was rumoured to have had affairs with lovers including Peter Sellers and, more improbably, Dusty Springfield."

Plans had been made by the BBC to screen the Royal Albert Hall concert over the following Christmas period but it never materialized. One source suggested that this was due to the predominantly gay audience which, on one occasion, tried to encourage Dusty to join them in the stalls. Or perhaps the company objected to her style of singing, as one reviewer, Glen Platt, noticed during "Wishin' & Hopin'" when she had sung the line "each night of his charms" and laughed, "His or hers, I don't give a damn!" Whatever anyone thought, it marked the last time she would perform in concert in Britain.

Recorded at The Factory in Surrey, "Your Love Still Brings Me To My Knees" was the first single of the new decade. It was co-writer Roger Cook's ambition to write a song for Dusty and, with Bobby Wood, this was it. Chugging along at an even pace, the single was her swansong for Phonogram Records. An uplifting tune, it was a radio turntable hit only; in fact it topped London's Capital Radio's Hit Line. "Submissive nonsense" was one critic's view, although to her fans it was it was manna from heaven. It was another huge disappointment for an already disillusioned artist – "I'm a lady who has learned not to expect too much from life."

Having suffered one failure too many, she now hired Jack Stein to replace Kevin Hunter, and parted from Polygram to sign with 20th Century Fox Records in America. Ironically, that company was later taken over by Phonogram so she ended up back where she started. An emotionally delivered "It Goes Like It Goes" in July 1980 was her only single released under the deal, and was the theme from the *Norma Rae* movie, performed by Jennifer Warnes in the film and voted the Best New Song in the 1979 Academy Awards. Quite why Dusty recorded it remains to be seen.

Spending less time in the studio meant she could plough her energies into the Wildlife Way Station situated in 160 acres in California's Angeles National Forest. Internationally known for its ongoing charitable efforts to rescue and rehabilitate wild and exotic animals, Dusty explained at the time, "Exotic means anything you should not keep as a household pet, anything from a snake or an otter, a racoon or a large Siberian tiger... The point is most of the animals are abused out of ignorance rather than a sense of cruelty, there are some who have been beaten up by crowbars... tiger cubs are fine except they're going to grow up to be 450lb, so they're de-fanged and de-clawed, so they can never go back into the wild again." Being a passionate animal lover, she was on the board of directors and was able to raise awareness of the barbaric life some of these animals had endured at the hands of the Californian wealthy, which in turn raised funds for the Station.

After being a one-time guest vocalist four years previously for Peter Allen, Dusty now supported him at The Greek Theatre, Los Angeles, during August 1980. "I was very nervous about performing live again but the ice had been broken by performing in England. The Greek thing wasn't as difficult as I thought it would be." From Los Angeles she switched to New York to appear twice nightly for two weeks at the Grand Finale nightclub, her first dates in the city for eight years. She opened on 7 October before an audience that included Billie Jean King, Nona Hendryx and Rock Hudson. And it was pictures of him cuddling Dusty that were splashed across New York newspapers, with headings like "Dusty's rocking back". "Your wonderful city gives me colds and laryngitis," she told her audience part-way through her act. "But I love it!" "This combination of honesty and good public relations has always been typical of Miss Springfield, an English pop singer whose best work is both directly emotional and polished to a high gloss," wrote Robert Palmer in the *New York Times*. "...Aside from her cold ... there are other problems with her show. She hasn't been able to find enough new material that really suits her. She sings flag-wavers ... contemporary pop ballads and none of these show off her tonal variety... as effectively as the pop rock trifles that are crammed into her medley of hits."

A short engagement at Lake Tahoe, followed by selective television appearances took Dusty through to the end of the year. It was March before she re-emerged as a guest on the 1981 Canadian series *Tom Jones Now*, before participating in a Datsun car sales promotion in Melbourne Australia. While there she crammed in some radio and press interviews.

"I never got enough love from my beautiful, blonde, unattainable mother," wrote Carole Pope in her autobiography *Anti Diva*. Dusty met her in 1981 following an introduction from Vicki Wickham, who managed Carole's group Rough Trade. By May, Carole and Dusty lived in the Cabbagetown area of Toronto. The couple visited London and met up for a drink with Simon Bell. Dusty had kept in touch with him via middle-of-the-night phone calls which worried him senseless. "Everything would be fine, though. She was testing me to see if I really would do anything for her. It was a strange time, but I really cared about her. She had this thing that she thought she'd lose the people she cared about. Quite often she did... when she behaved badly. She didn't do that with me. At least, not until she was dying and then she didn't care. I was the only one around, so nothing mattered except her."

Dusty trusted Pat Rhodes with her life but it took years for Dusty to feel the same way about Simon. He knew he'd gained that trust when he saw her for the first time without make-up. Meantime, he cherished the times he spent with her and Carole, explaining "She was a very nice person and Dusty was in good spirits!"

However, it didn't take long for Carole Pope to realize her partner was on the road to destruction. Dusty turned down job offers as she preferred to drink her way through life. It was fun for a time, but Carole Pope admitted the real horror started when she started checking Dusty into hospital. One time with drug abuse, another when Dusty had sliced her arms with a kitchen knife. In time, the bad times outweighed the good, and within six months Dusty and her cats had returned alone to Los Angeles.

In November, she began working on her next album *White Heat* and, a year later, the first single from the sessions was issued. Titled "Donnez Moi (Give It To Me)", it was synthesized pop/funk, ideal for the current music climate, but as 20th Century Fox was purchased by Polygram US, the single and album were released carrying a Casablanca label. Their impact was lost. Dusty later moaned that "There was a point where I began to feel I was just some company's tax loss!" Although she was adamant that *White Heat* should be released in Europe, that wasn't to happen until 2002 when it was released in CD format. Yet when it was originally released, she held back permission for the London promotion company Eyes & Ears to remix the 12 inch version of "Donnez Moi (Give It To Me)." The company knew there was a waiting niche in the disco market for her and guaranteed her a dance-floor, and possible crossover hit, but she still declined.

Fred Perry was involved in the album's recording sessions. He collected and drove her to the studio in North Hollywood, then returned hours later, he wrote, to "pick up the pieces and take her home and repeat it night after night." For being at her side, Fred was credited on the album sleeve, which in itself caused controversy. A drawing of Dusty's bleached face, with two shards of light shining from her pupils, filled the front cover, while she wore a football helmet on the back cover. Rumours were strong in the British music industry that she had fallen off stage into the orchestra pit, leaving her with a disfigured face. Whatever the reason for the helmet, Dusty would actually become a victim of violence in 1983.

The *Daily Mail* reported in August 2006 that she had been hit in the face with a saucepan, knocking out her front teeth. She had subsequently had plastic surgery and dental work to repair the damage. In 1985 she told *Gay Times'* Kris Kirk that she had been beaten up more than once by the same person: "... and the second time I experienced what battered wives often came up against, where they're not only afraid to talk because they'll be beaten up again, but the relationship was so disapproved of anyway that people... say, 'We told you so.'" She also had a scar on her mouth, she said, after being kicked by a cowboy boot.

She first heard the dance floor opener "Donnez Moi (Give It To Me)" in Jean Roussel's Montreal basement. Although it was unfinished at the time, Dusty liked it enough to record it. Roussel was also responsible for "I Don't Think We Could Ever Be Friends" which he co-wrote with Sting. The song boasted a repeated hookline and compulsive beat, and from this Dusty progressed to rock, where her aggressive approach on "Blind Sheep" was surprisingly equal to anything recorded by female rockers of the time. Next came pop music with a lazy feeling, for example "Don't Call It Love", also recorded by Kim "Bette Davis Eyes" Carnes in 1981 and four years later by Dolly Parton. Dusty remembered her roots with "Time And Time Again" as she weaved her way through the emotions of love until the chorus and strings climaxed together. On "I Am Curious" she compared herself to a volcano close to eruption: addicted to lethal sexuality, embodying desire and urgency. Born from the same mould as "Blind Sheep" Dusty once again distorted her phrasing on "Sooner Or Later" as she rocked with Tommy Faragher's synthesizers belting their hard rhythm. "Losing You (Just A Memory)" was Elvis Costello's tribute. Paul Howes wrote that in her performance of the ballad, "The mimic in Dusty comes to the fore with a vocal that's obviously intended as an Elvis Costello soundalike." From the smooth she moved to searing high energy with "Gotta Get Used To You", where Dusty tackled the sexual dilemma of comparing her lovers' abilities to please her. But many believed "Soft Core" – the closing track, written by Carole Pope and Kevin Staples – to be the project's highlight. Memorable because of Dusty's Marlene Dietrich delivery about the reality of a dysfunctional relationship, it was said to be an indictment of her relationship with Carole.

Released in November 1982, the album thrived on tension; stark ballads blundered along ungraciously against rock excess, and there was too much sex and not enough Springfield. Without a doubt, *White Heat*, also co-produced by Dusty, was a personal risk.

She promoted tracks from the album during a low-key Canadian concert, and made plans to tour Australia to support its release there. When that was aborted, she had nowhere else to go, so she stayed at home and concentrated on getting her teeth fixed. While her career was on hold, Dusty took a major step in her personal life, one she obviously hoped would remain secreted away in America. Dressed in a second-hand, full-length white gown, long lace gloves and a veil hanging down the back of a white bowler perched on her head, she married American actress Teda Bracci, whom she had met at an Alcoholics Anonymous meeting in 1982. The ceremony took place on the ranch of Dusty's friend, and fellow AA veteran, Helene Sellery in the San Fernando Valley, and the guests were close friends. The wedding photos were published by the *Daily Mail* in August 2006 under the headline "The day Dusty vowed: I only want to be with you." Also, according to the newspaper, it was a tempestuous relationship and they parted within two years of the ceremony.

Sixteen years previously, in 1968, Stax artists William Bell and Judy Clay released the soul classic "Private Number". It stood the test of time and was a one-off single Dusty recorded with Spencer Davis, now A&R head of Allegiance Records. Spencer Davis had been a regular guest on *Ready, Steady, Go!* and had his own group which boasted Steve Winwood in its line-up. They recorded a host of hit singles from 1964 through to 1968 like "Keep On Running", "Somebody Help Me" and "Gimme Some Loving". Spencer Davis's manager invited Dusty to visit a studio in the San Fernando

Valley where Spencer was recording an album. While there, they recorded "Private Number" together. Dusty said "It's a song I had known for (years) and for some unknown reason they've decided to put it out as a single." When released in Britain during March 1984, very few people actually heard it, but it was a highlight on Spencer Davis's *Crossfire* album.

Dusty may have been struggling for success on vinyl but she triumphed on stage at The Royal Albert Hall with Anne Murray in October. Looking like a member of the *Dallas* cast, Dusty was dressed in green (Anne was in pink) as she sang "You Don't Have To Say You Love Me" and duetted with Anne on "Son-Of-A Preacher Man". As Dusty was late arriving, Anne referred throughout the show to her guest, asking her audience to be patient before graciously adding, "I realize you're here to see her and not me."

Even when she did arrive the act didn't go according to plan because Dusty caught her earring on the sequins of her padded shoulders of her long jacket. Without thinking, she whipped the earring off and threw it over her shoulder. The American film crew decided this was too messy for television and re-shot the performance. For some reason the re-shoot was also omitted from the CBS special. Eight years after Dusty's death, Anne released the album *Anne Murray Duets: Legends & Friends*. Included on that was "I Just Fall In Love Again", a track from the *Living Without Your Love* album. Anne wrote to Dusty's estate to secure permission to use her friend's vocals: "I explained that we did have a friendship, even though maybe five years would go by and I wouldn't talk to her. A woman from the estate emailed back and said 'absolutely'." The duet was magical, Anne added. "However, I couldn't believe how eerie it was singing with Dusty in the studio knowing she was no longer with us. She was my hero."

Following months of speculation thoughout the latter part of 1984, Dusty signed with Hippodrome Records in a deal worth £100,000 for three singles and one album. The label's owner, Peter Stringfellow, was overjoyed.

Chapter Ten

WHAT HAVE I DONE TO DESERVE THIS?

"Sometimes I look like a ten cent hooker, at other times a drag queen."

Following the television coverage of horrendous scenes of starving and dying people in Ethiopa, the Boomtown Rats' lead singer, Bob Geldof, was moved to approach the cream of British rock/pop to record a single about the tragedy and dedicate all the royalties to Ethiopia. The British public flocked to buy "Do They Know It's Christmas?" released under the collective name of Band Aid to become a 1984 Christmas number one and a huge international seller. The British project prompted singer Harry Belafonte to organize a similar recording session in America, whereupon "We Are The World" by USA For Africa was issued to repeat the British single's success. A decision was then taken to mount an international television-linked pop/rock benefit marathon to include both countries, and Live Aid was born. The 12-hour festival in July 1985 included 28 of the world's biggest stars. The British section was staged at Wembley Stadium while the JFK Stadium in Philadelphia showcased the American contingent. The music world was dominated by Bob Geldof's determination to make the world a little better for those who couldn't help themselves.

Around this time, Dusty was due to record in Britain for a London-based company. Her deal with Peter Stringfellow sounded exciting and promising but it was a deal doomed from the first note. However, for the time being, expectations – and adrenalin – were running high. The combination of money and talent was always intriguing. Peter Stringfellow had pursued Dusty for a year to sign to his newly formed record company. He said he found her doing nothing in Los Angeles and was warned she had a fearsome reputation, "But I liked her and I enjoyed her music." Dusty said "He wined and dined me and told me these stories about how wonderful it would be." She longed to be visible again, to join the British music scene, although she wasn't sure if it still wanted her. But this was her chance. To celebrate the deal, Dusty flew from Los Angeles to London to guest on *Saturday Night Out* at The Hippodrome.

Before she could concentrate on the future, however, Dusty had to deal with a blast from the past, in the form of the commercial release on video of volumes 1–3 of *Ready, Steady Go!* This included *The Sounds Of Motown* which incorporated the original show plus a special tribute to the late Marvin Gaye (hence the slight title change) who wasn't on the original broadcast. "I'm embarrassed about how badly I mimed... looking at the shows now makes me very grateful that I'm still around making records when so many of the performers aren't." Confirming that she had watched the videos, she confessed she now had little affection for the *Ready, Steady Go!* programmes, except perhaps the New Year's Eve shows. "I'm glad I was there and glad I did them. It was very good exposure because I did so many of them. I remember the cameramen were essentially news people and would have covered a war really well. I mean, it was very unflattering, they had no idea of how to glamorize anyone – it was always up the nose. People wouldn't show up or be there on time to sing their songs. I remember when Sandie Shaw went missing I had to sing her 'There's Always Something There To Remind Me'. Nobody cared, and that was one of the wonderful atmospheres about the programme."

With that out of the way, she concentrated on her future, which was "Sometimes Like Butterflies", the flipside to the Donna Summer hit "Finger On The Trigger". It was written by Bruce Roberts, who had worked with The Pointer Sisters and Sam Harris.

The original intention was for Dusty to record with Jolley and Swain, who had penned a song with her in mind, but when she arrived in London they were in the studio with Bananarama and, as Dusty's schedule was tight, she couldn't wait for them to be free. Peter chose "Sometimes Like Butterflies" instead. "It was his personal crusade, there was no listening to anything else." Recorded in London in May 1985, with Simon Bell and Stevie Vann joining Dusty on backing vocals, "Sometimes Like Butterflies" was recorded "one hundred times", utilizing several producers, before Peter Stringfellow decided to release the first take, which he also remixed without telling Dusty. "I could strangle the fucker!" she said when she heard the news. Fans were alarmed to hear her voice crack and groan through an inferior song which she said Peter had released because he liked the rawness in her voice. However, a label spokesperson said the real reason that particular take was issued "was because subsequent versions were worse."

As if to make matters worse, selecting a Donna Summer song was unwise because Dusty had a huge gay following and, in a misguided move, Summer had publicly stated that homosexuals brought AIDS upon themselves. Her records were subsequently burned in huge bonfires across America and her future selling power was considerably weakened.

Advertised as her second comeback, Dusty dumped her natural look of 1978 in favour of silk and sequins and candy flossed hair. Her make-up was still heavily applied, although her black eye colour of the sixties was toned down to purple and mauve, and it was clear she'd had plastic surgery which had altered quite severely the shape of her nose, lips, mouth and chin. Her high cheekbones remained the same, defining the outline of her eyebrows above her green eyes and high forehead. The roundness of her face may have gone, but the mischief in her eyes lived on. "Sometimes I look like a ten cent hooker," she said, "at other times a drag queen!"

On 31 July 1985, Dusty – or Madame Butterfly as she was nicknamed – hosted a champagne lunch and photo shoot at The

Hippodrome, or rather she nearly did. After hearing her music and watching videos of her performances, Peter Stringfellow assured fidgeting journalists that his newest star would indeed join them. Radio DJ John Peel attended on behalf of the *Observer* and said, "... veterans of record company receptions smiled knowingly. Dusty wasn't going to show up... But a screen (rose) out of the stage and a dry ice machine (produced) billows of smoke. Behind this and flapping her arms in mock alarm was our Dusty. Clad in silver ... and clearly in high spirits, she mimed to her new single and forgot the lyrics!" Peel also reported her silver suit made her look like "a minicab driver in Bacofoil". Dusty later replied "I don't know how I got my reputation for not showing up. I always show up. And I'm going to wrap his car in Bacofoil for him!" She fended off the usual barrage of questions about her sexuality, to concentrate on promoting her record deal, insisting "I feel now I want to be with a small label that can give me individual attention. I think Peter and I make an explosive combination." She also confirmed her return to British music wasn't financially motivated either. "I did very well in the sixties. I was always rather extravagant but I've never been less than comfortable. And I'm still receiving royalty cheques for songs I sang 20 years ago. I'll never go short."

Two weeks after the reception "Sometimes Like Butterflies" was issued, but it was fated from the start. Reviews were far from flattering, and despite a number of television appearances by Dusty, it only scraped into the Top 90. The competition was tough. Girl power was alive and kicking with the top three best-selling singles of the year from Jennifer Rush ("The Power Of Love"), Elaine Paige and Barbara Dixon ("I Know Him So Well") and Madonna ("In The Groove"), while Sister Sledge, Phyllis Nelson, Chrissie Hynde and Whitney Houston figured in the Top 20. Leading the male contingent was Paul Hardcastle and "19", followed by David Bowie and Mick Jagger's version of "Dancing In The Street", recorded for the Live Aid gala; Feargal Sharkey ("A Good Heart") and Philip Bailey and Phil Collins ("Easy Lover"), among others.

The short life of "Sometimes Like Butterflies" was, Peter Stringfellow explained, due to Dusty's refusal to be interviewed – "... and she even refused to sing it in public, claiming it was too difficult. How can you possibly get a hit ... when the artist won't perform it." Apparently, Dusty's dislike of being in nightclubs led to her turning down a chance to appear at The Hippodrome's heaving gay night, yet ten months earlier she had visited The Entertainer gay pub, where members of her fan club were holding a convention. Peter Stringfellow further told the *Sun*, "I did scream and shout at her, but then again I'm not the sort of person who's going to take all that sort of nonsense from anybody... I did what would make her happy and I couldn't get any enthusiasm out of her whatsoever."

While in the studio recording "Sometimes Like Butterflies", Dusty also worked on a second song with David Martin and one with Biddu titled "My Love Is A Disaster", later called "My Love Life Is A Disaster". Hot on the hi–nrg (high energy) feel, this fast-moving dance track held an incredibly hypnotic hookline that elevated the song into the compulsive listening category. Dusty said "It was such a great title, but it just didn't work out. It was never finished because halfway through it I realized it was just the wrong thing to do. There was a real gem of an idea and I was just unhappy with the whole situation... my heart wasn't in any of it. I just wasn't committed to the whole idea of being Peter Stringfellow's disco queen, it didn't strike me as being valid." Another credible version of the song was recorded, and not officially released, by ex-Surpreme Mary Wilson, with British singer Dotty Green on backing vocals. When Dusty later heard this vital interpretation, it inspired her to think again: "I think it could be made into something but at the time it struck me as being too dancey." It never happened because Dusty became locked into the Pet Shop Boys project with EMI Records where the material was chosen for her. Interestingly, during the time Dusty was signed to Hippodrome, Peter Stringfellow asked her to perform with the Pet Shop Boys but she refused, saying "They weren't the sort of group I wanted to be associated with." Imagine Stringfellow's anger when, two years later, she enjoyed real success at their hands.

Dusty's most significant interview at this time was with Jean Rook for the *Daily Express* in August, in which the much-read and respected Fleet Street journalist surprised the unsuspecting singer.

Dusty: "You're going to ask me if I'm gay. I'm not going to tell you."

Rook: "Then tell me you're not."

Dusty: "God, you've got me into a corner haven't you, coming straight out with it like that... Let's just say I've experimented with most things in life..."

Jean Rook closed her interview with the words, "I'd known her five minutes and I like Dusty Springfield. I could love Dusty Springfield."

By October 1985 a saddened Peter Stringfellow announced Dusty had fled her rented Mayfair apartment for New York. "This experience has cost me a fortune. Legends don't come cheap!" He added that it had taken six months of difficult negotiations, four months recording and two months promotion, and all he had got at the end of it was one poor-selling single! Dusty said "Peter knew fuck all about the record industry... and my relationship with him was one of the incidents that made me so fed up with the business, I nearly gave it up for good..." Despite her attitude, she was still signed to Hippodrome. David Martin told the media that she had gone to New York to discuss the possibility of working with new producers. A new single and album were expected to be delivered in January 1986. It was a pipedream. In the three years Dusty was signed to his label, Stringfellow spent £1 million. "I did single-handedly ruin his wonderful label," Dusty admitted.

The new year started on a bittersweet note when Dusty performed the *White Heat* track "Soft Core" live at several concerts in Rough Trade's farewell tour. Dusty fan, James Russell, wrote in *The Dusty Springfield Bulletin* that he saw her in Toronto on 29

January 1986. "The club was a cavernous renovated warehouse on the Lake Ontario waterfront... a sort of rave atmosphere. Despite the venue and despite having never been a fan of Rough Trade, I had to be there. I remember the chest-pounding noise of Rough Trade and the raucous swell of the audience. Then... halfway through the concert everything calmed and became dark, except for stage right where one pale spotlight shone on Dusty, perched on a stool. She began to sing 'Soft Core' and I watched transfixed...There was never really absolute silence from the crowd during her performance and when she finished singing, I remember a... polite but somewhat reserved applause... I felt sorry for her... a bittersweet pill."

Whatever else the next two years threw at Dusty, they marked a turning point in her career thanks to two duets, one of which gave her another chance to crack the British music scene. The first duet was recorded at London's Advision Studios during February 1987 and released the following August. Titled "What Have I Done To Deserve This?" it was written in 1986 by Neil Tennant and Chris Lowe, the Pet Shop Boys, with the American composer, Alee Willis, who had numerous hits to her credit including Earth Wind & Fire's "Boogie Wonderland". When the song was completed, Tennant flew to New York to conduct his final interview for *Smash Hits* magazine. He played the song non-stop on the flight, but needed someone to sing it with. "Nikke Slight, who worked in our management office, said 'you're always going on about how much you like Dusty Springfield – why don't you ask her?'" Neil Tennant told *Literally*, the Pet Shop Boys' fanzine, "And we thought 'what a great idea' and we stormed out of the office. Orders were issued. And then it didn't happen. It was going to be on (our) first album. Ages later, we got a call saying that Dusty would do it." Vicki Wickham had contacted Dusty while she was staying with Helen Sellery and told her the Pet Shop Boys wanted her to record with them. Dusty was unsure; she didn't know who they were, and it was unclear just what her involvement would be. Vicki, then Dusty's manager, gave her a tape of "What Have I Done To Deserve This?" to listen to and that was enough to convince her. Vicki told *Music Week*'s Robin Katz in 1990 that she was tired of Dusty's constant complaining about her career and management, "Plus, I wanted to kick her in the behind because she sat vegetating in Los Angeles for so long. I'm a vocal freak... and singers like her shouldn't get lost."

Wearing a black leather designer jacket and high-heeled boots, matching her black eye make-up, Dusty arrived at the Advision Studios where Neil Tennant and Chris Lowe were working. Carrying the song's lyric sheet, annotated and underscored, they put down some guidelines. Neil said "When she sang her solo part, 'since you went away...' everyone in the control room smiled. She sounded just like she used to, breathy, warm, thrilling. Like Dusty Springfield."

"Is that the sort of thing you want?" she asked a stunned Pet Shop Boy. Neil then got the idea to include the "we don't have to fall apart..." line at the song's close. "Dusty was a little alarmed. She thought she'd finished, but she did it marvellously."

The single was a departure for the Pet Shop Boys. Neil Tennant, added "I can't believe we made it, to be honest. It's not like the records we've made before. It's very grown up." Dusty said, "It's a bit more me than them...They write songs that don't take a lot of interpretation... I had to unlearn my vocal mannerisms to get it right, because that's how Neil sings. He's very flat and you almost have to talk it." The fusing of the two talents had been an uphill struggle for Neil Tennant; he'd been told she was difficult to work with, her voice was shot and an EMI Records' executive insisted that no-one was interested in her any more. Tennant stood his ground and the executive, and others, ate their words when the single passed silver status to shoot to Number two in the British chart in August 1987, and Number one in the American Cashbox chart. Dusty had last enjoyed an American hit with "Silly Silly Fool" in 1970. It was the Pet Shop Boys' sixth British hit single and

Dusty's first top five entrant since "I Close My Eyes And Count To Ten" in 1968.

Advertised as "camp meets camp", the single's bag showed the insignificant Pet Shop Boys astride a motorbike in one corner, totally overshadowed by a Dusty pose from the sixties. That's unashamed fan worship in anyone's eyes. *Record Mirror*'s reviewer noted "...the first moments of this collaboration are disappointing, with Neil Tennant's deadpan vocals tugging things downwards, but when Dusty takes over, the tune quickly livens."

Dusty did nothing to promote her new hit single, except appear on the promotional video. Not only had the Pet Shop Boys returned Dusty to the charts but they had also introduced her to the wacky world of music videos. Shot in Brixton's Academy Theatre, she found it a nervous experience, but thankfully Pat Rhodes' calming influence got her through the ordeal. At one point, though, Dusty holed herself up in the dressing room while lanky dancing girls and bored extras stood around. It was said Dusty couldn't decide what to wear, or had misplaced her make-up. When she did appear, a spikey grey/blonde in rippling purple sequins, the look was perfect. But when Neil Tennant asked her to promote its American release, she cried off saying she was needed elsewhere. However, she made a surprise appearance with Neil and Chris at the BPI Awards ceremony staged at The Royal Albert Hall on 8 February 1988. But the whole significance of her returning triumphantly to the music business was tarnished with newspaper headlines, "Star Neil Dwarfed By A Giant Of Pop". True, Dusty was carrying a little weight at 12 stone, and it was general knowledge she'd had a life-long battle against the flab, but never in her wildest dreams had she believed she would attract such adverse publicity. Whatever anyone thought about the musical merging, the single introduced Dusty to a new generation of record buyers. Following this performance, she booked herself into the Henlow Health Resort in Bedfordshire.

The second duet was due for British release in September 1987.

She went into the A&M Studios in Los Angeles a year earlier to record "Something In Your Eyes", a track due for Richard Carpenter's *Time* album, his first since the tragic death of his sister, Karen. The high-octane ballad, in typical Carpenters' style, was smooth and melodic, so suitable for Dusty's soft vocals. But she fell foul of her demons of insecurity, believing she was unworthy of stepping into the huge void left by Karen Carpenter. As it was, she suffered from bronchitis when she recorded the song, and was unhappy with her vocals and, of course, wanted to change them. Richard took no notice and released "Something In Your Eyes" as the album's first single. "Karen and I always enjoyed (Dusty's) music, and I was looking for a vocalist who had her own unique sound." To this end, he had sent Dusty a demo tape and received word that she liked it sufficiently to work with him. "She has a great sense of humour, and is an absolutely terrific singer. I remain very pleased with the finished product." The song was a perfect showcase for Dusty, yet it faltered at Number 84 in the British chart. A&M Records had hoped she would help promote it, particularly on chat shows, but she wouldn't. Instead, she agreed to appear in a promotional video where she abandoned her harsh hairstyle of late for a soft, waspish shoulder-length style, similar to her early seventies' look. Dressed in a black smock, she appeared relaxed, and interacted comfortably with Richard Carpenter. It was a shame the video received so little television exposure. It was an enjoyable experience, Dusty admitted, before pointing out that her name wasn't on the record label – "Really dumb. It's obvious. I'm on the video, unless it's Richard in drag..."

Dusty's debut solo single "I Only Want To Be With You" was responsible for her spearheading a television advertisement during December 1987 for the sparkling orange drink Britvic 55. Shot in grainy black and white, the advertisement was a pastiche on Carnaby Street during the sixties. It showed Dusty getting into an open-top sports car and driving off. She switched on the radio to hear "I Only Want To Be With You". In rapid succession viewers saw Sandie Shaw, resplendent in a white mini-skirt, while The Tremeloes cavorted around a phone box. The Animals' Eric Burdon was walking a ferocious-looking bulldog, while a chap wearing dark shades and sitting at a table in a café was easily identified as Scott Walker. Other cast members included Georgie Fame and Dave Dee. The storyline ended with Dusty alighting from the car surrounded by admiring fans, and walking into Phonogram's head office. As she reached the top of the stairs, she turned, smiled and held a can of Britvic. Although viewers didn't see Dusty full-on there were a number of clues, including "I Only Want To Be With You" of course. Prior to the advertisement being shown, the *Sun* newspaper reported that it would feature black-and-white footage of Dusty in her sixties' blonde beehive, driving along in a car, while singing "I Only Want To Be With You". A gust of wind would then blow off the wig to reveal the present-day Dusty in colour, holding a can of the drink. Britvic denied this was ever considered. A spokesman added, "As there is a sixties' revival... the theme of the advertisement was unmistakenly real. The idea was to use real stars from the 1960s in real settings, drinking real fruit juice."

To coincide with the single's exposure, it was re-issued and Dusty agreed to promote it if it starting selling. At the end of the first week, it broke into the Top 100 and showed all the signs of becoming a Top 20 entrant. However, that didn't happen because the single was virtually unobtainable around the country. Even in central London, stores like the Virgin Megastore carried fewer than ten copies and it took over a week for the shops to restock. Fans blamed the record company.

With the recent exposure with the Pet Shop Boys and the Britvic advertisement, Dusty had been introduced to a whole new generation of record buyers who boosted the legions of her loyal fan base. Her record company, Phonogram, was quick to recognize this expanded market and planned to release a compilation of her greatest work, not only to acknowledge her return but to celebrate her twenty-fifth anniversary in the music business.

Chapter Eleven

NOTHING HAS BEEN PROVED

"And I am a survivor."

In a flurry of publicity *The Silver Collection* was released on 18 January 1988, and was welcomed by record buyers. Her record company took no chances, throwing money into pre-publicity, marketing campaigns including record store window displays and television advertising. Everyone was talking about the 22-track album with the fake Andy Warhol cover design. Each track was a gem, from the opening "I Only Want To Be With You" through the big sellers like "I Just Don't Know What To Do With Myself", "Losing You", "Son-Of-A Preacher Man" which nestled cosily with "The Look Of Love", "My Colouring Book" and "Twenty Four Hours From Tulsa", to the closing track "Goin' Back".

The *Collection* jumped straight into the chart at Number 31, going silver within three weeks of release, and gold after that. At its peak it was outselling albums by George Michael, Rick Astley and the Pet Shop Boys themselves. The reviews were ecstatic. *Music Week* said "Britain still has no homegrown singer even approaching her stature and owning the LP in at least one format should be obligatory for anyone connected with the music industry." *Melody Maker*'s Paul Mathur wrote, "If Dusty Springfield didn't exist, it would naturally be necessary to invent her... This album is a better document than most of what British pop can do so well, of how to maintain a dignity and a force in the face of feckless celebrity. We should treasure it with our lives..." And Roger Holland in *Sounds* added, "When Dusty Springfield gives herself to a song, the earth moves and dolphins dance. Because she has a voice which is beyond good or evil... She's an icon, a living metaphor..."

And the singer herself? "I'm amazed at the success. It's also iron-ic. It proves what can happen when a record company takes an in-terest in something. At one point I was tempted to fit in with what the company wanted – which was to come over (from Holland) and plug it for them. But… thinking about it… I thought that may sell a few extra copies but basically it has a life of its own… I think enough is enough now on the old stuff. It went gold and I couldn't have wished for anything better."

To capitalize on her emerging new career, Dusty sold her house in Los Angeles and moved to Herengracht 125 in Amsterdam, Holland. She had friends there but, more importantly, Holland had no quarantine laws. If she moved to Britain from America, her cats would be quarantined for six months. "I'm obviously going to be working a lot more in Europe… and of course I can't bring my cats into England. I totally agree with the quarantine laws but I don't want to put my cats through it, and I wouldn't dream of trying to smuggle them in, that would be foolish."

Among the possessions she left in America was her record col-lection. "It's still in somebody's garage," she sighed. "I got rid of a lot of it but I'll get it eventually when I've paid the tax to get it through Customs. All my paintings are there too, with other bits and pieces that are precious but I miss my music most of all. It was crippling before I left California. I had to make a lot of deci-sions and it took me weeks to go through my record collection. I started to go mad because as I pulled a record out I'd look at titles… 'Where the hell did I get this? Why did I keep it, there has to be a reason?' Then I had to play it because there was a song on it I must have wanted to keep, knowing in my mind it would be a good one to record sometime.

"It took months to get out of that house because of the amount of decisions over that bloody record collection. It's like a huge thing… in the end there's this gibbering idiot in the corner going 'I can't make one more decision.' Everything else got thrown in trucks, but when it came to the collection… oh my God!"

Dusty was quick to appreciate she had been given a second chance by the Pet Shop Boys and, although she feared new studio technology and had a growing reluctance to perform, grabbed the opportunity to re-establish herself in Britain. This time, thankfully, her return wasn't considered a "comeback" she said, "because it implies you want back everything you once had, but I don't. I want something different. I'm a different person from that blonde with a beehive..."

Pat Rhodes visited her friend in Amsterdam, deciding it was a good place to visit but not to live. "It's difficult to shop there. You can't find our lovely big supermarkets or stores. You have to try all the little shops and they have strange things in shops... it's really weird trying to find out where to buy things and then when you do, they only have one brand and that's that." Travel agent and friend, Leon Shaier, was another visitor. He first met Dusty when she was filming her third television series at the Golders Green Hippodrome in 1969. Dusty stayed in touch, and they would meet occasionally for afternoon tea. On one occasion she invited him to join her, Tom and Helene Sellery. "She always squeezed my shoulder and said 'lovely to see you.' There was something magical about her." When she was playing around with the idea of moving to Amsterdam, Pat Rhodes gave her Leon's phone number to arrange flights and so on. Dusty phoned him at 11.10 pm, he said, "and I nearly fell on the floor in shock." Once in Amsterdam, she then spent weeks persuading him to visit her. Eventually, he gave in, on the condition he stayed in a hotel near to her home, but the second time she gave him her bedroom which overlooked the Herengracht canal. "She had an upstairs one-bedroom apartment, and it was lovely but not how she'd have had it. The house was owned by a couple of guys," he remembered. "Dusty collected me from the airport, took us shopping, saying she wouldn't be cooking, thank you. 'Stick some things that you like in the basket,' she said. She always wanted to pay for everything. She may have had her faults but she was very generous." They talked away five days and Leon returned to London. His memories included her regularly falling out with her brother, Tom, and Madeline Bell, "... and Dusty could take exception to something that meant nothing. You could say something to her in all innocence and she would get annoyed. I never experienced it personally." He also loved her humour. "She was really funny, she had a very dark humour, and wasn't the sad person people thought she was."

When Dusty visited London, Leon would often collect her from Heathrow. One trip in particular stuck in his mind because it reflected her humour. "I had an old Mini Clubman and as we were travelling another car full of passengers recognized her. They were all waving furiously and Dusty waved back. I remember feeling mortified that she was seen in my old car. She thought it very funny and laughed abut it. She really wasn't bothered at all!"

While glowing in her silver success, Dusty agreed to participate in a *Home Box Office* special starring Waylon Jennings. America's most successful movie cable channel had recently diversified into producing its own programmes and this was to be the first of three to feature Dusty. In the end, all three were shelved with no reason being given. However, she did record a duet with B J Thomas, despite never meeting him. The track, "As Long As We Got Each Other", was originally sung by B J Thomas and Jennifer Warnes in the American sitcom *Growing Pains*. Steve Dorff, who penned the song with John Bettis, felt the song had too much of a country and western sound to it with Jennifer and BJ, and when it was decided to release the song as a single he wanted Dusty to sing it, having worked with her before. "If you think Dusty's a perfectionist, you haven't met BJ," said Steve Dorff. "The two of them in the studio together would have done me in!" Instead, Thomas laid down his vocals first, while Dusty sang along to the tape in a small studio in the San Fernando Valley. The studio was near Steve Dorff's home and they spent several hours while she "put those little nuances and sounds that only Dusty can give to a recording." To her surprise, the track was released as a single in November 1988 but, she pointed out, "I did it as a personal favour for a friend... I wouldn't get too hot around the collar about it because a lot of times they put these things out and they don't push them for reasons of their own. It's nothing to do with me, but I wish it good luck." She blocked its British release fearing it would interfere with her EMI work.

Also in November, Dusty flew from Amsterdam at her own expense, while nursing a virulent strain of flu, to attend her fan club Silver Convention held at The Central Park Hotel, London. It started at 7.30 pm with a DJ playing her music as nearly 300 fans mingled and networked. Then he broke into his programme to announce Dusty was on the premises and would perform. The audience's disbelief was shown by the silence that descended, but when the star walked on stage her welcome was deafening. After a short, good-natured rapport with her fans, Dusty introduced Simon Bell to launch into George Michael and Aretha Franklin's hit duet "I Knew You Were Waiting For Me". That led to a handful of her hits as she walked the stage delivering her best. When songs were requested, she obliged until the performance closed to a standing ovation and she was presented with a large bouquet. She then agreed to autograph photos and memorabilia, in return for donations towards a seal sanctuary run by Brenda and Allan Giles of Kings Lynn. ("Food and medicine costs so much for those little flippers.") Dusty left the convention at 1.00 am, after being reminded she had an early return flight to Amsterdam, and should have returned to her hotel room. Instead, she asked Leon Shaier if she could stay with him in his Hanger Lane apartment. "She was really low that night, saying nobody wanted her. She hadn't got a recording contract, and was at a low ebb."

Dusty retreated from the public spotlight once again, to settle into her new lifestyle. She admitted that, although Amsterdam was closer to Britain, it wasn't the most ideal place for her because "it closes early and is very conservative... It's basically a place to retreat to from activity, but for me not a great place to be when I'm on hold. It's even a quiet place when there are a lot of people around... The cats like it but I wish it would stop raining." She was bored, although she did put the time to good use by meeting her accountants and embarking on what she called "daily maintenance" like getting her teeth polished. Her fans told her she was lazy and was disinterested in progressing her career. Peter Collins, for one, wrote her an open letter published in *The Dusty Springfield Bulletin*: "If you want to do nothing then that's up to you, but it does not take anywhere the length of time that you keep saying it does to get your act together. You have had ample time to negotiate a recording contract, and ample time to record an album... If it's to be another year or two then you will miss what has become the greatest opportunity you will ever get to achieve large scale popularity." John McElroy, founder of the magazine, also wrote, "It appears that Dusty is not really interested in a successful long-term comeback, but simply does occasional 'one-offs' that provide enough money to live on in return for relatively little work. If that's the case then of course that is her decision, but why can't she be a little more honest with her fans?"

Writing in the *Dusty Springfield International* fanzine, an extremely annoyed singer responded, "I am aware of and have read letters... that very much seem to reflect the opinion that I find very negative... What I read – and this is only from a few people, most people are understanding – is that the few people base their opinions on ignorance of the reality of the situation. I know that when you're not in this business it is very hard to understand why everything takes so long... If they don't have information about me they must think I'm not doing anything. Well, I am... A true indication of my commitment to this coming year is the fact that I moved lock, stock and barrel. It's all part of a great plot and some of it is slow... I'm doing everything in my power to move my career along. There is piss all I can do about it... but driving myself crazy in the process is going to be no use to anyone. There would be this hollow shell of a woman who shows up in the recording studio... It's crashingly boring for me. Even my cats are bored. I tell you the three of us are looking at each other like you wouldn't believe... I get to throw a lot of balls around – if you'll pardon the expression." In fact, Dusty did turn down many work opportunities, so perhaps her fans' claims were vindicated.

It took a year before a deal was struck with EMI Records to release product via its Parlophone label. It also enabled her to begin "officially" working on a new album, her first British release for over ten years, and her first since 1982's *White Heat*. "The reality of it is," she explained with honesty, "I'm considered a risk in this business. If a record company is going to put up £150,000 to do an album, they want to be really very sure. Accountants and lawyers run record companies. The music people are always full of immense praise for me and are very supportive but when it comes down to the accountancy level the element of risk comes in." The details of the contract were never publicized but it did cover one album and, in line with other companies' recording contracts, an option to renew once the fate of the album was known. It was initially thought she would work with producer Stuart Levine, best known at this time for his work with Simply Red, and megastar Phil Collins whom Dusty idolized, describing him as "intensely musical". She further said, "If it happens we have to wait for him to finish his own album... it's now down to paper work but he definitely said he would like to do something with me." Nothing came of the negotiations.

Meantime, she worked with the Pet Shop Boys on a song Neil Tennant had written several years previously and which he now believed to be the perfect vehicle for her. The song, "Nothing Has Been Proved", told the tale of the Profumo affair which had rocked Harold Macmillan's government in 1963 when a young showgirl romped about with a cabinet minister. The affair had threatened the country's security, and the names Jack Profumo, Stephen Ward, Mandy Rice-Davis and Christine Keeler (and her infamous pose of sitting naked astride a chair) had become the topic of household gossip. Twenty-six years later, film producer Steve

Wooley approached the Pet Shop Boys to write the theme for the *Scandal* movie based on the affair. The British film starred Joanne Whalley as Christine Keeler and John Hurt as Stephen Ward, with co-stars of Ian McKellen, Britt Ekland, Bridget Fonda and Leslie Phillips. Neil Tennant was intrigued by the suggestion because years before he had met Chris Lowe he had actually written a song about the Profumo affair, but the music wasn't to his liking. He subsequently re-wrote most of the song, and put his idea of Dusty recording it to Steve Wooley, who agreed instantly because "she had been around at the time." Dusty said "I remember seeing it in all the papers but I wasn't really aware of what it was all about. I understood that people got very excited about it all, but that was a period of my life when I was extremely innocent." She recorded her vocals very slowly, often syllable by syllable, although the end result flowed together seamlessly. The first line of "Nothing Has Been Proved" was "Mandy's in the papers". Neil Tennant wrote in *Literally*, "She got the track started and her cigarette and her cup of coffee, and she gets to 'Ma–' and stops. Wind the tape back and start again. I just looked at all these words – two sheets of them, and we had to double-track them – and I thought I'd go insane. But we got through it." When Dusty reached the end chorus, she grabbed it by the scruff of its neck – "It may be false, it may be true" – and stamped her mark on it. Dusty explained "...they waited patiently, and they don't say very much and it's sort of like 'let's let Dusty flail around until she gets it right'." The original demo she worked from was more "out there" she said, "...and I was a bit pissed that when it came to my recording it, they wanted it smoother."

"Triumphantly brilliant" and "Atmospheric, orchestrated kitsch with Dusty's breathy tones going from a whisper to a scream..." greeted the release of "Nothing Has Been Proved" in February 1989. "I know the Pet Shop Boys wanted it out as a single. I think it's wonderful for the film although I'm very scared about it as single because it's a quiet record..." Despite this, it roared up the singles chart to Number 16 within two weeks of its release, firmly re-establishing her in the British music scene that included high-flying, mega-sellers like Michael Jackson, Madonna, Kylie Minogue and, of course, Kylie's one-time singing partner, Jason Donovan. Sales of "Nothing Has Been Proved" were helped by Dusty's non-stop promotion that included an appearance on the British Academy Awards ceremony, and later *Top Of The Pops*, which she found a strange experience because "it was such a long time since I'd been on that show." Pat Rhodes said, "Having been around with her, she hasn't stopped for the two weeks she's been here. For instance, the Monday after the awards ceremony in Manchester, she had to be up at the crack of dawn, rush off to Liverpool to appear live on *This Morning*, and then dash back to Manchester to put down the tracks of *Top Of The Pops* and then back to London. From there we dashed off to the Greenwood Theatre in south-east London for her to appear on *Juke Box Jury*. Some days she's done between four and six interviews interspersed with radio and television shows. I have no idea how she managed to cope with it all, but she has." Dusty added, "I find living normally a problem now!"

She also starred in a classy promotional video where, against a nightclub backdrop, she sang the song while the Pet Shop Boys, dressed as reporters, were interviewing "Christine Keeler". These shots were interspliced with black-and-white newsreel footage from 1963 with colour clips from the movie. Dusty, wearing black gloves, was featured in monochrome although her jacket was vivid purple, highlighted by light blue spotlights... She injected life into the lyrics in her own inimitable style – a flick of the wrist, or a pointed forefinger and, for the more observant, she was superimposed over a short sequence from the film starring Jean Alexander, better known as *Coronation Street's* Hilda Ogden. The video was the perfect companion for the single.

"I must say the single did more than I expected it to. I didn't give it a light basically, but I'm delighted. It's funny because I wake up every day and it's blasting across the rooftops of Amsterdam. Last week I was on a boat with some friends going past the red light district and the biggest, brightest, pinkest, most purple of houses of ill repute was blasting it out across the canals. I just heard 'Mandy's in the bedroom' and I burst out laughing. We all cheered and the ladies in the windows wondered what we were cheering at!"

In June, she promoted the single and the *Scandal* soundtrack in New York. While there, fan Tony Leong heard her interview on a live local chat show. "I knew I wanted to meet her, so I did the unbelievable," he recalled. "I rang a couple of hotels near the studio and asked for Mary O'Brien. On the second try at the Parker Meridian, I got her and explained I was a fan and wanted her autograph. She was in the middle of interviews at the time, but said she was coming out at 4 pm and she could meet me in the lobby.

"As I spotted her, she lit up (Dusty had been smoking for four years now) and we sat to chat. She mentioned she had had trouble with the booking because she only had 200 US dollars, but Vicki had made a deal with the night manager. Among the things we discussed were Motown, girl groups, current New Wave, and her hopes for her new songs... Dusty was more animated when she discussed other people's songs. Walking down 57th Street, Dusty and I stopped in a shop so she could try on boxing boots, but they didn't have her size. She was so energetic and electric, what a character. At 5th Avenue we hailed a cab because she had to get to the Village to get cat medicine on 13th Street... What I remember vividly was that as we got to the place she had to go, she put on her glasses to see the name on the intercom. She put her face real close to read the thing. She then thanked me for the cab ride. I gave her an index card with my name and address on it and a request for an autographed photo. Dusty's last words before she entered the building were 'perhaps we'll cross paths again'. Sometime later, two autographed photos came in the mail."

Her next single "In Private" was also written for *Scandal* but this time the Pet Shop Boys started from scratch. Chris Lowe wrote the melody and as soon as he played a particular section of the song, they knew Dusty had to sing it. It was under-produced and cut in four days, but Neil Tennant was annoyed when she changed the emphasis on a lyric by adding the word "and". "I said to her 'why are you singing 'and'? She just blatantly ignored me, because she wanted that pick-up note before she went into the chorus, so it's still there." Once again the public loved it, and following its release in November 1989, it shot to Number 14, two rungs higher than "Nothing Has Been Proved". Once more, Dusty starred in a promotional video and the single reviews were mixed but this was typical: "The revitalized Dusty works her way through another Tennant/Lowe composition with the duo's characteristically mournful keyboards giving the song a somewhat tragic feel. It works perfectly for Dusty, probably because their songwriting has always harked back to her heyday in any case... 'In Private' is a comparatively slight (that's compared to the genius of 'What Have I Done To Deserve This') but wholly satisfying orchestrated sigh, Springfield's voice is knowing and effortless as ever." It was never issued in America, despite being heavily supported on the nightclub scene.

During August 1989, Dusty left Amsterdam because of her increasing work commitments and had no choice but to put her two cats, Nicholas Alexi, named after the last Russian Tsar's son ("because he's constantly ill!") and Malaysia ("I don't know why I called her that because she looks like a Friesian cow") into quarantine. It was left to Pat Rhodes regularly to drive her to see them at the quarantine kennels in Chingford and, when Dusty was working, Pat went alone because she couldn't bear them to think they'd been abandoned. "I wasn't able to plan a holiday in 1989 because I spent the summer visiting. They hardly missed one day's visit for the whole six months they were there. I felt so sorry for many of the animals who didn't get a visitor at all, as many people send their animals on in advance of returning to this country themselves."

Dusty moved in with Pat and her husband, Tony, in their London home. She slept in the little front bedroom that once belonged to their son. "She said all she needed was a bed and a television. She often came down in the middle of the night and would leave notes for me in the morning like 'iou chocolate digestives'." As Dusty loved Indian food, she would often eat in local restaurants with Leon Shaier, much to the diners' surprise. "She just wanted to be like everyone else," he said. "To do things other people did. Y'know, if there were any problems on the underground, she would phone me to see if I was OK. She got upset when she lost touch." And when she rented an apartment near to Pat, she was often spotted by disbelieving shoppers in the local Asda in Southgate, or when she popped into the local fish and chip shop. Some people asked for autographs, others walked by because they weren't sure if it was her or not.

From Asda to The Springfields housing estate, Saltash, Plymouth. Dusty said, "I travelled to Cornwall in October to open a housing estate, partly because it had been named after me and partly because I'd seen the British Rail ad on TV – where they take off their shoes and relax – and I thought it would be a great journey. But there wasn't even a buffet car on the train!" It was a fun-packed day, nevertheless, with jazz bands, aerobatic and parachute displays (John Fisher dropped from a light aircraft at 5,000 ft above Saltash, carrying a bouquet for Dusty), children's entertainment, and a presentation of a £500 cheque to The Saltash Youth Centre. Dusty, who arrived by herself, was introduced and then she signed autographs. The public flocked to share the occasion with her. A trio of fans led by Patrick Kent met her in one of the show houses, where she chatted and autographed items. When photos were taken, Dusty put her arm around Patrick's waist and he realized she was trembling. "She is a very nervous lady," he said, "and it confirmed that Dusty is like an exposed nerve..."

From October 1989 Dusty was back in the studios recording three tracks ("Daydreaming", "I Want To Stay Here" and "Occupy Your Mind") with the Pet Shop Boys for her new album. They didn't produce the whole project as it had taken Dusty so long to secure the EMI deal and they needed to complete the Liza

Minnelli album on which they had been working. Besides, Dusty had other songs she wanted to record, because, she said, she felt stifled doing exactly what they told her, with little input of her own. In the end, Neil Tennant and Chris Lowe were the album's executive producers.

As if that wasn't stressful enough, Dusty moved house yet again in December to spend her first Christmas in a £100,000 two-bedroomed house near the village post office in sleepy Taplow, Buckinghamshire. Suffering from bronchitis, which she blamed on the stress of the move, she admitted that she'd bought it in a hurry and wasn't really that fond of it at all. "It needs work but I just haven't had the opportunity to do anything. It's not structural work that needs doing, it's cosmetic stuff but I'm sure I'll feel better about the house when the builders put up wallpaper and I get new carpets. As long as I look out of the window I'm fine."

Pat Rhodes was riddled with guilt. "This is the time I felt really bad about her being so far away from me..." and "I obviously can't start popping in and out to feed the cats and see that she is OK. It's a lovely home and a very pretty place to live but I feel she's somewhat isolated out there. She has... her car... and has bought herself a bike which she hopes to ride around to the shops... but I wonder what people will say when she comes flying down the country lanes on a bike!" Dusty's neighbours called her Mary because that was how she presented herself. "It's interesting that they can't accept the professional me, but much prefer the one who goes running around looking for her cat outside, with no eye make-up on," she told a *Melody Maker* journalist. "The few times they've seen me in the full works, the full war paint, after a video or something, they kinda reel back. They're used to seeing the slob!"

Dusty survived Christmas and the New Year and, after a trip to New York in February 1990 to record the vocal for "Born This Way", the final song on her pending album, she geared herself up to promote her first single of the year. Titled "Reputation" and released in May, it was the title track from the album due for June release. Originally recorded by its composer, Brian Spence, it was a strange choice for Dusty. It displayed a type of campness which she liked and, of course, it was a word associated with Dusty throughout her career. It was a soft rock song with a catchy, heavy hookline, and high attitude. Her vocals hit echo valley to bounce off the music, that itself hit patches of hard drumming and deep breathing. At times she strained and struggled with the depth of the song. "There was a gem of an idea in the original," she said, "...once (producer) Andy Richards started making his noises, it suddenly occurred to me there was a form to the song... I managed to make some kind of semblance of order out of the chaos." *NME*'s reviewer disagreed: "It's a terrible way to trip back under the spotlight", while the *Sounds'* critic wrote, "Harmless, lifeless, and characterless, somebody of Dusty's experience ought to know better."

What was an added attraction on the single was her whispering, "I don't care what they're whispering", about which she later explained, "But that's not true, I do care about what other people think about me, although I pretend not to. I'm very paranoid. If someone gives me a funny look, I think they're looking at a spot on my face and I disintegrate within a moment. I'd love to be one of those people who don't give a damn." Not as big a hit as "In Private" but a respectable showing at Number 38 was sufficient to launch the album bearing the same name.

How could someone who was responsible for the sound of the sixties and who smacked purist soul fans between the eyes with her visit to Memphis, now work again with the Pet Shop Boys, the gay scene's darlings of extreme sounds? This album was a cross between her experience, her fragility and the genius of Neil Tennant and Chris Lowe which was confined to side one of the album. On the other side was Dusty with Brian Spence, Dan Hartman and Rupert Hine. They weren't in competition, rather complementary, and the balance worked.

Omitting the singles, Dusty used her fanzine to write her own review of the album, with which she appeared to be delighted. "The second track 'Send It To Me' is my favourite… because it's simple and I think it has a warmth to it rather like some of the more obscure stuff I did on albums before… It's got some wit and makes me smile. 'Arrested By You'… was sent to me by a Dutch publishing company and was written by Rupert Hine and Jeannette [Obstij], whose surname I can't pronounce, let alone spell… Rupert's done a lot of great production on some of the early stuff with Howard Jones… I thought it had a real quality to it; a hypnotic quality and a strangeness I look for in a song, so I was delighted to do it." Neil Tennant admitted they tinkered with the track by removing the saxophone solo and replacing it with a sequence on an Emulator. "I did it without even telling Dusty!" he later confessed.

"'Time Waits For No One', written and produced by Dan Hartman, is a nice… slick… light song. It was relatively easy and a truly cheery song so I wanted to do it," Dusty continued. "The next track, 'Born This Way', also produced by Dan Hartman, was written by Geoffrey Williams … he's so wonderful that I couldn't fail to be impressed as I love everything he does. It wasn't an easy song to do… we originally set it in a key that was too high for me, but by the time I got to do it at the end of the album I had no voice at all, so it sounds low… it's got a real grittiness. I have a real fondness for the song." Dusty flew to Dan Hartman's home studio to complete the song, where she thoroughly enjoyed herself, saying, "I could look out the window and see wild geese, and it was snowing, and it was all toasty and warm in the studio." She loved the oddness of "Daydreaming" which included a Dusty-rap. "What happened was Neil couldn't quite fit the words he had thought of and the tune together. I walked into the studio one night, and he said that it wasn't quite right so why didn't I talk it, giving me no warning whatsoever. 'I Want To Stay Here', well, I did that song to please Neil. I find it a little frou-frou, light and fluffy… I don't like it. I was looking for a little more substance, but hey, I trust the Pet Shop Boys and that's why I did it. 'Occupy Your Mind' was extraordinary. I could have phoned that in… it's not really a song, it's a sound. It's quite a meditation in itself, but half the time I didn't know what the hell I was singing about. Written and produced by the Pet Shop Boys, and like 'I Want To Stay Here' it was produced by them also, and it was Neil's idea, not mine."

Leon Shaier visited the London studios several times when Dusty was recording the album, with Simon Bell amongst others as session singers. He tucked himself away in a corner to listen and watch. There was one track in particular which was intended for the album but didn't make it because, he recalled, Dusty was having problems with the vocal. "She kept going over and over the same lines but it wasn't working out. It was a shame because she loved that Diane Warren song." Seven years later "Any Other Fool" would be one of four rarities on the re-issue of *Reputation*.

The album's release was delayed because there was a sleeve design problem. "I did another photo session," Dusty explained at the time, "then EMI didn't like those, so we've gone back to a photo from the first session which I'm not altogether happy with." The resulting front cover was dark and incongruous and did little to attract the casual buyer. John McElroy confirmed, "Whatever did they do to her nose... it's nothing like that in real life... makes her look like a Neanderthal woman. A large version of the cover in HMV, Oxford Street, looks rather better, mainly because the photo has a sepia tint to it."

The album was dedicated to Dusty's cat, Malaysia, who was run over and killed by a car in the road outside her Taplow home. She was devastated. "It's a great shame because she came all the way from America to get squashed. The whole thing was a black comedy. I brought her in and put her in a baking tin. I never realized how quickly animals stiffen when they die ... Nikolai was sad for a couple of days, but since then he's never been happier. He just wanted her out of the way. Cats have their own morality and it's not like ours."

Woolworths also sponsored a series of television advertisements for the album, showing video clips of each of the three singles, set against a black background, with captions: "After 20 years at the top/What can you say?/Dusty/We mean the singer/The album's brand new/Dusty Springfield's *Reputation*". Most of the press reviews were upbeat, like *NME* – "A thing of dignity and charm. The sound of two decades colliding and nobody getting hurt." While *The Times* believed it was "polished and sure-footed" and the *Daily Telegraph* noted "It was an impressive return by a true original." Laura Lee Davies wrote in *Time Out* that "... from the title track in, Springfield's sassy cynicism, her wit and style have no problems proving that this is where she wants to be, and that she's having a bloody good time."

In press interviews, she admitted recording the album was a nightmare because she was paralysed by studios. "I feel trapped and I feel tested. I'm not as bad as I used to be but I doubt I will ever lose that moment of sheer, unadulterated terror when you close that thick door behind you." Yet that terror didn't show in the finished album which sold 60,000 copies in three weeks, was certified silver and peaked in the British Top 20, delighting its owner beyond words – well, not quite. "I feel as if this is happening to someone else... This is never going to happen again and I'm not fool enough to think this will last."

Alas, she was right. "Arrested By You" was the second extracted single in November and despite her concentrated promotion, including a video featuring a couple strolling by a lake, was not a great success. In keeping with the song's atmosphere, it was shot in sepia tint, and struggled to Number 70 in the British chart. It was an unwise move by EMI Records because the obvious choice for a single was "Daydreaming", which could have shot up the singles chart. Before the dust settled on that argument, Dusty severed her ties with EMI Records in December 1990 "because the financial terms weren't very advantageous to me. There comes a time when you have to say, hey, wait a minute. I've got to make some money out of this. It's nice having fun and making music, but we all have expenses in life. Had I stayed with EMI, it would have been on the same terms and that's not viable and it would be very stupid."

Perhaps if she had promoted the whole project with a little more enthusiasm, EMI Records might have supported her with a more advantageous deal, but it wasn't to be. And once more Dusty floundered until 1993 when, following the breakdown in negotiations with MCA Records in America, she signed with Sony/Columbia Records. But fate was to play an even crueller game with her; three months after joining her new record company she was diagnosed with breast cancer. "When you've been around as long as I have, you get used to the ups and downs in this business, and you learn how to survive. And I am a survivor..."

Chapter Twelve

SOMEONE TO WATCH
OVER ME

"It's not going to get me…"

A fter spending a quiet family Christmas with her neighbours in Sunningdale, 1991 started badly for Dusty when she watched comedian Bobby Davro portray her as a drunk in a three-minute sketch on his ITV television show on 23 March. While sitting at her home in Taplow, she saw him stumbling on stage, dressed like her in high heels and a frizzy wig. He swigged from a bottle, before falling over after singing a slurred parody of "What Have I Done To Deserve This?" While admitting that alcohol, usually vodka with coca cola or in champagne (because she couldn't taste it) had been her crutch for 20 years, she felt humiliated and angry by Davro's portrayal; so much so that she sued ITV for libel and the case went to court on 26 November.

Dusty's counsel, Hilary Heilbron QC, described Davro's portrayal as "vivid and graphic and depicting Dusty as being so intoxicated by alcohol that she was unable to control her own actions… She has never in the whole of her career performed on stage when her performance has been impaired by alcohol and she is deeply offended at being depicted in this way. The distress to Dusty has been made even more acute because she does not drink and has not for eight years drunk any alcohol." Dusty accepted an out-of-court settlement of £75,000. Wearing a black suit and pink sweater she told journalists waiting outside court that she wasn't seeking publicity with the case and wished the action hadn't been necessary, although was delighted with the outcome. "I have never been upset by the mimicry or satire of me which has occurred on

numerous occasions and which I have... found highly amusing...
But this particular portrayal went to the heart of my personality and
was deeply hurtful."

For their part, ITV offered to apologize and acknowledged that
the portrayal of the singer as a drunk on stage was false, while stress-
ing Bobby Davro wasn't named in the action nor was he liable for
costs. The *Sun* newspaper rushed to Davro's defence by reporting
that comic Freddie Starr had said, "Bobby is so good at mimicking me I have asked him how I am!"; that footballer Paul Gasgo-
ine, previously portrayed by Davro as a blubbering fool, said, "His
impression of me is very funny and I'm not offended"; and that
Jonathan Ross was quoted as saying, "When Bobby does me I see
it as a form of flattery. Any other star should see it the same way."
However, apparently Dusty had the final say, "I have no quarrel
personally with Bobby Davro. The only thing I liked about the
sketch was (his) hair when he was portraying me. I'd like to know
the name of that hairdresser!"

Meanwhile, with no news about a new recording deal, Dusty
once more strongly defended her position to her fans, pointing out
that she had been engaged in talks with interested parties for some
time. "... I can push and shove as much as I like, but there's no
point in moving a record deal sideways. It has to be a better one
and at the moment the (music) business is extremely slow..." She
further wrote in her fanzine, "What bothers me is that some people
think that I'm too expensive, but if they only knew the truth of
what artists get paid they'd probably think again. It's a misconcep-
tion that because you sell some records you make a lot of money.
It's not true, it's a job like anything else."

To take her mind off her musical frustrations and to fill her
time, Dusty would have a flutter on the horses, either choosing
by name or form, or catch up on her various animal charities. She
supported Redwings Horse Sanctuary, for one, by adopting a horse
called Albert. Of course, the Redwings' administration team may
not have been aware of this because she always used her real name.

Pat Rhodes smiled as she recalled another of her friend's adoption schemes. "She decided to adopt a granny through Help The Aged... A short while later she rang me... laughing... 'I never get anything quite right, I've got a granddad! Isn't that typical!'" She also supported The Cat's Protection League and The Celia Hammond Trust. To this end, Dusty spent an evening with Celia collecting stray cats. "Dusty was a great giver," Pat concluded. "That's why she never had any money."

Dusty was also house hunting again. Although she had only recently moved to Taplow, a quiet area where her right to be private would be respected, she had been hounded by fans. She believed her address was leaked to the press by the estate agents, so she had little choice but to move on. Generally speaking, she said, she loved her public. "It goes with the job, except that for some reason I'm finding it rather difficult to handle. I went through so much before on that level that I was sort of naïve to think that anybody would want to do that again. And they do, and I actually find it upsetting. I'm not flattered by it at all because some very nasty things have happened in terms of people being abused by that, and people get killed... I try not to get paranoid.

"But when people turn up in the dead of night, I really consider that's dangerous because you're caught between a rock and a hard place. If you're too nice to them or if you're nice at all, they take that and run with it. If you're nasty to them, they say 'fuck-off'. You don't know what kind of fine balance they're working on mentally. I mean that's how bad things happen... I seem to attract that obsessive quality.

"I have no way of closing myself in... I feel like a prisoner, and that's why I went there. My neighbours try to rally round as much as they can but it seems people pick the times when they are either asleep or they're not in. A friend of mine, a manager in the States, who manages a young actress who is very popular – an ABC blonde type... and she had a fan who kept showing up and she tried to be nice to him and he wouldn't take no for an answer. He kept asking her out and she said no. She had ordered a pizza and the pizza arrived, except it wasn't the pizza man, it was this guy with a gun. So, if people do show up at night, it's getting creepy and it's beginning to really upset me. I don't want to have to live in a mansion with a porter... The reason I went to the country was because I thought I'd get some peace and quiet. Maybe that's very naïve of me."

When Dusty first moved to Wellbank, Taplow, her immediate neighbours didn't know who she was. Anthony Husher told the *Maidenhead Advertiser*, "She didn't wear her famous make-up... that was for the stage. I didn't recognize her the first time I saw her. She was a very private person..." Her reputation as a cat lover quickly spread, and he would often see her at night time walking round her garden with a torch calling for her cats. He added, "Our cat used to get Christmas presents of Harrods pet stockings from her cat." Dusty wasn't the only pop singer in the locality either. Sandie Shaw was collecting names for a petition concerning the village's traffic problems when she knocked on Dusty's door. Both being short sighted, they failed to recognize each other straight away.

When the press printed Dusty's intention to move was due to her cat Malaysia being killed by a car outside her home, Pat Rhodes retaliated: "This is garbage as usual. The only reason she wants to leave... is because the press have tracked her down and knock on the door and then get annoyed because she won't answer them... How would we feel if we wanted to slop around occasionally in something not looking particularly smart because we were weeding the garden, turning out cupboards or whatever, and we were con-fronted by a grinning photographer wanting to plaster a picture all over the tabloid press? I can just see the headlines – 'Dusty Spring-field In Hiding (Because) She Doesn't Look Good Anymore' or some such drivel."

Within a short time Dusty was impressed with two prop-erties, but while she made up her mind which to purchase, she was gazumped – twice. "This means I have to start all over again digging out old newspapers with pictures of houses and keep driving around," she sighed at the time. "If I hadn't got Nicholas [Nicholai], I'd move into a hotel until I could find the right property." In 1992 she found one: Frogmore in Hurley, and told readers of *Dusty Springfield International* "I'm living on a building site at the moment as the house is being done around me. I always vowed that I'd never be in a house when there were workmen in, but that didn't quite work out... It's all terribly unglamorous and I hate it!" Pat Rhodes – "I can quite understand why she is having so much hassle with the builders and decorators. Dusty daren't leave anyone alone to do what she asks as they constantly get it wrong. She's really tied to the house until all the work is completed." Dusty said "The only thing I knew about Christmas this year was I kept playing the Phil Spector Christmas album... I am so tired. If I had the chance – if I had a carpet – I'd roll it up and crawl underneath. But it's very difficult with a wooden floor."

Pat, who continued to work with Dusty under all manner of guises, still handled her fan mail despite the actual club being closed years previously. She had made regular visits to Taplow with letters, gifts and requests for autographs whereupon Dusty would spend hours signing photographs, usually with personal notations. When writing to Dusty, fans sent their mail to Pat's address, enclosing their letters for the singer but they were asked to write Ms M O'Brien on the envelope, enabling Pat merely to add Dusty's address. This cut down on the huge postage bill Dusty paid each month.

During the year Dusty was offered the part of Grizabella in the touring cast of *Cats*, the highly entertaining, visually exciting feline musical which was one of Andrew Lloyd Webber's finest scores. "I would have made a lot of money... [but] it would have taken me away from this country for nearly a year. I had to think long and hard because in my heart I know I was born to play the part of Grizabella, the glamour cat. To be offered it was a fantastic honour." She declined the offer because plans were afoot for a BBC rockumentary based on her career which would, she insisted, command her full co-operation. "… I made the choice to take the risk although I'm quite sure I'd make more money doing *Cats*, but I do have some feelings about where I want to be and what I want to do… it was one of the hardest decisions I will ever have to make."

With the decision made, Dusty was at the mercy of the television company where the wheels move very slowly. Meanwhile, she became involved in another project, that of a proposed CD boxed set. The intention was for her to approve the final track listing but this was taking longer than expected because of her preference for rare material in the form of B-sides and American releases. She cited tracks from *Cameo* and *White Heat*. "I'm not with Phonogram anymore and when they keep bringing out the same stuff over and over again, I can only assume that's because they make more money on it, whereas my choice would be to give people less of the same." Ideas were bounced back and forth with Phonogram until Dusty said, "I get very upset when people think I don't care because I care a lot… My aim is to try to put together a boxed set which has some rarities on it or, at least, some less exposed things." Her main concern was the intention to release tracks that were discarded the first time around due to a variety of reasons. "That happens on sessions, people over-record and they pick out the best ones, just like you pick the nicest chocolates out of a box." She also criticized her record company for insisting on releasing different takes and alternative versions, or tracks with bum notes. Yet, she must have realized the financial viability in releasing these tracks because, if nothing else, it was the perfect marketing ploy to persuade her faithful public to purchase familiar material. And, of course, these tracks proved she was human after all.

The Legend Of Dusty Springfield boxed set was issued in June 1994. The four discs covered 92 tracks including 14 previously unreleased items, like "Heartbeat", "Time After Time" and "Meditation".

To celebrate Cilla Black's thirtieth anniversary in the music business in 1993, Sony/Columbia Records released a 12-track duets album *Through The Years* featuring her singing with Cliff Richard, Barry Manilow and Dusty. Cilla also starred in her own television special, where Dusty was among her guests. "The TV show was great fun... Naturally I would have liked the lighting to be better, but, hey, what can I say? I have no control over these things which is absolutely maddening..." Dusty wrote in her fanzine. "[Cilla] and I have worked together in the past and we've always worked together well... We're two people who have lasted one way or another through all sorts of things. One went away, one didn't, and we've both survived it all."

The gals intended recording "Nineties Ladies", originally called "Eighties Ladies", written by country artist K T Oslin. When the writer wouldn't agree to the changes, another song, "Heart And Soul", was written specifically for them by Rick Blaskey and Charlie Skarber, who also produced, with Dusty assisting in the mixing. "They were nice enough to give me credit for that – the first time anyone has," she said. They also devoured copious amounts of Thai food. Support singers included Simon Bell, Katie Kissoon, Tessa Niles and Mac Kissoon, and during the session Dusty insisted on an extra-long cable on her headphones to enable her to dance while she sang. They intended to sing it as a proper duet but, as they couldn't hear themselves think, decided to record the song separately. Cilla said "I'm supposed to have the heart, and she's got the soul. It's a crib of every Motown song you've ever heard and I've got all the worst lines, all the ones to do with age." Dusty added "I've done my bit. I showed up, had fun... I'm just a guest on the record and view myself as such. A very polite guest at a very nice party, and if it's a successful party, I shall be very happy."

"Heart And Soul", the second single extracted from *Through The Years*, released in October 1993, reached Number 75 in the British chart. Its distribution was limited, so it was a small wonder it charted at all.

Shortly after Dusty's recording with Cilla Black, the highly-respected journalist David Wigg wrote in the *Daily Express* that

Dusty had signed a recording deal with Sony Records. True, there had been a deal on offer, but it wasn't signed. The story, therefore, caused her considerable embarrassment at the time but, by the end of 1993, the deal had been struck.

For some time now Dusty had made no secret of the fact that she wanted to opt out of the pop world after her huge success with the Pet Shop Boys had ended as quickly as it had begun. She admitted she had felt uncomfortable singing for a young generation; it was stressful deciding the right clothes to wear and tiresome fielding questions about her past – although she was extremely proud of her achievements – rather than her potential in the future. She wanted to record an album with a Country and Western flavour, perhaps influenced by her work with The Springfields during the early sixties, but definitely influenced by the market showing no age limit. When the chance came to work in Nashville with producer Tom Shapiro during January 1994, she jumped at it. "I truly believe there are no coincidences in life. I feel as though I left something of myself back there (when The Springfields recorded there) and I got the chance to go back and claim it."

The trip got off to a bad start when Dusty arrived to the worst winter for 15 years. Pat Rhodes travelled to Nashville with her, and when they arrived at Dulles Airport, Washington, the weather was horrendous. Their baggage was held up due to ice on the machinery, arriving two hours later with not a porter to be found in the airport. They then had a 60-mile cab drive to catch a plane for the final two hours to Nashville, where a welcoming, warm limousine collected them from the airport. "Nashville… is a strange place as the city itself doesn't consist of much except hotels, business buildings, hundreds of churches, restaurants and, of course, the State Capitol building," recalled Pat Rhodes. "To go shopping you go to any one of the numerous malls which are situated all over the place… supermarkets are open 24 hours which is great when you need to shop on the way home from the recording studios."

During their stay, originally planned for six weeks and later extended to -10, there was an ice storm which uprooted trees, taking down the power lines. There was no electricity and people couldn't get to work. Those with previous experience of such storms simply moved themselves into whatever hotels had power but, by the time Pat and Dusty realized this, the nearest hotel they could find was 60 miles away. There they stayed for three days until the power was restored, allowing them to start recording again. "It was a period of major snow and ice, which meant you were taking your life in your hands just getting back and forth," Dusty reported. "But somehow that contributed to a kind of trench mentality. Everyone involved maintained incredibly good humour throughout." Pat Rhodes added "Most of the recording studios are in houses, although there are some normal type ones… Dusty really worked hard with all the recording and the video she had to do, despite contracting a nasty throat virus with all the bad weather." She also remembered that they couldn't smoke in the studios, and had to light up outside in the snow in the freezing weather.

Dusty invited Leon Shaier to join them. He stayed in a hotel near the studio and they collected him in their chauffeur-driven car each day. He also noted that Dusty had problems with her voice and that she appeared unwell: "She was clearly sickening for an illness of some type, and of course at the time, we had no idea what it was." Dusty eventually sought medical help, had an endoscopy and was prescribed medication. She "ate like a hog", hoping to build up resistance to further infection – but nothing seemed to work.

The bulk of the songs were recorded live, or with a minimum of overdubs, in the high-ceilinged dining room of Bennett House, in the heritage community of Franklin, just outside Nashville. The remainder were completed in Nashville proper at Recording Arts, again an actual house rather than a purpose-built studio. Dusty said that working with Tom Shapiro was a joy. Twice named Songwriter of the Year by the Country Music Association, he was much in demand. Yet it was his work in Los Angeles with the likes of Labi Siffre and George Benson that had attracted Dusty. "Neither he nor our engineer, Brian Tankersley, are exclusively Country in their grounding. Their sensibilities turned out to work really well with mine... I was blessed with the people I worked with because it wasn't easy."

Once she returned home, Dusty started dieting to shed the pounds she had piled on in Nashville. The first place she lost weight was on the top of her breasts and this revealed a large indentation. She had private insurance and immediately arranged to see a doctor in London, who the next day arranged for her to see a diagnostic doctor at The Royal Marsden Hospital in the Fulham Road. The biopsy showed a tumour, "and it's one we don't want" the doctor told her. Dusty burst into tears. The shock was enormous but, thanks to the private consultations, she knew within three days what she had to deal with in the future. "I was pretty enraged that this was happening to Miss Springfield," she said, "and it was highly inconvenient because I had this record to promote, for God's sake. Yes, I was angry that it was happening to her." She shed a few more tears in the corridor before saying to her brother, Tom, Pat, and others who had accompanied her, "Let's have lunch!" It was when she returned home that evening that she suffered the blackest of thoughts; the damning moments of an early death. Then she saw her cat Nicholas lying asleep, and realized he wouldn't have a mum if she died. It was the kick she needed – "It's not going to get me ... and I never entertained the notion again." And when her doctor advised her to return to work for two weeks during which time a plan of treatment would be worked out, she understood that she wasn't going to die straight away. Being part of a team at The Royal Marsden meant Dusty didn't have to face her demons alone. She had a lumpectomy and the chemotherapy thinned her hair but she didn't lose it all, and for that she thanked the hospital's ice cap which froze her hair follicles before the drug hit them. There was no pain but Dusty felt very nauseous, which she believed was more through terror than the drug itself. "My body seemed to like the chemicals. I've poisoned it so many times in the past that it went,

'Yes please! Poison!'" Radiotheraphy was more difficult for her because it was tiring, but she faced this with an inner strength that she
described as "the Irish fighter who wasn't going to be beaten."

News of her fight with cancer didn't hit the newspapers until November 1994 when an announcement was made through
Sony's press office that "Dusty discovered she had breast cancer in
the spring and has been having treatment throughout the year."
Publicist Jo Donnelly also told journalists, "The doctors are extremely pleased with her and the prognosis is very good... Dusty is
a very private person and we are leaving her alone to get completely better." Neil Tennant, Cilla Black, Dawn French and Jennifer
Saunders were among hundreds of fans who sent her messages of
support, gifts and flowers. By Christmas 1994 Dusty had completed
six months of treatment. "She's doing really well but is a little tired
still as the effects of radiotherapy can take as long as a year for the
body to fully recover," Pat Rhodes explained at the time. Dusty
eased herself back into work by completing the album she had
started in Nashville. Not wanting to let her record company down
plagued her because she had signed a contract agreeing to complete
an album within a certain time limit, but had been unable to honour that. She expected to be fired and for the album to be scrapped.
Instead it was put on hold – and she was sent flowers.

After Dusty had finished recording in Nashville from January to
April, the BBC screened *Dusty – Full Circle* on 2 May, the rockumentary she chose to do instead of taking the part of Grizabella,
the glamour cat. The 60-minute profile included a skit with Dawn
French playing a smarmy interviewer, and Jennifer Saunders a diz-
zy publicist. Not everyone enjoyed this element of the show. *The
Times'* reviewer summed it up: "The whole thing was in danger of
becoming an extended French and Saunders sketch, with Springfield making a cameo appearance. It seemed not just distracting but
a little insulting. Can you imagine a documentary on Pavarotti being punctuated by Bob Monkhouse." To be fair, Dusty wasn't the
easiest of people to approach about this type of personal documen-

tary because she would not be comfortable talking about herself. "Some people… didn't care much for the French and Saunders' thing, but I liked it… so I'm well pleased with that… I wanted to take the Mickey out of myself." She had hoped viewers would see more obscure clips from her past, but due to the cost being "up to $300,000 a second or something ridiculous", familiar archive footage was included instead. On the positive side, viewers welcomed the sight of "Mockingbird", a fragmented television duet between Dusty and Jimi Hendrix provided by a fan who had recorded it on 8mm film. And it was interesting to hear contributions from Martha Reeves, Neil Tennant, Elvis Costello, Dionne Warwick and Burt Bacharach. The programme's producer, Brendan Hughes, said, "I wasn't shy about asking her about her sexuality or alcohol or drugs, I just wasn't interested. What's interesting about her is the music." Subsequently, very little was learnt about the lady behind the voice, which was exactly what Dusty had intended.

As she had fused her feel for soul with the best Nashville musicians for her next album, many felt the album should have been titled *Dusty In Nashville* but the singer wanted to avoid being stereotyped. The decision was taken to call it *A Very Fine Love*, the spiritual successor to *Dusty In Memphis*, and in May 1995 Diane Warren's composition "Wherever Would I Be?" was the first track to be issued as a single. Originally intended to be a solo song and recorded by Dusty as such, it was later decided to bring in Daryl Hall, the blonde half of Hall & Oates, to add his vocals to the track. "I called Diane up and she played me a few things," Dusty explained in the album's press release. "'Wherever Would I Be?' was among them. At the time I wasn't really looking for a ballad, but she's a very persistent lady and sent me over a tape of it. And she was right, it was too good to miss." Then followed the suggestion of recording it with Daryl Hall, a voice she'd always worshipped. "We did the vocals in London, but separately. After meeting up I went away for a while, gave him the privacy he needed. Then it was just a case of coming back afterwards and giving him big hugs because he'd done such a wonderful job."

The single's release was supported by a rather strange video that featured the occasional shot of a television screen showing the two singers performing while the bulk of the camera work concentrated on somebody leaping about over rooftops. "Wherever Would I Be?" peaked at Number 44 in the singles' chart. Its poor sales were a tremendous blow. Everything had been geared towards its release with Sony Records' concentrated promotion, and Dusty's broadsheet interviews (where she smoked as she talked – "the doctors would be very upset if they knew") in preference to music newspapers, but radio play, which was prolific prior to the single's relaease, had stopped. The single was featured in the closing credits of the movie *While You Were Sleeping* starring Sandra Bullock, due for British release soon after. If the film had enjoyed the same success as it did in America, Dusty would easily have scored a high-charting single.

"I'm very proud of the work I've done in the past, but there's more to me than that," Dusty told journalists in support of *A Very Fine Love* being released on both sides of the Atlantic in June, her first studio album for five years. "I don't want to rest on my laurels. It's not true that you can't make anything other than a country album in Nashville. Their skills in pop and R&B are equally well developed." And the new album proved it. Will Jennings and Marlee Lebow penned the opening track "Roll Away", which should have been the first single. Dusty's plaintiff vocal against a highly melodic tune that was instantly memorable was perfect chart fodder. The album's title track, by comparison, lacked the quick attraction and ease of melody. The Dipiero/Photoglo composition was saved by tight rhythm and horn sections while the marked change in Dusty's vocals that became apparent during the late eighties was quite noticeable. Yet, she excelled beyond words on the introspective ballad "Go Easy On Me", a magnificent track penned by John Jarvis and Randy Goodrum. Heart-tugging lyrics were delivered in true Springfield style, despite a certain weariness in her voice. The same applied to Berg/Samoset's "You Are The Storm" where the help-lessness in her voice against a guitar-based backdrop turned a medi-ocre song into something musically special. Producer Tom Shapiro co-penned "I Can't Help The Way I Don't Feel" which was the closest Dusty came to a country and western influenced song. Sim-ply constructed, relatively mundane, it was only heightened by her vocal presence. The same can be said for Craig Wiseman's "All I Have To Offer You Is Love". Diane Warren's second contribution here was likened to Dusty's tribute to the Motown sound. R&B in style, previously recorded by Celine Dion, the catchy song "Lovin' Proof" relied too heavily on its hookline. The penultimate pop track "Old Habits Die Hard" from Graham Lyle and Terry Brit-ten (who successfully wrote for Tina Turner) was high on chorus, but little else. Thankfully, the soulful closer "Where Is A Woman To Go?", which Dusty considered to be the most adult track on the album, was truly stunning. At their initial meeting in Watford, both Dusty and Tom Shapiro turned up with a copy of the K T Oslin track. Dusty said "Then he suggested that we ask both K T and Mary Chapin Carpenter to sing on it. I never thought it would happen, but it did. They were both so great; no egos, no attitude, just women helping each other out... after recording, we took ourselves off for a long, long lunch. The whole thing was just a joy." It took a lot of courage for Dusty to sing this song, and when she performed it on the television show *Later With Jools Holland*, it was note true and faultless. This was true of the whole album, although it was unfortunate that some of the material let her down, particularly as this was to be her very last.

Her record company launched a two-pronged marketing cam-paign to attract new audiences, and reach her existing fans, includ-ing television and radio advertising in selected areas, an extensive press campaign in the national newspapers, a four-sheet poster campaign and in-store displays. Dusty commented "This is my last shot. Dear God, how many times can you make a comeback?"

The reviews were critical. "Twenty-six years ago she released the classic *Dusty In Memphis*. So it seemed a good idea for England's blue eyed soul queen to record her first album in Nashville. Too bad it sounds more like 'Dusty In Hell'" wrote Jim Farber. "Hackneyed and dull" penned the *Pink Paper*'s Jonathan Chandler. *NME*'s reviewer was kinder: "It's beautifully made soul/pop with a couple of country-style moments. Dusty can still sing better than anyone else..." And another said, "...the grande dame of white soul returns, mellower but still licensed to chill ... age shall not wither her." The album peaked at Number 43, a poor showing particularly in view of the high profile Dusty was attracting at this time.

With the British promotion behind her, she flew to America where, in contrast to her visit to Nashville, the weather was distressingly hot. As she was there for a short time only, interviews were crammed in. "You do what's in front of you..." she told *Dusty Springfield International* readers, "...which is usually lots of press and satellite television where they sit you in a room with a camera on you with nobody there, and these people come on long distance and you have to pretend they're there. You do a different interview every two minutes. By the time you've finished you're so punch drunk you should be arrested." While she was promoting *A Very Fine Love* a package arrived on Dusty's doorstep and, as she was an avid catalogue customer at Innovations and Laura Ashley, she assumed it was an item she had ordered and forgotten about. Inside the package was a platinum disc for "Son-Of-A Preacher Man", representing sales of the soundtrack from *Pulp Fiction*, the Academy Award-winning film, directed by Quentin Tarantino and featuring John Travolta, Samuel L Jackson and Uma Thurman. "I was really very touched that the film company bothered to go to all that trouble. It's not up on the wall because it's the wrong colour. The platinum part's terrific but that's only the bottom, the rest is orange and that's the problem." It was the first platinum disc of her career and she had done nothing towards it!

Released in October 1995, "Roll Away" was the second extracted single and once again Dusty threw herself into promoting it. A lot had gone on in her life since she had recorded the album, and she felt quite estranged from the whole project. It was, therefore, a constant surprise to her to hear music from those sessions, as she later explained: "I was talking to this station in San Francisco and they go... 'here's "Roll Away"' ... and they start playing it and it brought tears to my eyes because I thought, 'gosh, it really sounds good'... It was hard work doing it all, and then I got ill, and there they were playing it. The thrill has not gone on that level."

Once again, she promoted the release by filming a video, this time along the windswept Atlantic coastline of Ireland. "It was a lot of fun making it, although it was total chaos because of the time pressure." Directed by Sean O'Hagan and Seamus McGarvey, it was inspired by the film *Into The West* where Ellen Barkin and Gabriel Byrne trailed a white horse and two children across an Irish landscape. They chose their site for the two-and-a-half day stay and happily prepared for the routine of a video shoot. Dusty, on the other hand, had other ideas. She didn't trust the video process, banned close-ups, and left the Gregg Castle hotel in Corrandulla at noon for the 40ft Winnebago which was hired at her insistence. Sean O'Hagan wrote in the *Observer*, "I still have nightmares about that Winnebago. The half-mile tailbacks it left in its wake; the stand-offs between the driver and tractors, lorries and herds of cows." The strong wind that blew from the Atlantic affected Dusty's concentration and played with her hair which, he said, necessitated constant re-shooting by a panicking film crew who, at one point, had endless footage of two children and a horse but not Dusty. With one day left for shooting, Sean O'Hagan and Seamus McGarvey spent the previous evening in the local bar. Dusty joined them and together they enjoyed an affable evening. Next day, she gave her all. "Ever the diva, she'd waited until the eleventh hour, then performed faultlessly for the camera." She was filmed alongside standing stones, flowing streams, the Celtic ruins of County Clare and the Galway coast. Shots featured her looking whiter-than-white with a soft hairstyle, wearing her much-favoured black trouser suit. It was apparent she was at ease with herself and had come to face and accept the ambiguities of life. One wondered if she suspected that this was to be her last video. "(The song means a lot to me) because of the line 'roll away... it's only time and the river...'" she explained at the time. "For the last year I'd been obsessed with going to the Shenandoah River. And I did it this year in the snow. I don't know whether it was in a previous life, or whatever, but I had to be there... I stood there and wept, and I have no idea why. I felt so still, so happy (and) the tears were not sad at all... This last year has been pure shit, but... I've done the record and the cancer is over... That was a genuine spiritual experience, watching the flow in utter silence."

When the shoot ended, Dusty bought chilled champagne for the crew before signing autographs and posing for photographs. She then stayed behind at Cregg Castle after the crew had left for a short holiday. She relaxed, joined the family for meals and bar-beques, became smitten with a sheep called Ziggy, who was also a bit of a loner, and walked the dogs through the nearby meadows. Before Dusty left she wrote in the visitors' book, "All of you will be etched in my memory forever, and I will see you again for sure. Love to you and all the animals, especially Flash and Ziggy and A[indecipherable], Dusty". Despite all the hard work, "Roll Away" sold poorly and crawled into the British Top 70.

Five years after the shoot, Carole Gibson and her husband stayed at Cregg Castle, a large house with a handful of guest rooms and a slightly faded elegance. They slept in the same room as Dusty, with a large bathroom, but no television or phone. "Almost below the bathroom window was the 'green door' which was featured in the video, used, I was told, on the last day of filming when they were running out of time," recalled Carole. "It was really in the back yard, surrounded by bins and empty bottles – the true glamour of filming!"

Ann Marie, who ran the hotel, remembered that Dusty had been particularly stressed out by the whole process of the filming, because every day they travelled in the Winnebago to different locations. Carole Gibson explained "One of the sites was the Poulnabrone dolmen, the large stones that Dusty sits on and stands in front of towards the end of the video. I had visions of that Winnebago being parked on the very narrow lane, causing absolute chaos and of Dusty making her way over the very rugged landscape that nearly resulted in me breaking an ankle or two. At the end of the video, when Dusty is silhouetted by the setting sun, she nearly didn't make the shot. The director wanted to film her as the sun was setting, but Dusty needed a loo break and when you gotta go, you gotta go! She took about an hour and the director was apparently in tears!"

After wandering around the Cregg estate, Carole quickly understood why Dusty wanted to stay there. It was the perfect place for someone who wanted to escape from the world for a while, where she could walk unhindered and be herself without being bothered by the media.

Upon her return from the Galway coast, it was business as usual for Dusty. She recorded various television appearances, including *Des O'Connor Tonight*, which was the last show she ever appeared on. And she recorded her final song, ironically titled "Someone To Watch Over Me", from the 1926 stage musical *Oh, Kay!* composed by Ira and George Gershwin. It was for a television advertisement for PPP (Private Pension Plan). Recorded during an afternoon in a London studio, and accompanied by Paul Hart on piano, Dusty took three hours to complete the session. Several versions were recorded, none lasting longer than 60 seconds. It was eventually made available in 2000 on the lavish *Simply Dusty* CD anthology that she helped to plan but did not live to see released. Paul Howes added "Dusty sang two verses and hummed another and out of that several versions were made to tie in with the visuals of the commercials." Her voice was vulnerable, personal and, Paul noted, the very antithesis of what she strove to achieve with her earliest records.

Chapter Thirteen

GOIN' BACK

"...She was the greatest white singer there has ever been."
– Elton John

Early in 1996 Dusty returned to Cregg Castle with Helene Sellery for a short holiday. This time her comment in the visitors' book read, "Fantastic as usual – my healing place – thank you for everything." In fact, far from being her "healing place" it was during this trip to Cregg Castle that Dusty felt her cancer return. "She wasn't feeling well when she came back from Ireland," remembered Simon Bell. "She went to see a Harley Street specialist. Vicki, Pat and I went with her. We had coffee, then she came out and said the cancer had returned."

Dusty was given an appointment at The Royal Marsden Hospital the following day to plan another course of treatment. "Dusty was pretty strong," Simon continued. "She wanted to live. She had never used a computer and one of the things she liked was getting information off the internet, particularly the American websites for cancer treatment. I took pages and pages of stuff to her which she then took to the doctors, asking them why weren't they treating her with this or that." It was ironic that in her past life she went through a phase of caring little about living, now she was fighting to keep her life. When the tests showed that the cancer had spread to her bones, she knew the prognosis was bad.

Pat Rhodes added, "Sometimes she'd say 'why now?' because she wanted to work. But basically she felt 'well, if it's going to happen, I've just got to make the best of it'. Then she said to me there's no point in giving up smoking now is there!?"

To ensure she could live comfortably while she fought the killer disease, she agreed to sell the rights to 275 of her songs to Prudential Insurance. The selling price was said to be £6.25 million, but in reality it was a much lesser figure. A company spokesperson said the deal was a one-off and "Dusty just felt the time was right." Up to this point, Dusty had never written a will. "We laughed about it and talked seriously about it," Vicki Wickham remembered. "And I pushed her into it (but) she had no idea what it really meant." It was hard for Vicki to talk to Dusty about how she wanted her affairs handled following her death. "For me to question her about these things when she was dying, when you have to keep hope alive, (was) very difficult." Some issues, therefore, which should have been addressed with Dusty before she died were pushed aside for fear of upsetting her. In the end, Dusty decided to ask her neighbours, Lorna and Gib Hancock, to be her executors. She was seduced by the middle-classes and her neighbours fitted the bill.

"We had been in Africa during the sixties," explained Lorna. "We knew who The Beatles were but the name Dusty Springfield didn't mean a lot to me. Gib worked for ICI and we were out of the country for 28 years." Lorna first met Dusty when Sam, Lorna's little dog, first met Nicholas, the cat. "She said, 'Hi, I'm your neighbour. I'm Dusty' and in the course of the conversation I realized I knew 'Son-Of-A Preacher Man'."

The Hancocks lived opposite Dusty, who lived in a converted granary, and all the residents looked out over the courtyard. "We were often in each other's houses. I used to cook for her a lot. She'd phone over and ask what we were having for dinner. Sometimes it would only be bangers and mash, but she'd join us. Dusty felt at ease with us because we weren't part of her history. She was a fantastic human being with a huge sense of fun… a middle-class lady. She had her standards and always insisted on good manners. She had a small circle of friends, and Tom came by occasionally to see her. Helene came too, she was a dear lady and very protective of Dusty." Sadly, Helene died before she inherited one of Dusty's favourite pictures.

One evening, Dusty and Lorna sat down to discuss wills and lawyers which, Lorna noted, Dusty didn't really want to do. A meeting was then arranged for Dusty to talk through her personal wishes with a lawyer, who made the legal procedure painless for her. She also arranged for a confidentiality agreement to be drawn up to be signed by Simon Bell, Vicki Wickham and Pat Rhodes, among others. This was to guarantee that nobody would openly discuss her illness or business affairs after her death. When Dusty had asked Lorna to be executor of her will, she declined, saying she hadn't known her long enough. "The second time she asked me, I knew she really meant it. I asked my husband what should I do. He said 'you can't turn her down again.' So I said to Dusty I'd do it but only if Gib helped me. David was the third executor. When I was doing business things with her, she would open a bottle of champagne. She'd drink diet coke because she never touched alcohol. She was immensely proud of her success with AA, but she had her standards to uphold." The downside to this business arrangement was that the Hancocks knew nothing about the music business, nor how Dusty's "legend" should be protected, which would inevitably cause them concern after her death. Simon Bell explained "I can understand why she made them executors of her estate. She trusted them, and didn't trust anybody in the business. And she wasn't close to her brother."

Dusty also arranged her funeral with Lorna Hancock. She discussed the order of service and the hymns to be included; she didn't want a Catholic church, having never returned to the faith, preferring St Mary's Church with its pretty setting. Black horses had to pull a carriage holding her coffin, and she wanted to bring Henley to a standstill while they did so. For her last journey, she would wear a cashmere suit which she'd purchased specifically for this purpose. It was very upsetting for Lorna but she knew that without her help Dusty would flounder and arrangements would be left unfinished.

The first the public knew of Dusty's returning cancer was during February 1998 when compère, Ben Elton, told the audience at the BRITS award ceremony that she was too ill to attend the evening's celebrations. Dusty had been scheduled to present Bjork with the Best International Female award. Ben Elton said, "We had hoped that Dusty Springfield, that icon of music, would be here tonight. I know everybody in the industry will send her their love and very best wishes." Almost overnight, the media camped outside her front door. "It was awful to live like that," Lorna Hancock recalled. Dusty became a prisoner in her own home, venturing out after dark, often taking refuge in the Hancock household. "She had to move," Lee Everett told the *Mail On Sunday* in 1999. "The Granary was too public and it was becoming clear she needed live-in staff." Lee found her a sprawling family house in Harpsden Bottom, Henley-on-Thames which Dusty adored on sight, thanks to its sloping gardens, towering fir trees and woodland where deer roamed. The house was shielded by evergreen holly and an electric fence. The double gates were padlocked from the inside. A bolted wooden gate barred the track leading to the back door. Dusty felt she would be secure there, while Lee Everett believed her being there added a year to her life.

So, it was from Harpsden Bottom that Dusty began two three-month long treatments of chemotherapy. During her trips to The Royal Marsden Hospital she often persuaded the paramedics to stop the ambulance on the way home so that she could pop into Heals or Jerry's Home Store. On another occasion, legendary racehorse trainer, Jenny Pitman, chanced to meet her in the hospital's waiting room. Dusty placed her hand on Jenny's head, gently ruffling her hair and whispered "good luck". The two had never previously met and Jenny doubted that Dusty knew who she was, "but when she stopped to wish me luck, it moved me to the core."

Simon Bell put his life on hold to live with Dusty during her final months. "I can't remember whether I offered to move in with her or whether she asked me. Anyway, it was a quiet time for me.

Dusty knew I was booked to tour with James Last later in 1999 and said she'd better be gone by then. And she was. Doctors said she had four months to live, but she lived for fourteen. She didn't know quite what to do when she was told this. I prayed she'd say 'I'm going round the world' but all she wanted to do was stay at home. She would be very ill, then rally, but throughout she was incredibly strong. Because of the abuse given to her body over the years, she felt real guilty about taking any medication." Towards the end, however, she welcomed the morphine to help ease the agonizing pain.

Dusty refused to use an upstairs bedroom, fearing that would have isolated her. Instead, she chose to have her bed in the centre of the sitting room which looked out onto her splendid garden. Simon couldn't be ill either, "...because she'd say 'you wanna be ill, you try cancer!' It was the tyranny of the sick. My friends thought it would make me ill looking after her because, apart from everything else, I often thought she'd contemplate suicide given her history." When he came downstairs each morning, the first thing he did was check on Dusty. Quite often he'd be alarmed because she had the knack of "sleeping with her eyes open".

When she was well enough, Simon would take her out for the day, otherwise they'd listen to music, discuss world affairs or watch videos. It was while they were watching Bette Midler in *Diva Las Vegas* that Dusty asked Simon to sing at her funeral. "Dusty was in bed and I was sitting in a chair at the foot of her bed. We both cried when Bette sang 'Wind Beneath My Wings' and Dusty said 'I want you to sing that at my funeral.' She knew I'd already sung it at a funeral of a friend who'd died from AIDS. To lighten the moment, I said, 'No. I'd rather sing "By The Light Of The Silvery Moon"!'"

Dusty also shopped and, as ill as she was, the urge to spend money never left her. She ordered items from catalogues and scoured the fashion magazines for new ideas. "She was a compulsive shopper," Pat Rhodes said. "She shopped on-line. Bought loads of stuff from Land's End – five pairs of identical chinos, and her loose black tops and black trousers which she wore latterly on TV." Staying awake during the night watching news programmes and sports, particularly the 1998 World Cup, was another favourite pastime. Simon administered her medicine and fielded the countless phone calls. Dusty quickly realized that people were phoning to say goodbye and she was unable to deal with this, although she constantly spoke with Linda McCartney who was diagnosed with breast cancer in 1995. She put Dusty in touch with her own American consultant, who agreed with the treatment Dusty was receiving from The Royal Marsden. Linda was a huge support, sending her flowers and gifts each week, but no-one knew just how ill Linda was. Her death on 17 April 1998 devastated Dusty because she never believed her friend's cancer to be terminal. After all, she had beaten it before, why couldn't Linda? Paul took over from his late wife by phoning and sending gifts.

Carole King, Burt Bacharach and Martha Reeves were among the many trying to talk to Dusty. Although they hadn't been in contact for several years, when Martha learned of her friend's illness, she attempted to contact her by phone and letter. Dusty didn't return the calls, and when Pat Rhodes gave her Martha's letters, she wouldn't read them because they upset her too much. A distraught Martha never had the chance to say goodbye to a lady who had meant so much to her. Carole Pope, however, spoke to Dusty, and so did Leon Shaier. She had phoned him immediately the cancer had returned because she didn't want him to find out from elsewhere. "I spoke to her every week until she got pretty ill... I sent her funny cards and flowers... I had just lost my business and she wanted to know how much in debt I was. I told her and she told me not to worry, she would sort it out. I thought I'd be a beneficiary. She rang me six weeks before she died to say goodbye and 'I love you Leon'."

Meanwhile, outside the Henley retreat, Vicki Wickham attempted to allay fears about Dusty's deteriorating health. She told *USA Today*, "She is in remarkably good spirits... she loves life and she's not giving up yet. She's not in hospital but is receiving treatment and is recovering at home... she has had to put everything on hold for now." Then, during a star-studded event at The Metropole Hotel, Brighton, East Sussex, organized by the Variety Club of Great Britain, the media were informed that famous people associated with the area would be immortalized in the Walk Of Fame at Brighton's Marina. Modelled on the famous Hollywood attraction, it was due to be opened in September 1998. As her parents had lived in Hove, Dusty was one of several to be honoured, including Leo Sayer, Norman Wisdom, Lewis Carroll and Dora Bryan. A year later, Dusty was one of 14 celebrities who had brand new buses named after them in a project inspired by David Courtney, responsible for the Marina's Walk of Fame. On a much grander scale though, during November 1998, it was publicly announced that Dusty was to be inducted into the prestigious Rock And Roll Hall of Fame in a ceremony at New York's Waldorf Astoria Hotel, due to be held on 15 March 1999. An optimistic reply to the invitation was sent to the effect that Dusty hoped to attend the event and that she was honoured the Hall of Fame wanted to pay her this respect.

Meanwhile, everyday life at Henley slowed down. Sometimes it wasn't easy living with Dusty, particularly when she plunged into the blackest periods of frustration and despair. Feeling totally inadequate, Simon Bell obviously made allowances but admitted to "biting his tongue" on several occasions. They were the best of friends, soul mates, but when he moved in as her carer, the relationship changed. It had to because, sadly, Dusty was no longer in control. She didn't have a partner during this time to take her through to her next journey, so Simon and her cat Nicholas became the centre of her life. And it was this trio who spent the last Christmas together. He cooked dinner and they pulled crackers and laughed a lot. Pat Rhodes was a regular visitor, of course, and, as well as bearing gifts and cards from fans, looked after Dusty's finances. She was one of the few who knew Dusty's monetary worth.

Five days after Christmas Day, Dusty was awarded an OBE in the New Year's Honours list. "She was thrilled to bits," Vicki Wickham said at the time. "I said to her how surprised I was because she was never really into that sort of thing." As Dusty's health was deteriorating quickly, Buckingham Palace officials agreed with representatives of the Central Chancery (the government department in charge of the honours) that Dusty could receive her OBE without having to attend the Palace. Generally speaking, recipients of awards waited two hours at the Palace before seeing the Queen, but special arrangements were made for the sick to ensure their wait was reduced and in comfort. Alas, Dusty was too ill to do this. Finally, it was agreed that Vicki Wickham could collect the award from the Palace and deliver it to Dusty who was now in The Royal Marsden. A few nurses and close friends had gathered with Dusty in her room to celebrate her achievement with cups of tea as Vicki arrived with the OBE inside a Fortnum and Mason plastic carrier bag. It was an upbeat occasion, where Dusty was laughing, "What would the Queen think about an OBE being presented in a plastic carrier!" Tom Springfield later gave the OBE to Pat Rhodes because she deserved it more than anyone else he knew. She also gave a home to Dusty's dog-eared, but much adored, Einstein teddy bear.

When Dusty returned home, two nurses, her housekeeper, Eileen Hurley and Simon Bell were her lifeline. A month before she died, Dusty asked her hairdresser to colour her silver hair, "I'm going out blonde!" she declared. Simon Bell added "She looked incredible to the end. She had lost weight but still had wonderful skin..." Pat Rhodes visited Dusty and found her restless. She asked if a vicar could be called to give her a blessing to calm her. The local vicar, who would jointly conduct Dusty's funeral service, attended. Pat had no idea that Dusty would die that night.

At approximately 10.40 on Tuesday evening, 2 March 1999, Dusty Springfield died in her sleep, weeks before her sixtieth birthday. The cause of death was carcinomatosis and carcinoma of the breast, and her death was registered in Henley the day after by her brother.

When Pat Rhodes arrived at Dusty's home the following morning, her possessions were being bagged up in black bin bags. She had no input into clearing the house and was unsure of what actually went where. However, the whereabouts of several gowns was known because over a period of time, when she had arranged for them to be cleaned, Dusty insisted they be stored at Pat's house. The cashmere suit that Dusty wanted to be buried in couldn't be found, so she left this world in night attire lovingly bought for her in life by Eileen Hurley. Paperwork, including letters and cards from friends like Martha Reeves and Linda McCartney, was burned. Vast quantities of her everyday clothes, including her much-loved black designer suits, items she had ordered from catalogues and not worn, went to Cancer Research, while some of the remaining stage clothes, jewellery, records, awards, personal videos and tapes, and photographs were put up for auction by Sotheby's in the September Rock 'n' Roll Memorabilia sale. The £25,000 proceeds from this auction went to The Cat's Protection League and The Royal Marsden Hospital.

Close friends had been told by Dusty that she would remember them in death. A discretionary trust was attached to her will which, generally speaking, meant trustees had discretion over who received what. In this case, Dusty's wishes had been logged with her lawyer and trustees and, in effect, it was left to them to administer it. Some were indeed remembered although not, perhaps, in the way they had expected. But others weren't, like Leon Shaier whom Dusty had already assured would benefit, and Pat Rhodes's son, who was Dusty's godson. In 2002 the *Sunday Express*'s David Wigg reported that the taxman wanted a huge slice of the money she had left to be distributed among her closest friends, and that her executors were fighting against this because, "If the taxman won, Dusty had left nothing at all. There was no property to sell because she rented her last house…" The outcome was never made public.

Nicholas was "willed" to Lee Everett. The Californian rag doll cat and Dusty had been inseparable for 13 years, and to ensure the transfer was as painless as possible, Dusty had arranged for a year's supply of Gerber's tinned baby food to be flown in from Los Angeles on a regular basis. He slept on one of her pillow slips from her deathbed and one of her nightgowns which she wore until she died. The cat's home went with him to Lee's Berkshire bungalow. Standing seven feet high, the indoor wooden tree house studded with hearts, with its garden of foliage and carpeted apartments, was so heavy it took two men to carry it. Nicholas was put to sleep in 2004 following a long illness.

It was originally thought that Dusty wanted to be buried as Mary O'Brien and that her funeral service would reflect this wish. When she discussed her wishes with Lorna Hancock, however, Dusty made it clear that wasn't the case. "Arranging the funeral was unbelievably complicated. Anything going on in Henley brings things to a standstill. However, the police were very co-operative, buses had to be re-routed and the road closed. We had to hire crash barriers to prevent people running into the road or being hurt, and the service needed to be relayed over tanoys outside the church. At the end of it, I said 'Dusty, I hope you're pleased with this.'"

While Gib and Lorna Hancock were engrossed in these arrangements, lists of people were being contacted. Vicki Wickham and Pat Rhodes spent hours on the phone telling people of Dusty's passing and inviting them to the funeral. Vickie phoned Carole Pope, who immediately made arrangements to say farewell to her ex-partner. She wrote in her autobiography *Anti Diva* that she hated to think of Dusty suffering, that she was so resilient and strong, that she believed Dusty would outlive her. Admitting she had been caressed by her voice long before they met, Carole wrote that she begged Dusty to sing to her when they were in bed. "She would put her mouth up to my ear. The sound of her voice, so intimate and close, washed over me like waves of pure pleasure." On the other hand, Gene Pitney declined to attend, saying, "It's going to be like a circus. I wouldn't go near the place. I just hope she rests in peace."

A public relations firm was hired to deal with the media and oversee the day's events. It was decided to hold the wake in Danesfield House, between Henley and Marlow, because it was nearby and security friendly. Dusty was happy with this, yet in an earlier conversation with Pat Rhodes, she had insisted she wanted her wake to be held in a huge marquee, with a Latin American band playing for all it was worth, while guests slowly got intoxicated by the music and alcohol. Pat Rhodes said, "I don't know why I wasn't an executor but they said it wasn't possible. It was a pity really because Dusty wanted to go out with a bang."

When visitors first arrived in Henley on Friday, 12 March 1999, there was a disarming quietness around Hart Street, while the air appeared tense with expectation. Gradually, people began milling around, cameras were set up and, Carole Gibson sadly remembered, "It was as if some mega media event had closed the centre of Henley." Everyday folk mingled with fans to stand on the pavements behind the barriers lining Hart Street. The funeral was due to start at 12.30 pm at the Parish Church of St Mary The Virgin, and as two black horses pulled Dusty's coffin inside a glass-sided hearse lined with pink and white floral letters spelling her name, the crowds ignored the rain to grieve the passing of one special lady. Little bunches of daisies had been tied to the railings outside the twelfth-century church and Dusty was carried inside to the strains of "You Don't Have To Say You Love Me". Invited mourners and celebrities like Madeline Bell, Kiki Dee, Neil Tennant, Chris Lowe, Elvis Costello, Pat Rhodes, Simon Bell, Vicki Wickham, Nona Hendryx, Lulu, Fred Perry, Leon Shaier and Carole Pope mingled with fans. It had been arranged that once the invited mourners were seated in the church, fans who were queuing outside could fill the empty seats. Among them was Carole Gibson who found herself in the front row, on the right-hand side of the altar. To her left were the chief mourners, Tom Springfield, Vicki and Nona, while Pat sat between the Pet Shop Boys. "It just didn't seem real. What am I doing here? When the service started and the vicar started talking, I was half expecting a service for Mary O'Brien. But everyone knew her as Dusty Springfield and referred to her as such throughout."

Neil Tennant wrote in *Literally*, "There was a silence and then suddenly in the church 'You Don't Have To Say You Love Me' started, and it was so unbelievable and the coffin came in. You didn't know whether to laugh or cry. Both really, because it was very camp and very moving at the same time." The 45-minute service was conducted by the Reverend David Pritchard, assisted by Father Anthony Wilcox from the Sacred Heart Roman Catholic Church. Reverend Pritchard said, "The service was a wonderful blend of her, her talents and the way she used those talents to reach our lives as well as the fact that she was a person for whom faith was important throughout her life."

Lulu gave a tearful eulogy that included, "She was always so brave... but of course if she was here now she'd say, 'No, I wasn't.' We are all here with great love and great respect to honour Dusty's life and to celebrate it." Simon Napier Bell read a message from Dionne Warwick, before Elvis Costello read a few words from Burt Bacharach. Simon Bell then sang a heart-wrenching version of "The Wind Beneath My Wings". Gib Hancock followed and spoke of the Dusty he and his wife knew. Written by Lorna, it was a moving and honest reflection about the lady they grew to love. "I wish I could say that we had known her for 20 years, or even for 10 years, but we were deprived of that. We didn't know Dusty the international star, so there is no way we can add anything to the huge tributes that rightly have been made to her contribution to the world of popular music. Lorna and I met her just five years ago, when she became our neighbour. She was a very private person, shy and retiring, who didn't flaunt her fame or push herself forward. As a result our friendship developed slowly. In many ways it was a very unlikely friendship...

"However, as her illness developed, our home offered her a safe refuge when she felt like company and a good natter. In spite of her initial shyness, she enjoyed conversation and had interesting views on most issues. Always her sharp sense of humour, some of which might not be repeatable here, would invariably bubble through. It was at this time that I learnt of one of our shared passions and was frequently... dispatched to the Kentucky Fried Chicken shop with an order that could have fed half the neighbourhood...

"Her kindness showed itself in many ways, none more so than in her love of animals. She found it impossible to be cruel to anybody or any thing. The love and affection she gave to Nicholas is almost as legendary as Dusty herself – there can be few cats that have been so adored. But it wasn't just Nicholas. She couldn't bear the thought of any kind of cruelty to any living thing. Flies and insects were not swatted or sprayed in Dusty's house. They were carefully collected and released into the wild...

"... Although she was proud of her Irish descent, she wasn't always happy at the way she believed her Irishness showed through. No tribute to Dusty would be complete without some reference to the more explosive side to her nature. Nobody who heard her in full flight will forget it. Volatile seems a very inadequate word to describe it. I've even seen Nicholas' hair stand on end as he ran for cover. However, as day follows night, her remorse would follow every outburst. She used to come into our house distraught and ashamed. 'You'll never believe what I've just said to so-and-so,' she'd say. Or 'I don't know what has just come over me, but I've had an enormous run-in with you know who.' Genuine regret led to a potted plant or a carefully selected small gift, and an abject apology...

"We used to think that the magic of Dusty was the result of her being a big star. Nothing could be further from the truth. It takes more than a voice to make a star and her star qualities remained with her to the end. It is hard to say goodbye to someone so special. But she leaves us, and many more like us, with her music and the memories of the time we shared with her. She affected the lives of thousands of people she could never have known. Their lives, our lives, will be the poorer for her passing, but much the richer for having known her."

Silence followed. Father Wilcox took over and then the strains of "Goin' Back" filled the church. The choir began singing "Take My Soul" and the coffin was slowly carried to the waiting limousine hearse to the applause of the congregation, led by Madeline Bell. Pat Rhodes was dismayed that she wasn't asked to deliver a personal eulogy but, she said, in retrospect her grief was so enormous that she doubted she could have done Dusty justice. "When she died a part of me died. She was just always there and suddenly she wasn't."

When Carole Gibson left the church, she joined others to look at the hearse with the coffin inside. "All the cameras were pointed at the church and Dusty was left on her own on the other side. The car then drove off on its own. Nobody followed, they'd all gone to the wake. People applauded when the hearse drove past them." She stood around, not sure what to do, before deciding to join fellow fans at The Red Lion to toast Dusty and her life. Neil Tennant also shared Carole's view, saying, "…There'd been a huge funeral, everyone was there, and the press, and then suddenly there was the coffin by itself, speeding through the streets of Henley. It seemed rather sad. It suddenly seemed a very lonely moment." Dusty's body was taken for private cremation. A casket containing some of her ashes was interned in St Mary's churchyard, while Tom followed his sister's wishes and scattered the rest in the sea at the Cliffs of Moher in County Clare. Tour guide Noel Curtin gave Tom a lift from his hotel to the Cliffs, and told the *Sunday Tribune* that he was understandably upset during the journey and had said little. "He was a friendly man. He had a cup of coffee and I told him about the history of the place, that it had been for many generations in the O'Brien family and so was a fitting resting place for his sister."

Floral tributes placed outside St Mary's Church reflected just how much Dusty was revered. "To the Greatest, love Elton and David" was attached to a heart-shaped wreath of yellow roses. "Dearest Dusty, I'm so glad I had the chance to tell you what a classic you were. We love you. Paul McCartney and the kids" was another. Others included "Your sun drove out our rain" from one of many fans, together with floral tributes from The Rolling Stones, Rod Stewart, Tom Jones, and Cilla Black, among others. Fred Perry's tribute was different. He remembered Dusty always favoured bright and "tarty" colours. "I found a florist in Henley High Street and bought just two flowers. One from me... a particularly nasty shade of orange, and one from Susan (Cameron, who was unable to attend) in a taxing pink shade. I placed them on the ground in front of where the cortege carried her out... I like to think that Dusty was chuckling to herself knowing full well exactly why I had chosen that colour scheme. I am happy to report that my instincts were perfect – they managed to clash with every other colour in the church. I did my girl proud!"

Two weeks after her death, Elton John inducted Dusty into the Rock And Roll Hall of Fame. She was one of 10 inductees to be honoured before 1,500 people at the fourteenth event at the Waldorf Astoria Hotel in New York. They included Bruce Springsteen, Paul McCartney (who was making his first major public appearance since the death of his wife, Linda), the late Del Shannon, Curtis Mayfield (who was unable to attend through ill health), the Staple Singers and Billy Joel. Representing Dusty, Elton recalled how he was a member of her fan club and had pinned pictures of her on his bedroom wall, while his tribute was what rock 'n' roll was all about: irreverent and quotable – "She was enough to turn the gay boys straight!" He then struggled to find the perfect words of praise but the truest way to honour her was to experience her music – "I'm biased because I just think she was the greatest white singer there has ever been. Every song she sang, she claimed as her own." Lesley Gore, whose composition "Love Me By Name" Dusty had recorded, remarked, "It's sad that she should pass just before she was to be inducted. But she'll be there I'm sure, so the rhythm section had better be tight!"

Inductees are then featured in the Rock And Roll Hall of Fame Museum in Cleveland, Ohio, which exists to "preserve, exhibit and interpret the living heritage of rock and roll."

Seven years later Dusty was honoured by her British peers, when she was inducted into the UK Music Hall of Fame during a ceremony at the Alexandra Palace. Patti Labelle, dressed in white, sang a magnificently soulful version of "You Don't Have To Say You Love Me". A red-haired Joss Stone, a committed Dusty fan, inducted her heroine into the Hall of Fame with a short speech that included, "Once upon a time it was a man's world (making reference to an earlier spot by James Brown) but every so often a wonderful woman comes along who is so talented and determined that men have to sit up and take notice... Dusty was one such woman with an incredible ear for music... she took control in recording sessions until she was one hundred per cent satisfied... More than anyone she took a song and made it her own, pouring her heart and soul into it, and her performance was as intense as it was invigorating... and I owe her so much..."

Tributes from Martha Reeves, Tom Jones, Cilla Black and Burt Bacharach followed, before Patti Labelle and Nona Hendryx collected Dusty's award. Joss Stone, who had also named her dog Dusty Springfield, then launched into a credible version of "Son-Of-A Preacher Man", reminding the audience that a new generation of British singers relied on artists like Dusty for inspiration. However, if she had been alive to hear Joss Stone, Dusty would, doubtless, have wondered what all the fuss was all about. She never believed her compliments, and never believed she was more than a so-so singer who got lucky.

Dusty Springfield was one of the finest white soul singers of all time, a singer who sang with the same depth and emotion as black Americans, and for that she was held in the greatest esteem by many of her black peers like Aretha Franklin and Martha Reeves.

Her influence is boundless and legendary; her music timeless. Not bad for a shy, awkward convent school girl whose ambition was to be a blues singer, without knowing what it meant. Not bad for a fledgling Lana Sister who defied showbusiness rules and traditions, and who then became the chirpiest of Springfields with the cheekiest smile and the craziest American twang when she sang.

Dusty's life was great fun but also tragic, and despite having at one time seemed intent on self-destruction, she survived. That cancer should claim her was not in her game plan. As Gib Hancock noted in his eulogy, Dusty affected the lives of thousands of people she could never have known, "Their lives, our lives, will be the poorer for her passing, but much the richer for having known her."

"A legend?" is how Dusty put it. "I suspect I am to some people but frankly it's nothing special."

The legend, however, will live on forever.

BIBLIOGRAPHY

The following publications, newspapers, magazines, articles, fanzines and websites proved to be invaluable reference sources during the writing of this book. I am extremely grateful to all those authors, journalists and website owners but unfortunately there are some that I cannot thank because some of the memorabilia and newspaper clippings date back to 1959 and are in a very poor state. Some of the publications are of unknown origin. And if anyone is omitted from this list I do apologise.

Frank Allen – *Travelling Man-On The Road With The Searchers* (Aureus Publishing 1999)

Joe Ashton – *Red Rose Blues* (MacMillan Publishing 2000)

Jack Ashford – *Motown:The View From The Bottom* (Bank House Books 2003)

Cilla Black – *What's It All About?* (Ebury Press 2003)

Jill Gardiner – *From The Closet To The Screen* (Pandora Publishing 2002)

Paul Howes – *The Complete Dusty Springfield* (Reynolds & Hearn Ltd 2001)

Lucy O'Brien – *Dusty* (Sidgwick & Jackson 1989)

Philip Norman – *Sir Elton: The Definitive Biography Of Elton John* (Pan Books 2000)

Carole Pope – *Anti Diva* (Random House Canada 2001)

Martha Reeves – *Dancing In The Street: Confessions Of A Motown Diva* (Hyperion New York 1994)

Ronnie Spector – *Be My Baby* (Onyx Publishing 1991)

Barbara Windsor – *All Of Me* (Headline Publishing 2000)

Vickie Wright – *Motown From The Background:The Authorized Biography Of The Andantes* (Bank House Books 2007)

Blues & Soul, Disc and Music Echo, New Musical Express,
Melody Maker, Record Mirror, Record Collector and Sounds –
selected quotes from 1960 to 2000 from journalists including
Keith Altham, Ian Birch, Tony Bromley, Bill Buckley, Bob
Dawbarn, Roger Hollands, Peter Jones, Mike Ledgerwood,
Paul Mathur, Tom Springfield, and Penny Valentine
Billboard magazine – Peter Hartz (date unknown)
Cashbox magazine (journalist/date unknown)
Daily Express – Jean Rook 1985
Daily Mirror – Anton Antonowicz 1999
Daily Mail – (journalist unknown) 2006
Evening Standard 1966: Ray Connelly 1970: Ray Coleman
Ladies Of Soul – Chris Williams (date unknown)
The Maidenhead Advertiser – Anthony Husher 1999
The Mail On Sunday – Peter Sheridan 1999
Music Week – Robin Katz 1990
Gay News – Kris Kirk 1985
New York Times – Robert Palmer 1980
The Observer – Marcelle Bernstein: John Peel 1985: Sean
    O'Hagan 1999
Q Magazine – 1988
Rolling Stone magazine (journalist/date unknown)
The Sun – (journalist unknown) 1985: 1991
Time Out – Laura Lee Davies 1990
The Times (journalist unknown) 1995
You magazine – Louette Harding (1995)

Websites
The Beatles Ultimate Experience
Dusty Devotedly
Let's Talk Dusty
David Redfern

Radio programmes
Any Peebles – 1989
Roger Scott – 1989

Important miscellaneous items

Dave Godin – emails

David McGrath – emails

Fred Perry – articles and letters

The Dusty Springfield Bulletin – the pages of which are crammed with a wealth of information, thanks to the dedication of Paul Howes.

Dusty Springfield International, to which Dusty contributed on a regular basis. This excellent service for fans was headed by (the late) Lynne Jackson.

Pet Shop Boys Fanzine – *Literally*

And all the reviewers, critics and journalists who helped shape the rich tapestry that was the public life of Dusty Springfield.

BY THE SAME AUTHOR

Marvin Gaye (1984)

Motown:The History (1988)

Marvin Gaye: I Heard It Through The Grapevine (1991)

Every Chart-Topper Tells A Story – Sixties (1997)

Every Chart-Topper Tells A Story – Seventies (1998)

Every Chart-Topper Tells A Story – Eighties (1999)

Diana Ross: A Legend In Focus (2000)

Stevie Wonder: Rhythms Of Wonder (2003)

Chinwaggin: The Classic Interviews (2006)

Lionel Richie: Hello (2007)

INDEX